Prime Ministers and the Media

Issues of Power and Control

Colin Seymour-Ure

Blackwell
Publishing

© 2003 by Colin Seymour-Ure

350 Main Street, Malden, MA 02148-5020, USA
108 Cowley Road, Oxford OX4 1JF, UK
550 Swanston Street, Carlton, Victoria 3053, Australia

First published 2003 by Blackwell Publishing Ltd

Library of Congress Cataloging-in-Publication Data

Seymour-Ure, Colin, 1938–
    Prime ministers and the media : issues of power and control / Colin
Seymour-Ure.
        p. cm.
Includes bibliographical references and index.
    ISBN 0-631-16687-4 (alk. paper) – ISBN 0-631-18767-7 (alk. paper)
    1. Press and politics – Great Britain – History – 20th century.   2. Great
Britain – Politics and government – 20th century.   I. Title.

PN5124.P6S43 2003
070.4′493209′41 – dc21

2003001709

A catalogue record for this title is available from the British Library.

Set in 10.5 on 12.5 pt Sabon
by SNP Best-set Typesetter Ltd., Hong Kong
Printed and bound in the United Kingdom
by MPG Books Ltd, Bodmin, Cornwall

Picture research: Jane Taylor

For further information on
Blackwell Publishing, visit our website:
http://www.blackwellpublishing.com

Prime Ministers and the Media

For Alessio and Asha

Contents

Figures

Maps

Tables

Preface

Most of the essays in this book are about subjects in which I have been interested for a long time, as the Introduction explains in greater detail. My debts of gratitude are correspondingly numerous and, to some extent, diffused by time. For funding and/or hospitality, once the idea for the collection began to take shape in the mid-1980s, I am grateful to the Woodrow Wilson Center in Washington; the Australian National University; Carleton University, Ottawa; the Joan Shorenstein Center, Harvard University; the Canadian High Commission, London; and the Economic and Social Research Council (award number E00232197). Early versions of most of the chapters benefited from the opportunity to give lectures or seminars under the auspices of the institutions in that list, and of the European Consortium for Political Research, the Institute of Contemporary British History, the Political Communications Group of the Political Studies Association, the Reuter Foundation Programme at Oxford, the American Political Science Association, the Wissenschaftszentrum in Berlin, the London School of Economics and the Universities of Essex and Kent.

My colleague Graham Thomas generously read nearly all the book in draft; and I am very grateful also to the following for their comments on one or more individual chapters: Steven Barnett, Nick Garland, John Hart, Bill Jenkins, George Jones, Martin Rowson and Jeremy Tunstall. Others whose comments and encouragement about one or another topic have been much appreciated include Tony Barker, Richard Bourne, Mark Bryant, Dick Crampton, Virginia Crowe, Eric Einhorn, Bill Fox, Bob Franklin, David Goldsworthy, Peter Hennessy, Nick Hiley, Godfrey Hodgson, John Jensen, Tony King, Michael Lee, Peter Mellini, Ralph Negrine, Eric Neveu, Jane Newton, Pippa Norris, Barbara Pfetsch, Michael Rush, Maggie Scammell, Jean Seaton, Adrian Smith, Dominic Wring, and colleagues at the University of Kent in the Departments of Politics and International Relations and of History.

Warm thanks are due to the persons who agreed to be interviewed for the book, the great majority of whom, in contrast to the era when I was a graduate student, do not now mind that they are identified in footnotes. They include political correspondents back to the 1960s (such as the *Guardian* veteran Francis Boyd, and his contemporaries such as David Wood, Harry Boyne and Ronald Butt), and almost all the Downing Street Chief Press Secretaries since then or surviving at that time. Corresponding groups were interviewed in Washington at various times during the Ford, Carter, Reagan and Clinton presidencies, in Ottawa in 1961–2 and 1987, and in Canberra in 1981 and 1987.

I am grateful to Lord Hemingford and the Bodleian Library, Oxford, for permission to quote from the papers of William Clark; and to John Williams, Mrs E. F. Thomson, the Churchill Archives Centre (Churchill College, Cambridge) and Her Majesty's Stationery Office for permission to quote a letter from C. R. Attlee to Francis Williams. For permission to reproduce cartoons, thanks go to Steve Bell, Nick Garland and Chris Riddell, and to Atlantic Syndication Partners, Express Newspapers, Mirror Syndication and the Telegraph Group Ltd. For information about media peerages I am grateful to Steven Kennedy, Senior Library Clerk in the House of Lords.

Alison Chapman and Nicola Huxtable have given invaluable help in the preparation of the manuscript, especially the tables.

Last in these acknowledgements I pay special tribute to David Butler. His influence both set me on an academic career and spurred me to specialize in political communication and mass media. In 1962 I returned from an MA course in Ottawa, fully expecting to take up a deferred appointment as Assistant Principal in the Ministry of Agriculture. David, I suspect, was decisive in getting me a postgraduate studentship at Nuffield College. So but for him I might have ended up, figuratively speaking, not going gently to seed but with foot-and-mouth disease, incinerated on a pyre, with my feet sticking stiffly out of the smoke. (You retire from the civil service at age 60, so the dates are about right for the disastrous 2001 outbreak.) Some people say, of course, that this is what has been happening in academic life anyway.

Last of all I thank my wife Judy, as always, for her constant support.

Canterbury
New Year's Day 2003

Introduction: Prime Minister, Communication, Power, Control

This book is about prime ministers and public communication. Its themes are power and control. Some of the research dates back to 1962, when I started interviewing for a study of Westminster political correspondents. At that time 'communication' did not figure much as a topic in books and courses about British politics. 'Media', used to denote both technologies and the organizations employing them, had barely entered the popular vocabulary (and was always treated as a plural word). 'The press' implicitly included broadcasters. There were few if any undergraduate optional courses about politics and media, and certainly not whole degrees.

The growth of communication as a field of study in the last forty years is a major development in British political studies – a natural consequence of the spread of electronic media and of politicians' access to them. It increasingly dawned on politicians from the late 1960s that the television studio was as much a debating chamber as the House of Commons and a far better way of reaching voters. Media, to put it glibly, used to be regarded as an instrument applied *to* politics: they have become part of the environment *within* which politics is carried on.

The early 1960s were a time, too, when the orthodox accounts of cabinet government were challenged. Too long snug between the pages of constitutional historians and lawyers, they were rudely disturbed in 1962 by the Labour shadow cabinet minister and former Oxford don, Richard Crossman. Crossman was a bewitching lecturer. His thesis that cabinet had been supplanted by prime ministerial government was delivered, with a conviction possibly strengthened by not yet having served in a cabinet, to a room of entranced graduate students. The lectures were published as a long introduction to Bagehot's *The English Con-*

stitution.[1] They started an argument that was played out for some twenty years in text books, essays, exam papers, lecture theatres and the further reflections of Crossman himself (after actually being a cabinet minister under Harold Wilson).

The argument about prime ministerial power eventually became frustrating, because it concentrated on comparing the prime minister with his cabinet colleagues, it strayed into superficial comparisons with the American president, and there was little hard evidence. It soon went round and round. Questions about how much power would be appropriate for the tasks expected of a prime minister, or about how Downing Street and the cabinet office should be organized, were relatively neglected – partly, no doubt, because everybody outside Downing Street and Whitehall had so little to go on. Not until the 1980s and 1990s did these conditions change and a substantial new literature develop (see chapter 1). At the same time the broadsheet press began to take a more detailed interest than before in the workings of Downing Street. Parliamentary select committees became more curious too. The result was that during Tony Blair's premiership the organization and staffing of Downing Street were subjected to a continuing public critique on a scale inconceivable twenty years earlier, and Blair's pre-eminence was made plain. Blair, so it appeared, was a centralizing prime minister who, in Richard Rose's phrase, was a first without equal – not a first among equals.[2]

The growth of media and the growth of the premiership come together in a puzzle about the nature and extent of prime ministerial power. We tend to believe that media are powerful simply because they saturate our daily lives. It is the attitude of the mouse confronted by an elephant. Thus we may instinctively assume that the media have significant power over the prime minister's fortunes – for good or ill. More than in the days before media glut, the prime minister has to take into account the 'communication implications' of what he says and does and how he says and does it – and of where and when, and in whose company, and what he wears, and his body language in addition to his words. All can come under the media spotlight and all can affect his public image.

A paradox of media glut, moreover, is that the reality of the personal prime minister – the man his friends and colleagues know – is eclipsed

---

[1]   Walter Bagehot, *The English Constitution*, Introduction by R. H. S. Crossman, London: C. A. Watts, 1964. Crossman's lectures were delivered to David Butler's graduate seminar at Nuffield College, Oxford.
[2]   Richard Rose, *The Prime Minister in a Shrinking World*, London: Polity, 2001, p. 3.

by the unreality of the media version. The change is symbolized in the photograph in chapter 4 (figure 4.1) of Tony Blair giving a doorstep press conference outside Downing Street. Blair is distanced from the journalists by the intrusiveness of the technology which appears to bring him closer. In the same way security at Westminster or party conferences (places to which a graduate student had easy access forty years ago) distances and mystifies the person of a political leader.

None of that makes the prime minister a passive object of the media. Their very potential to harm him obliges the prime minister to use media as an instrument of his own power. Blair and his entourage put unprecedented efforts into nurturing key journalists, editors and proprietors, and into coordinating and trying to manage the news agenda, first in opposition and then in Downing Street.

Powerful media, then, mix with a powerful premiership. Which is the dominant force? How much did the efforts of the Blair 'spin machine' produce the desired results? In principle, the achievement of a landslide in 2001 almost identical to the 1997 general election victory could have been despite, not because of, all the news operations. The very complexity and pervasiveness of media, however, make questions such as those impossible to answer. Contrary to our instincts the impact of media is rarely that of the elephant treading on a mouse. The variables affecting people's attitudes and behaviour, whether as voters, taxpayers and motorists, or in their jobs, are subject to a multitude of factors. The direct or indirect influence of media can rarely be isolated.

In the musical about the New York underworld in the 1930s, *Guys and Dolls*, the gambler Big Julie wins at dice every time, because the dice are blank and he has scared everyone into agreeing that he has memorized where the spots were. Media do not give prime ministers such powers of control. I gave this book the working title of *Heads and Tales*, so as to emphasize the elements of chance which bedevil a prime minister.[3] 'Chance' is the product of all those variables which a prime minister cannot control or has not even discerned, and which may be more influential than those which he can. So press secretaries slave away, nuancing their stories; ghostwriters hone paragraphs for publication under the prime minister's byline; style advisers match his suit to the occasion. But all are ants beneath the hooves of history.

The relationship between the prime minister's public communication and the media through which he carries it out, on the one hand, and the effectiveness of his power on the other, is thus inherently unstable.

---

[3] Titles must clearly indicate a book's content, the publishers rightly say. *Heads and Tales* had to go.

A prime minister ideally wants *focused* power – in other words, control. His news operations pit him in a continuous struggle to be understood as he would wish. The same is true to an even greater extent of the American president (who features in several of the chapters that follow). From a distance the president seems uniquely powerful: directly elected, independent of Congress and his cabinet. Yet the constitution gives him almost no uncontrolled power, and his effectiveness depends heavily on uncertain powers of persuasion.

The prime minister's efforts to control his public communication cover, potentially, as wide a range as media themselves. The chapters in this book have been chosen to illustrate the sometimes elusive significance of places, persons, organizations and types of media. Except where it is obvious (chapters 1 to 3; chapters 6 and 7) the chapters stand by themselves. The three opening chapters develop some of the points made here, exploring the links between the prime minister's public communication and his power. Chapter 4 examines the distinctive impact of places – specifically capital cities – upon the communication patterns of the prime ministers or presidents who work in them. 'Harlots Revisited' (chapter 5) looks at the phenomenon of the frequently reviled 'media baron'. The example of Rupert Murdoch, most reviled of all in the last twenty years of the twentieth century, exemplifies the crude belief in the elephant theory of media power. The two chapters on the Downing Street press secretary (6 and 7) trace the attempts of prime ministers to meet the challenge of an expanding media (especially broadcasting) across half a century, and to control their public communication on a daily basis. Chapter 8 analyses the specific device of the prime ministerial press conference – a forum of exchange which British prime ministers were much slower to use than American presidents. The last two chapters – on political rumours and political cartoons – deal with peculiar kinds of communication which are exceptionally difficult to control. Rumours are harder to swat than houseflies. Complaining about cartoons plays into the cartoonist's hands.

This summary encapsulates the range and point of the selection but does not account for the specific choices. These require a personal explanation. The subject in general, as earlier indicated, goes back to my experience as a graduate student and a junior lecturer. (I started teaching an undergraduate option on political communication and mass media – presumably one of the first – in 1967.) A doctoral thesis on Westminster political correspondents proved too daunting in the early 1960s. Journalists lunched me in Westminster and Pall Mall and talked off the record, but in those days footnotes needed chapter and verse, and so I wrote a tedious thesis about the press and parliamentary privilege. However, the subject of political journalism – increasingly viewed from the Downing Street press office perspective, not the journalists' – remained a continuing interest, and I wrote about it in *The Press, Politics and the Public* (Methuen, 1968) and when working for the Royal Commission on the Press in 1974–6.

Purpose-built capital cities intrigued me from the time of a year-long visit to Ottawa – essentially then a company town – in 1961–2, when you could roam the corridors of the parliament buildings free and easy. But the broader implications of cities as news environments came much later. I learnt casually in 1995 that the White House in Washington had been located one-and-a-half miles from Congress by design, to symbolize the separation of executive and legislative powers. This, for some reason, I assumed almost no one else realized. To a student of political communication its implications were very exciting. Then I found everyone realized (in Cambridge, Mass., at least), but that made it none the less fascinating. Moreover 10 Downing Street (as chapter 4 suggests) is likewise such an epitome of the higgledy-piggledy British constitution. Earlier, in 1986–7, there had also been an experience with feral cats around the parliament buildings of Ottawa and then, to my delight, around those of Canberra. Far from exterminating them, the authorities looked on these cats benignly as one more element in the emblematic national patchworks which those cities had by then become – capital cities, not company towns, in which a cat may look at a king.

No one needs an excuse for studying media barons. If their influence were all it is sometimes cracked up to be (which I doubt), that would be reason enough. If it is not, then their eccentricities and occasional self-importance make them emperors with no more clothes than the girls on the inside pages of their papers. Similarly Tony Blair's adoption of a form of traditional American presidential press conference – at a time when American presidents were using them less frequently than for seventy years – was a good reason to explore why British prime ministers had not done so earlier.

Political rumours tend to be about health, sex or money. As a student journalist I listened agog to a predecessor, infinitely wise with the experience of a few years in Fleet Street, retailing scurrilous rumours about royalty. Then in the 1964 general election everyone seemed to know about 'the rumour' – and that the authors of a campaign history had been threatened with legal action if they so much as mentioned it. The rumour was about Harold Wilson's private life. How efficiently and privily, it struck me, do rumours work. Where rumours are a special kind of news, political cartoons are a special kind of comment. The two topics match. Rumours are easily disregarded by the student of communication because there is no hard copy or tape, cartoons because of the false assumption that a humorous medium cannot have serious consequences. For researching cartoons I had the great advantage of being involved in the development of the impressively catalogued cartoon archive at the University of Kent.

Part of the strength and weakness of political communication as a field is its breadth: a political system *is* a system of communication. Any selection for a book such as this will be idiosyncratic. Academics too are ants beneath the hooves of history, each labouring with its own crumbs. So here is my sample.

1

Public Communication and the Prime Minister's Tasks

Tony Blair's public communications, from the designer leisure wear to the designer accent and the designer press conferences, probably attracted more public interest than those of any previous British government. Apart from general claims that Blair was more concerned with 'style' than substance, much of the curiosity focused on the government's techniques of news management. 'Spin' – putting a tendentious interpretation on the news – and the 'spin doctors' who did it, became objects of suspicion and criticism in the later 1990s. The reason was partly a typical media obsession with media themselves: the dealings of Blair's press secretary Alastair Campbell with the Downing Street press corps were a recurring fascination. But the interest also reflected a growing curiosity about the links between communications and the prime minister's power. In what ways is public communication part of the prime minister's job? How far is it an instrument of prime ministerial power? How has it been treated in the literature about the prime minister?

The first three chapters of this book explore these questions. Chapter 1 starts by arguing the importance of the subject and examining its comparative neglect. The chapter then explores the prime minister's job description. Some of the prime minister's tasks involve public communication more or less as an end in itself: it is a form of accountability – of 'responsible government' in the literal sense of being answerable to the public, as in the theatricality of Prime Minister's Question Time. Other tasks involve communication as a means to achieve some separate goal, whether it be about American policy towards Saddam Hussein or the government's policy on the controversial MMR vaccination. Others again, such as chairing cabinet meetings, are supposed to be carried out in secrecy, with only the results (and by no means all of them) made public.

Chapter 2 discusses ways in which the prime minister's public communication fits in with his other resources. The prime minister's formal powers often guarantee only the minimum of success: good public communication can produce something better. For instance the prime minister has the formal power to reshuffle his cabinet. But whether the reshuffle is seen as a sign of weakness or strength, and what effect it has on his standing in his party and the polls, may depend on how it is publicly presented.

Chapter 3 takes this analysis further. It argues that public communication is a key resource for turning prime ministerial *authority* into *power*. The power may not be great enough to achieve much of what the prime minister wants. But his communication resources are normally better than those of any rival, inside or outside his party. If he does not use them, he spurns a potentially crucial weapon. In the foreword to his autobiography John Major writes eloquently about the distorting pressures of media attention: negligible response time, reductive soundbites, ritualistic rhetoric (often misleading), skeleton reporting (even in the broadsheets), pressure to produce sensational stories.[1] Major's public communication was extremely unsuccessful, judged by the scale of his defeat in 1997. His complaint was no doubt bred of frustration: he had used his communication resources, but they were simply not good enough to get results. Blair, in contrast, was extremely successful, throughout his first term and beyond.

Public Communication and Accounts of the Premiership

Awareness of public communication, both as a task for the prime minister and as a resource, grew with the rapid development of broadcast news media in the last thirty years of the twentieth century. In 1970 the group of political lobby correspondents covering Westminster and Downing Street (taking their name from the Commons lobby, to which they had privileged access) included only two broadcasters, one each for the BBC and ITN. From the 1980s, TV and radio channels proliferated and news was broadcast round the clock. By 2002, one-third of more than two hundred lobby correspondents were broadcasters.

Broadcast media had once been unobtrusively concerned just to report and interpret politics. Now they played an ever more substantial part in shaping the institutions and arenas within which politics is carried on. At the beginning of the new millennium the internet was having a similar effect. You could read or watch an interview with Tony Blair on the Number 10 website, as you might have done formerly in

---

[1] John Major, *John Major: the Autobiography*, London: HarperCollins, 1999, pp. xixff.

the papers or on TV. Politics was in an era of *electronic glut*. Almost everywhere the prime minister went became potentially a place for political communication. The 'publicity needs' of the prime minister's job grew correspondingly. Does the prime minister now do anything deliberate at all, without taking into account the communication implications? One simple measure of the development is the new prominence of the Downing Street press secretary. During the Thatcher era this hitherto unremarkable post changed from grub to butterfly. Bernard Ingham held it for eleven years and became an influential member of the prime minister's immediate entourage. Blair's press secretary, Alastair Campbell, elevated the job even further (see chapters 6 and 7).

The impact of electronic glut upon the prime minister's job was all the more important, secondly, because of the job's *flexibility*. Britain's famous lack of a written constitution – a single authoritative document – provides much of the explanation. The constitution is found in a mixed collection of statutes, precedents and conventions. Even the rule that the prime minister must be a member of the House of Commons is conventional. The prime minister's role is variable within the cabinet, and so is the cabinet's within the wider executive. Some of the classic one-liners about the prime minister stress the variability. The prime minister is 'first among equals' – which is a logical contradiction and can mean no more than that relations between ministers and prime minister vary. Asquith got into the constitutional textbooks by writing, 'The office of Prime Minister is what its holder chooses and is able to make of it'. George Jones, in a much quoted analysis of the job in 1965, drew the conclusion that the prime minister 'is only as strong as [his colleagues] let him be'.[2] None of the prime minister's powers is based in statute. The first statutes even to refer to the prime minister were minor laws in 1917 (providing Chequers as an official country residence) and in 1937 (setting ministerial salaries). The constitution can therefore change simply through behaviour changing without being challenged: unchallenged, the change then becomes a precedent. All that is the stuff of textbooks. For the prime minister, it makes possible an acute sensitiveness to the potential – and the dangers – of his media environment. When media change, in short, the premiership changes.

A third reason for looking at the relations between the prime minister's public communication and his job is that the literature on the premiership did not keep up with those developments. 'The British are

[2]   H. H. Asquith, *Fifty Years in Parliament*, London: Cassell, 2 vols, 1926, vol. 1, p. 185; George Jones, 'The Prime Minister's power', *Parliamentary Affairs*, 18.2, 1965, p. 185.

rather vague about their system of government' is the comment (equally British) with which Simon James began his own study, *British Cabinet Government*.[3] Except historically, there has been little depth of knowledge at all about the workings of the cabinet. Scholars used to get by with the not-quite-up-to-date reflections of elder statesmen, a few historically slanted textbooks, and a political journalism of circumlocution ('sources close to the prime minister'). The publication in 1975–7 of Richard Crossman's revealing and cheeky *Diaries of a Cabinet Minister* attracted disproportionate excitement precisely because they were unprecedented.[4]

For decades this lack of detail could be put down to the culture of secrecy in Whitehall and Downing Street.[5] Since the 1980s, however, 'the machinery at the heart of British government is gradually being demystified'.[6] Crossman's diaries were a landmark. The stock of information about the workings of the cabinet system steadily grew, stimulated by declining habits of loyalty among political colleagues and reticence among retired mandarins, more insistent investigative journalism, probing inquiries by parliamentary committees, TV documentaries, and big publishing advances for ministerial memoirs.

With this knowledge came a brightening in the climate of official secrecy. For example the rules were relaxed about publicity for the cabinet's engine room – its elaborate committee system. From a position where ministers were forbidden to disclose the very existence of the committees, attitudes shifted sufficiently that in 1992 John Major could without contention authorize the publication not only of the names of the committees but of their ministerial memberships. *Questions of Procedure for Ministers* – the Cabinet Office guide detailing 'the arrangements for the conduct of affairs by Ministers', and the authority for such rules – was made public too. By 2001 it was available, renamed

---

[3] Simon James, *British Cabinet Government*, London: Routledge, 1st edn, 1992, p. 1. The sentence is (disappointingly) omitted from the second edition (1999).

[4] R. H. S. Crossman, *The Diaries of a Cabinet Minister*, London: Hamish Hamilton and Jonathan Cape, 3 vols, 1975, 1976, 1977. For an account of the rigour with which secrecy rules were applied to prevent publication of the memoirs of the first secretary to the cabinet, Sir Maurice (later Lord) Hankey, up to twenty years after his retirement in 1938, see J. F. Naylor, *A Man and an Institution: Sir Maurice Hankey, the Cabinet Secretariat and the Custody of Cabinet Secrecy*, London: Cambridge University Press, 1984.

[5] Even in the comparatively open political culture of the USA, scholarly accounts of the presidency are anecdotal and unsystematic – mediaeval maps of the world, compared with the precise cartography of Congress.

[6] J. M. Lee, G. W. Jones and June Burnham, *At the Centre of Whitehall*, London: Macmillan, 1998, p. viii.

as *The Ministerial Code*, on the Cabinet Office website.[7] Whitehall in general became more receptive to academic inquiry.

The consequence of more detail about Downing Street and the Cabinet Office was an abandonment of the summary simplicities of traditional 'cabinet government' models. The system has come to be seen rather as comprising a large and changing group of people, among them the prime minister, whose relationships with each other fluctuate. The idea was popularized in the term 'core executive', defined by Rhodes as 'the complex web of institutions, networks and practices surrounding the prime minister, cabinet, cabinet committees and their official counterparts, less formalized ministerial "clubs" or meetings, bilateral negotiations and interdepartmental committees'.[8] As a result, concepts such as 'power' and 'decision-making' were visualized in terms of networks, coalitions, personal leverage, rival resources (knowledge, time, position); and they were seen as varying frequently with events, issues and personalities. In an early article Dunleavy and Rhodes were able to identify six different models even within the traditional institutionalist approach: prime ministerial government, prime ministerial cliques, cabinet government, ministerial government, segmented decision-making and bureaucratic coordination. In each, the prime minister's job was different.[9]

Although media relations were one of the factors distinguishing prime ministerial government (and the clique version) from others, none of those models said much about the prime minister's public communication. Later analyses in this warmer climate of inquiry do not necessarily say much either. For example Martin Smith, following Rhodes, builds a discussion of the premiership into an account based on structure, context and agents.[10] Within the structural constraints, the prime minister's power over his colleagues is seen as the outcome of an exchange of resources between them. Prime ministers have authority, staff and political influence; ministers have knowledge, time and networks of

[7]   The relaxation is traced by the historian Peter Hennessy, a major contributor to the stock of knowledge about the modern cabinet system, in *The Hidden Wiring*, London: Indigo, 1996, ch. 4.

[8]   R. A. W. Rhodes and Patrick Dunleavy (eds), *Prime Minister, Cabinet and Core Executive*, London: Macmillan, 1995, p. 12.

[9]   Patrick Dunleavy and R. A. W. Rhodes, 'Core executive studies in Britain', *Public Administration*, 68.1, 1990, pp. 3–28.

[10]   'All actors within the core executive have resources, but how they use them will depend on their tactics (agency); tactics, however, depend on the particular political and economic context and the limits of action as defined in the structures and processes of institutions.' Martin Smith, *The Core Executive in Britain*, London: Macmillan, 1999, p. 37.

support. Smith's categories and illustrations are informative. But his claim that 'a Prime Minister's authority can extend only as far as the cabinet will allow' could come straight out of the 1960s.[11] Only perfunctory attention is paid to such possibilities as the impact of structures upon the prime minister's communication, or the value of (say) a media campaign as a resource, or the use of leaks as a tactic.

Similar comments can be made about other studies, such as those by James or Burch and Holliday.[12] In general, although such works treat the cabinet/'core executive' in far greater breadth, depth and contemporary detail than before, they still do not build public communication categorically into their models. They fail explicitly and thoroughly to identify and evaluate the importance of public communication by or about the prime minister as a factor in the policy-making and administrative processes which the analyses and models describe. The political consequences of the enormous changes in the media environment of the prime minister during the last forty years of the twentieth century are insufficiently visible.

The same may be said about a second, less theoretically ambitious, strand of literature – historical, narrative and largely chronological. For instance Peter Hennessy takes a plain man's approach in *The Hidden Wiring*. Paraphrasing the Victorian child that asked its father, 'What is that lady for?', the lady in point being the Queen, he puts the question: 'What is the prime minister for?' As answer he lists thirty-three items. Only one directly involves communications: responsibility for the 'overall efficiency of the government's media strategy'.[13] But Hennessy is not concerned with how the tasks are carried out. Even though the remaining thirty-two are riddled with communication implications, media come into his discussion only in anecdote and parenthesis. His later and much longer study, *The Prime Minister: the Office and its Holders since 1945*, proceeds mainly prime minister by prime minister and uses essentially the same framework of analysis. Dennis Kavanagh

[11]   Smith, *The Core Executive in Britain*, p. 79.
[12]   Simon James, *British Cabinet Government*; Martin Burch and Ian Holliday, *The British Cabinet System*, London: Prentice Hall/Harvester Wheatsheaf, 1996. 'Most postwar developments have exalted the premier vis-à-vis other ministers,' James writes. 'Television, international summits and Prime Minister's question time have strengthened the public impression that in many ways the Prime Minister *is* the government.' Despite these promising remarks there is just half a page on the Downing Street press secretary and about the same on 'the prime minister's influence over the press'. The remark that 'presentation is now an integral part of policy-making' – a claim with crucial implications, surely, for the premiership – is mentioned almost in passing. James, *British Cabinet Government*, 2nd edn, 1999, pp. 207, 112, 95 and 112.
[13]   Hennessy, *The Hidden Wiring*, p. 89.

and Anthony Seldon organize *The Powers behind the Prime Minister: the Hidden Influence of Number Ten* on the same narrative and chronological basis. Their subject is the institutional premiership in Downing Street, so the scope is narrower and their comparisons are mostly summary.[14]

Two exceptions to these comments about the literature are books by Michael Foley and Richard Rose: *The Rise of the British Presidency* and *The Prime Minister in a Shrinking World*.[15] Foley comes close to a 'communications model' of the premiership, in that public communication is intrinsic to his key concepts and arguments. The analysis depends heavily on such ideas as 'leadership stretch' and 'spatial leadership'. The former applies to the vastly superior media attention and popular reputation of the prime minister compared with his colleagues, and the latter to his media-managed ability to distance himself helpfully from aspects of the institutional premiership. (Both are attributes shared with the American president.)

Foley's book is an extended argument, much of it about winning rather than holding office. He is more concerned with forms of communication-related activity by the prime minister than with the range of tasks to which they are applied. Rose, in comparison, is closer to the methods of the contemporary historians – but with a far greater sensitivity to public communication as a factor in the prime minister's performance across the board (including internationally) and in Tony Blair's populism. The book centres on five varying 'major political roles' essential to a prime minister's success, of which his communications are one. (The others concern party, electioneering, and managing parliament and the cabinet.) The discussion of communication (themed as 'from private to public government') is wide-ranging, subtle and historical. Communication is not an organizing or overarching concept applied systematically to the prime minister's tasks. But the approach is close to the one adopted – on a shorter scale – in the present study.

---

[14]   Peter Hennessy, *The Prime Minister: the Office and its Holders since 1945*, London: Penguin Books, 2000. Dennis Kavanagh and Anthony Seldon, *The Powers behind the Prime Minister: the Hidden Influence of Number Ten*, London: HarperCollins, 1999. Hennessy describes his book as not an 'essay in political science' but 'a work of political and administrative history with a large dash of biography' (p. 15). The job of the prime minister is defined principally in chapters 4 and 5. *The Hidden Wiring* is subtitled 'Unearthing the British Constitution' and covers much more than the prime minister.

[15]   Michael Foley, *The Rise of the British Presidency*, Manchester: Manchester University Press, 1993; Richard Rose, *The Prime Minister in a Shrinking World*, London: Polity, 2001.

The Prime Minister's Job in General

What, then, are the prime minister's tasks and activities? Which ones require public communication, and which may be assisted by it?

To explore these questions a number of distinctions can be made. First, the prime minister has three clear and overlapping roles in which to carry out his tasks as a public communicator. Most comprehensively he is a *source of news*. To project the news he wants, he is next a *communications manager*. President Eisenhower cheerfully but naively believed in 'letting the facts speak for themselves'. Perhaps a military hero turned politician could afford to take that view in the 1950s; but fortunately for him, his press secretary, Jim Hagerty, did not.[16] In an era of electronic glut, 'facts', more than ever, are manufactured, and they never speak for themselves. Third, the prime minister is a *public performer*. The locations are diverse. In the majority he will double as a news source, since the live audience will be supplemented by newspaper or broadcast audiences. When he takes part in a broadcast interview or 'writes' a newspaper column (a practice Tony Blair often used, through the medium of assistants), his performance is specific to news media but may be further spread by being discussed also as a source of news.

A fourth but rather different communications role is *media policy-maker*. It is different in that it directly involves substantive policy goals, whereas the other roles are principally means to the achievement of goals, not goals in themselves. By 2001 media policy was the responsibility of the Department of Media, Culture and Sport – a comparatively minor Whitehall player. But modern media impinge also on a wide range of other departments, including Trade and Industry, Education and Skills, the Home Office and the Foreign and Commonwealth Office. Most of these are run by cabinet ministers with more clout than the MCS minister. Media policy, in addition, can awaken passions. Increases in the TV licence fee are likely to irritate almost every household in the land; issues of privacy and censorship rouse editorialists. When governments tinker with media, moreover, they meddle with an instrument of their own public accountability – a 'free press'.

One result of these administrative and political complexities is that a distinction can be drawn in practice between policies based on ideology and those driven by expediency. Another result is that the prime minister tends to be drawn into media policy – of both types. For example,

[16]   See Elmer E. Cornwell, Jr, *Presidential Leadership of Public Opinion*, Bloomington: Indiana University Press, 1965.

in the late 1980s, as a matter of free market principle, Mrs Thatcher promoted the policy of allocating the periodically renewed Channel 3 ITV franchises by auction instead of by beauty contest – a radical shift of emphasis.[17] She was also determined to break the power of the newspaper production unions. In 2002 Tony Blair took a direct interest in the legislation establishing an umbrella broadcasting regulator, OFCOM, and relaxing media ownership rules.[18] But in his case the policy looked more like a pragmatic response to corporate pressure than the result of core Labour beliefs (new or old).

The prime minister's involvement is only occasional. But the fact that governments cannot avoid having media policies (in this substantive sense), as they very largely could until the 1980s, must colour his relationships with media entrepreneurs and the BBC. It is also a factor in his role as media manager. For example real or imaginary deals between Rupert Murdoch and Mrs Thatcher, and then Tony Blair, were a frequent source of public speculation – help with satellite and cross-ownership policy, in exchange for the partisanship of the *Sun*?

The prime minister's tasks are carried out, secondly, in a mixture of *formal* and *informal* roles, *institutional* and *personal* roles, and *governing* and *non-governing* roles. They reflect, again, the flexibility of the job. The prime minister's public communication can be an important factor in determining the range and balance within each pair. Electronic glut has increased the relative prominence of informal and personal roles and has made more difficult the isolation (and protection) of non-governing from governing roles.

Formal roles become so if they have constitutional definition, which gives them a predictable character and a gauge with which to judge how well they are carried out. The prime minister has the formal task of choosing whom to put in the cabinet, and the calibre of his appointments will be a factor in our evaluation of his premiership. Informal roles, independent of an external constitutional authority, may change at the whim of the officeholder. There are no formal rules, for instance, about exactly how much the prime minister must perform in parliament. In the absence of such rules Tony Blair had the flexibility to change Prime Minister's Question Time from two afternoons a week to one (but doubling its length). While there were grumbles of criticism, he could

---

[17]   The fifteen regional ITV franchises were allocated every ten years (but not in 2000) by the Independent Television Commission and its predecessors. Until the auction principle was introduced, the decisions were made on the basis of judgements about competence and quality.

[18]   *The Times*, 29 July 2002.

not be accused of behaving unconstitutionally, and nothing could be done about it.

Even if Britain had a written constitution detailing the prime minister's formal roles, their practice would still be modified and supplemented by informal roles. The American constitution defines the president's formal roles within a framework of the separation of executive, legislative and judicial powers. In order to exercise leadership, he tries in practice to join them together again through the performance of well-established informal roles such as party leader and mobilizer of opinion. The election of the president is formally carried out by the electoral college, but informally it is settled by the popular vote – and the difference between the two was sensationally highlighted in the contest between George W. Bush and Al Gore in 2000. That said, however, it is true that in Britain formal and informal roles are more easily blurred. What the prime minister must (and must not) do, and the procedures by which he must do it, are comparatively wide open to argument.

The distinction between *institutional* and *personal* roles separates the abstract and corporate from the personal and single prime minister. The United States comparison is again illuminating. The American president is in one sense a huge, formal, collective institution – 'the presidency'. The president is its symbolic head and, about most of its activities, an unknowing one. Even when limited to the White House staff, 'the president' is a formal institution, where many people speak and act in the president's name. But there is the personal officeholder – 'Mr President' – who, one hopes, knows exactly what he is doing. Finally, and informally, there is 'George W. Bush', not only the president but a human being.[19]

In Downing Street the distinctions are not as sharp. The collective premiership is in one sense the cabinet, united by the formal convention of collective responsibility. But, just as at the White House, there is a corporate premiership, employing around two hundred people in the various offices, including the press office, centred on Downing Street. Even here, however, the prime minister/cabinet connection is involved, since the largest office in Downing Street (strictly, it stretches along

---

[19] At different stages of the crisis over his relations with the White House intern Monica Lewinsky, and sometimes in different presidential roles at the same stage, Bill Clinton shifted from one version of the president to another. The affair was a private matter of the personal, informal president; impeachment would be harmful to the symbolic president, and so on. In the outcome, leaving Clinton secure in office, popular opinion may be said to have taken the view that it was a private and personal matter.

Whitehall) is the Cabinet Office, whose staff of more than two thousand serve the prime minister and cabinet collectively.[20]

The institutional/personal distinction gives the prime minister scope to try and achieve his objectives by switching between one 'version' and another, by the use of news management. The personal prime minister can hide behind the institutional: remarks can be sourced to 'cabinet sources' or 'Downing Street insiders'. The prime minister's chief formal surrogate is his press secretary. Informal surrogates, such as ministers and staff members whose formal jobs do not include media briefings, become familiar to journalists over time. A simple example of this process at work took place a few months after Blair took office in May 1997. Blair worked hard to distance himself personally from the earliest institutional embarrassment of his administration. The Labour party was exposed as having accepted a donation of at least one million pounds from the controllers of Formula One motor racing. Press briefings by the institutional premiership did not dissociate him sufficiently, so he sought to project a 'What, me?' pose of injured innocence through a prominent TV interview by Honest Tony, the people's premier. The businessmen would have lost heavily if a planned ban on tobacco sponsorship, subsequently cancelled, had gone ahead. Blair announced that the donation would be paid back.[21] Much later, at the end of 2002, Blair had to distance himself, with evident embarrassment, from a media frenzy ('Cheriegate') about his wife's association with a convicted fraudster.[22] Prime ministers obviously do not have complete control over the versions of themselves which the voters perceive. But part of their media management is the continual exercise of choice about what to attach themselves to and in what version.

The scope for switching between the two through media management is the point of the distinction also between the prime minister's *governing* and *non-governing* roles. It could perhaps be argued that across a decade Mrs Thatcher used public communication to remove certain governing roles from the sphere of government altogether, inasmuch as she helped shift public opinion towards a reduced role for government

[20]   Cabinet Office figures from Lee *et al.*, *At the Centre of Whitehall*. Number 10 figures from Kavanagh and Seldon, *The Powers behind the Prime Minister*, p. 306. Reliable figures for Number 10 are difficult to establish, since they depend on who is included (e.g. support staff). Two hundred sounds high, especially for late 1998.

[21]   Nicholas Jones, *Sultans of Spin*, London: Orion Books, 1999, pp. 107–19.

[22]   The conman, Peter Foster, was the partner of Cherie Blair's close friend Carole Caplin and had helped to negotiate the purchase of two flats for Mrs Blair in Bristol. One was student accommodation for Euan Blair and the other was for investment. See the national press *passim* for the first two weeks of December 2002.

in the public utilities, the prison service and various other traditional public sector undertakings. But more typically, media management is used the other way round, to turn non-governing roles to advantage in performing governing tasks. Spouse, parent, religion, occupation, and associated characteristics such as class and educational background, can be used both as symbols in their own right and to show the prime minister's governing capacities in the best light.

Bearing in mind these distinctions and the overall flexibility of the job, it is no simple matter to define the prime minister's tasks. James summarizes the job as 'running the key functions of government; fostering collective responsibility; giving strategic leadership; involving himself in individual policy issues'.[23] But general accounts do not get one far. Constitutional lawyers' textbooks are strong on such tasks as being First Lord of the Treasury and exercising what was historically the Crown's prerogative in various matters. In the different language of leadership analysis his tasks are managerial and executive (with much coordination, arbitration and decision-making), policy-making, and symbolic or expressive.

Hennessy's thirty-three answers to what the prime minister is 'for' are a job lot. Like the catalogue of a grand country house sale, they range from major items, such as the government's legislative programme, to attic trivia like the appointment of the Master of Trinity College, Cambridge. When informal tasks are brought in, such as the large number of activities carried out as party leader rather than as prime minister, the job lot approach becomes almost unavoidable. In addition, many tasks, including most of the prime minister's public performances, are carried out as means to some further end. Neither of these complications matters in the present analysis, provided that one avoids – as Hennessy to some extent does not – mixing objectives, functions, powers and positions (belonging to the prime minister either personally or institutionally).[24]

The Prime Minister's Formal Tasks and Activities

Some of the prime minister's formal tasks get called 'powers' (for example by Hennessy) precisely because there is no challenge to the

[23] James, *British Cabinet Government*, 2nd edn, p. 89.
[24] Hennessy, *The Hidden Wiring*, p. 90; *The Prime Minister*, p. 58. In the latter, 'hiring and firing', for example, is described first as a function then as a power – '*the* great twentieth century prime ministerial weapon'.

prime minister's right to perform them, although he obviously has to follow correct procedures. They include many *appointments*. First there are cabinet ministers (about twenty-one), non-cabinet ministers and all junior members of the government (totalling about one hundred). From among the ministers, the prime minister has to set up the standing and ad hoc cabinet committees, which traditionally have pre-digested or pre-determined most cabinet business, and to decide who will chair them.[25] The prime minister also appoints the Cabinet Secretary (and official head of the home civil service), the permanent secretaries in the departments, and other top appointments in the civil service – and also in the armed forces and the security services. He makes various other public sector appointments (such as heads of committees of inquiry), and he appoints most peers, certain clerics (notably bishops), and even a few regius professors. Inside his Downing Street entourage – greatly expanded by Blair in a move widely criticized as 'presidential' – he appoints staff to his private office and several other offices, including the press office; and usually he recruits a number of individual advisers. Many of all these will be political appointees.

How far into the business of making appointments does the personal prime minister go, before leaving the rest to the institutional premiership – the Cabinet Secretary for the civil servants; the whips or political members of his staff for others? Cabinet ministers are appointed by the prime minister personally – and he decides their specific portfolios. The personal prime minister dismisses them, too. One of the quainter instances of the prime minister as public performer is the customary formal letter of thanks to an outgoing minister, conventionally made public (with its reply) at the time of departure, and construed by journalists for its nuances and subtexts. (Most such letters are presumably drafted in fact by the institutional premiership.) The prime minister's involvement with diplomatic and armed services appointments is in collaboration with the Foreign and Defence Secretaries; and he gives only final approval to ministers' choices of parliamentary private secretaries and special advisers.[26] Even where his involvement is personal, he will seek or be given advice. Overall, there must be a large group of appointments, between the senior and more junior, with which successive prime ministers are personally involved to varying degrees. Mrs Thatcher became well known for asking whether proposed appointees were 'one

---

[25]   John Major chaired 9 out of 26 cabinet standing and subcommittees in 1992, Blair 5 out of 24 in 2000. R. A. W. Rhodes and P. Dunleavy (eds), *Prime Minister, Cabinet and Core Executive*, London: Macmillan, 1995, p. 305; www.number-10.gov.uk, 17 January 2000.

[26]   Hennessy, *The Hidden Wiring*, p. 89.

of us'. She also took a keen and direct interest in some ecclesiastical and academic appointments.[27]

When the prime minister is not personally involved in deciding an appointment, it seems less likely that anticipated public reaction will have been a significant factor in the decision. A few of the decisions – those concerned with intelligence and security – exclude publicity by their nature: they are not available even as news. But in this area too the warmer climate in the 1990s meant that the names of the heads of the intelligence services, for example, were freely disclosed. One lately retired head of MI5 published her memoirs.[28] For the rest, public reaction is most relevant to decisions about ministerial appointments.

A new prime minister takes over a going concern, but he may decide to change the *organization*. The cabinet's size, order of precedence and frequency of meeting are all flexible. So are the political parts of the Downing Street offices. The prime minister can also decide, on a larger scale, on the 'creation, abolition and merger of government departments and executive agencies'.[29] The main part of the machinery which formally involves the prime minister's role as a communications manager is the press office. (See chapters 6 and 7.) Its staff grew to ten in John Major's time and larger again under Blair. It was augmented by a Strategic Communications Unit and a Research and Information Unit, under the authority of a press secretary redesignated as Director of Communications and Strategy.[30] Although the press secretary/director generally has very close contact with the prime minister personally (both in non-governing and governing roles), the office itself is part of the institutional premiership. In this capacity it also quickly extended its reach, under Blair, into the Whitehall departments. Alastair Campbell added to his Downing Street job the headship of the Government Information Services in Whitehall. People in some other Downing Street offices also work formally, in part, as communication managers or sources for the prime minister. Blair's reorganization of Downing Street into three directorates in 2001 established a directorate for Government and Political Relations. This included units running prime ministerial 'events and visits' and relations with the Labour party.

---

[27]   Lee *et al.*, *At the Centre of Whitehall*, pp. 49–51. Mrs Thatcher's phrase, 'one of us', stuck to such an extent that Hugo Young made it the title of his biography of her (*One of Us*, London: Macmillan, 1989).

[28]   Stella Rimington, *Open Secret*, London: Arrow Books, 2001.

[29]   Hennessy, *The Hidden Wiring*, p. 89.

[30]   Lee *et al.*, *At the Centre of Whitehall*, ch. 5. The total cost of the Prime Minister's office by 1993, including such items as overseas travel, was more than £9,000,000.

One other formal piece of communications management served the institutional premiership at Downing Street during the last two years of the Major administration: a cabinet subcommittee chaired by Michael Heseltine, deputy prime minister, and charged with the coordination and presentation of government policy. It met daily at 8.30 a.m. 'Attended by ministers, party officials and civil servants, it considered day-to-day response to media interest, and coordination of policy in both the short and longer terms.' Its initials were EDCP, since it was a subcommittee of the economic and domestic policy committee, ED. It replaced a larger, unwieldy and less authoritative 'Number Twelve Committee' with similar functions, set up in 1991 under the chairmanship of the chief Whip. Under Tony Blair, this committee continued as an informal group chaired initially by a non-cabinet minister, Peter Mandelson.[31]

In sum, the tasks of organizing the Downing Street and Cabinet Office machinery and of making the associated appointments, both of ministers and of political and senior civil service staff, fall principally to the institutional prime minister. The necessary exception is the appointment of ministers themselves. In the orchestration of these appointments public communication can be important. It is managed chiefly through the institutional premiership, the Downing Street organization, and not by the prime minister himself, either as performer or personal source. The day-to-day work of coordination of media strategy and public communication is also handled by the institutional premiership.

Most of the prime minister's time is spent actually *working the machinery*, rather than organizing and staffing it. The scope for public communication varies. The prime minister chairs the cabinet and some cabinet committees, and meets with individual ministers, seeking agreement on decisions. From 1990 to 1997 John Major chaired 271 cabinets and 189 cabinet committees and had 911 recorded meetings with individual ministers. In his first two years Blair chaired 86 cabinets and 178 cabinet committees and had 783 meetings with individual ministers.[32] All that, depending on the detail, is potentially newsworthy activity. It is the stuff of routine news management but there is no public performance.

The prime minister reports regularly to the Queen and manages the general relationship between the government and the monarchy, much of which is confidential. The prime minister's dealings with opposition leaders (on a so-called 'Privy Counsellor basis') are confidential too –

---

[31] Anthony Seldon, *Major*, London: Phoenix Books, 1997, pp. 601–2; Burch and Holliday, *The British Cabinet System*, pp. 100–2.

[32] Seldon, *Major*, appendix III; Kavanagh and Seldon, *The Powers behind the Prime Minister*, p. 286.

giving William Hague grounds for complaint, when negotiations about one of his recommendations for an honour were leaked.[33] Probably not more than twice in any incumbency, the prime minister will advise the Queen to dissolve parliament – obviously a major news item. From time to time, also, the prime minister will, with the Defence Secretary, 'deploy Her Majesty's forces in action', as Hennessy puts it.[34]

The prime minister meets with heads of government at home and abroad, and attends more and more international meetings. Often overseas trips involve ceremonial and ritual. Thompson and Donoughue calculated that from 1974 to 1979 Wilson and Callaghan between them had 160 meetings and 120 formal meals with overseas dignitaries and made 35 official visits overseas, taking some 75 days. By John Major's time these numbers had swelled considerably. He had 662 foreign visitors and spent 251 days overseas between December 1990 and May 1997, on 96 separate visits. Under Blair the numbers continued to grow. He made 63 official visits overseas just in his first two years – nearly twice the Wilson/Callaghan total in less than half the time. In the six months after 11 September 2001 he visited twenty-two countries – though many of them briefly.[35]

Both at home and abroad, some ceremonial, such as big sporting occasions, elides governing/non-governing and formal/informal roles. Any of these types of event can involve the prime minister in public performance, ranging from a summit press conference to a silent wreath-laying at the Cenotaph. The latter type of event is primarily symbolic; but the symbolism generally has the potential for political advantage. Mrs Thatcher made a surprise visit to British troops in the Falkland Islands in January 1983, six months after the islands were recaptured and some months before a triumphant general election, and milked it for publicity.[36] John Major visited troops in the Gulf War of 1991 and was filmed in appropriate kit, addressing them from a military vehicle. Tony Blair made a similar visit to Kosovo in 1999.

[33] William Hague, 'What I learned about Tony – the hard way', *Guardian*, 26 April 2002.
[34] Hennessy, *The Hidden Wiring*, p. 90.
[35] Robert J. Thompson and Lord Donoughue of Ashton, *On the Treadmill: Presidents and Prime Ministers at Work*, University of Strathclyde, 1989, p. 23; Seldon, *Major*, appendix III; Kavanagh and Seldon, *The Powers behind the Prime Minister*, p. 286; *Guardian*, 15 December 2001, 26 April 2002. According to Hennessy (*The Hidden Wiring*, p. 91, quoting *The Economist*), some two-thirds of overseas trips during Major's first three-and-a-half years in office were to member states of the European Union.
[36] For details see Bernard Ingham, *Kill the Messenger*, London: HarperCollins, 1991, pp. 298–303.

The prime minister's diary includes, further, an unceasing round of visits, generally including a speech, to hospitals, schools, factories, conferences. Typically these will launch a policy or mark some achievement. Major undertook 1,359 such engagements, excluding personal, party and constituency engagements, according to his biographer. The *Guardian* reported that Blair had given 173 political speeches outside parliament during his first five years in office. He had spent 'a good deal of time attending carefully staged visits', commented Peter Riddell. 'There is hardly a school, hospital or rundown council estate within a couple of miles of Downing Street – and hence within easy reach of television cameras – that has not had such a media event.'[37] In the preparation for most of this public performance, the institutional premiership will have contributed, to a great or less extent. But the personal prime minister, inescapably, is the performer – unless he palms the task off on another minister. At least as likely, he will have taken over the task from another minister.

One must not forget, lastly, an archaic kind of public communication: letters. President Jimmy Carter got into trouble by campaigning in 1976 with the promise 'I'll never lie to you' and then, in office, using a signature-writing machine – not just a letter-writing machine. A prime minister, fortunately, can spread much of his correspondence round the Whitehall departments, or to his party headquarters. But some has to be done. The scale of New Labour's victory in 1997, and perhaps Blair's populism, were reflected in a surge of correspondence. Heath received an average of three hundred letters a week from the public in 1970–4, and Major four hundred in 1995. Blair was allegedly getting ten thousand – an estimated 500,000 a year – by 2000. A new unit in Downing Street, the Direct Communications Unit, was set up to cope with them.[38]

Away from Downing Street an important set of tasks is the prime minister's *formal parliamentary work*. It is a fundamental principle of parliamentary government that the prime minister must be a member of parliament, which in practice means the House of Commons. But although parliament is part of the very bedrock of the job, helping determine its entire shape and the rhythms of its timetable, this does not mean that the prime minister has to turn up very often. In the first six months of his premiership, for instance, Tony Blair voted in only two of eighty-six divisions in the Commons. Moreover, as party leader the

---

[37] Seldon, *Major*, appendix III; *Guardian*, 26 April 2002; Peter Riddell, ch. 2 in Anthony Seldon (ed.), *The Blair Effect*, London: Little, Brown, 2001, p. 35.
[38] Kavanagh and Seldon, *The Powers behind the Prime Minister*, p. xi; *Guardian*, 10 February 2000; Number 10 website, 14 July 2000.

prime minister has a separate set of tasks, which are also carried out *at*, one may appropriately say, rather than *in* parliament. These events sometimes gain as much publicity as the others – for example, after a stormy meeting with backbenchers – though they are not normally supposed to be public. These count as informal tasks of the premiership. The distinction may seem strained, because the connection between the constitutional office of premier and the party institution which enables it to work is at its closest in the parliamentary arena. Nevertheless, they can be discussed separately, since they take place separately.

When the prime minister does turn up, it is to carry out the task of public performer in the Commons chamber. He never appears before any of the standing (legislative) committees. Nor did Blair's predecessors appear before any of the select committees which shadow the Whitehall departments and which became increasingly prominent during the last twenty years of the twentieth century. Winston Churchill set a crucial precedent in 1940, by separating the jobs of prime minister and leader of the House. The prime minister was thereby removed from close contact with the practical management of parliamentary business. His performances now consist in periodic visitations to answer questions, make statements, deliver set piece speeches and very occasionally intervene in debates.[39]

From 1961 to 1997 prime ministers answered questions for fifteen minutes twice a week on Tuesdays and Thursdays. Tony Blair halved the frequency to once a week for thirty minutes on Wednesdays. This left the arithmetic unchanged at twelve to fourteen hours a year. Previously, even after 1940, there was variation between prime ministers: sometimes they answered questions on four days each week. Question Time in general became increasingly standardized and institutionalized. Questions grew more topical and less specific. Frequently they asked simply about 'the prime minister's schedule for the day', the object being to catch the prime minister out with a specific supplementary. The leader of the opposition became progressively more prominent in the exchanges, to the extent eventually of being expected to intervene in every one. Question Time is one of the opposition leader's main, regular, assured publicity opportunities, with the chance of (temporarily) seizing the news agenda. The intrusion of television in 1989 raised the stakes.

[39]   The following account draws for its details principally on Dunleavy and Jones, ch. 12 in R. A. W. Rhodes and Patrick Dunleavy (eds), *Prime Minister, Cabinet and Core Executive*, London: Macmillan, 1995, and on June Burnham and G. W. Jones, 'Accounting to Parliament by British Prime Ministers: trends and discontinuities; illusions and realities', paper for the Political Studies Association annual conference, April 2000.

It accentuated still further the trend towards a 'more topical, gladiatorial and stylized' Question Time.[40]

The prime minister comes to the chamber to make statements chiefly about international summits and crises (especially crises which might involve British military forces), and important developments in British politics with which he is personally associated. Compared with Question Time, their use is more flexible. Harold Wilson made statements on 106 days in the sessions from 1964 to 1969, relishing his mastery of the Commons and dramatizing his personal grip on policy issues. In the run-up to the 1970 election, the number declined sharply. Mrs Thatcher used statements largely for international issues (85 per cent compared with 42 per cent for Wilson and 24 per cent for Heath). But she made far fewer anyway – on only 79 days in her eleven-and-a-half years of office, including fewer than five per session in her last five years. John Major increased the number somewhat to 71 over six years and four months – but this figure includes speeches too. Blair made 41 statements in his first five years.[41]

Dunleavy and Jones found that Mrs Thatcher brought the amount of speech-making by the prime minister to a low point too. The decline had been going on since the 1920s, with exceptions during times of acute crisis, such as Eden in the Suez crisis. The prime minister's main routine performances are in the debate on the annual Queen's Speech, setting out the legislative programme for the new session, in debates on the most important pieces of legislation, and in emergency debates or no-confidence debates called by the Opposition. Mrs Thatcher made cabinet colleagues do all but the most unavoidable speeches. Half her own speeches were on foreign affairs. Apart from the debate on the Queen's Speech, she spoke for fifteen minutes or more only 23 times between 1979 and 1990. After 1987 she spoke on just one day per session. Major and Blair continued the trend. In his first year Blair made only one set-piece speech – in the debate on the Speech from the Throne setting out the government's legislative programme. Otherwise 'he seems to have shied away from speeches . . .'.[42]

The fourth type of performance, intervening in debates, is defined by Dunleavy and Jones to take account of the idea of debate as interactive. Their measure is anything which Hansard records – which excludes body language but includes points of order and interjections. Between 1974 and 1990 prime ministers intervened scarcely at all. Callaghan

[40]   Rhodes and Dunleavy (eds), *Prime Minister, Cabinet and Core Executive*, p. 282.
[41]   Rhodes and Dunleavy (eds), *Prime Minister, Cabinet and Core Executive*, pp. 284–5; Seldon, *Major*, appendix III; *Guardian*, 26 April 2002.
[42]   Burnham and Jones, 'Accounting to Parliament by British Prime Ministers', p. 15.

intervened only fifteen times in four sessions and Thatcher sixteen times in her first five sessions. From 1985 onwards she intervened only once, shortly before her resignation. Major and Blair barely intervened either.[43]

The exceptionally large Labour majority won in 1997 enabled Tony Blair to pay less heed to the Commons than John Major, and he quickly established a reputation for being uninterested.[44] The number of days in which he took some part in proceedings reached an all-time low of 25 per cent. It is clear that, at least for the time being, a prime minister no longer needs to appear in the Commons as often as even quite recent predecessors. He can use the rules of procedure, as did Major and Blair, to make written reports – in answer to planted written questions – on subjects such as summits and visits abroad, about which Churchill, say, reported in person and took questions. His performances are highly formalized. He need never speak without preparation and a script. He performs almost entirely on his own terms, starting with the decision whether to perform at all.

Apart from rare emergency or no-confidence debates, Question Time is the one exception to all that. Here, his control is severely limited. Indeed it is arguably the formal performance over which he has least control in any location, inside parliament or out. Its high priority for the prime minister is reflected in the fact that Blair missed only seven out of a possible 169 Question Times during his first five years, while being in other ways a comparatively poor attender. The pressure to attend was all the greater because the sessions now happened only once a week, and in 2003 the Commons rescheduled them to the still more newsworthy time of twelve noon.[45]

Some of the unpredictability of Question Time is removed by preparation and by party management – for example the planting of friendly questions (the institutional premiership at work).[46] When the prime minister is on his feet looking across the chamber, however, he is on his own. The fewer such performances, one might argue, the greater the H-bomb deterrent effect. The fact that a well-prepared prime minister with an adequate majority is extremely unlikely to put on a terminally disastrous performance at Question Time does not mean his preparation

[43]   Rhodes and Dunleavy (eds), *Prime Minister, Cabinet and Core Executive*, pp. 293–4.
[44]   William Hague, writing a year after the 2001 election, remarked that Blair's 'distaste for the House of Commons is all too evident to MPs'. Hague, 'What I learned about Tony – the hard way'.
[45]   *Guardian*, 26 April 2002. The timetable change was one of several 'modernizing' initiatives by the House Leader, Robin Cook.
[46]   See Gyles Brandreth, *Breaking the Code*, London: Phoenix Books, 1999, pp. 93–4.

will have taken no account of the need to minimize the possibility that this might happen. It is no surprise that prime ministers get nervous.[47] For such reasons it is difficult to know how far the largely quantitative decline of performance traced by Dunleavy and Jones reflects a lowering of prime ministers' priority for their parliamentary work. It is also difficult to fit the work clearly into categories of prime ministerial tasks. In some ways, it is activity devoted to the achievement of general goals: managing the government's policies and legislative programme; maintaining a majority; building the prime minister's vision. In others, performance is public communication as an end in itself. If one takes the 'stylization' point far enough, indeed, prime ministerial performance might now be regarded as one of the nineteenth-century commentator Bagehot's 'dignified' parts of the constitution and no longer one of the 'efficient' parts.

Ritual, however, can be highly functional. If one of the purposes of parliament is to symbolize representative and responsible government, then a ritual display may sustain the symbolism. It is probably in this way that one should judge Blair's agreement in 2002, after much urging, to attend, twice a year, sessions of the committee composed of twenty-five chairmen of the thirty-five departmental select committees.[48] But however one views it, the prime minister's parliamentary activity is the part of his formal work which most regularly shows him as a public performer.

The Prime Minister's Informal Tasks

By definition, there is even more flexibility about the prime minister's informal tasks than the formal ones, since there are no external authorities defining them. Even more of them, too, perhaps, are likely to be carried out privately, and any public accounts of them will not originate either from the prime minister personally or the institutional premiership. One should also expect more variation between prime ministers. For all those reasons there is no point in seeking to give more than an indicative account of them.

---

[47] 'If Britain ever had a prime minister who did not fear Questions, our parliamentary democracy would be in danger.' Harold Wilson, *The Governance of Britain*, London: Weidenfeld and Nicolson and Michael Joseph, 1976, p. 132.

[48] The first meeting took place on 16 July 2002 and lasted two-and-a-half hours. Blair described the discussion as 'less combative, more constructive' than Question Time. *Guardian*, 17 July 2002.

The prime minister undertakes innumerable *informal executive activities* linked to the formal work of running the machinery of government. For example, cabinet and cabinet committee meetings are supplemented by informal and casual meetings with ministers, civil servants and a variety of other persons involved in policy matters. Their purpose is to pre-digest, concert, bypass, undermine – that is, in one way and another to manage – the outcomes of the formal machinery. Their informality includes such features as spontaneity or irregularity, varying and informal locations (such as aircraft), lack of agenda and minutes, or even of a clear outcome, and changing and uncertain membership. They were a device much used by Blair and are well illustrated by the nature of his dealings with the Chancellor, Gordon Brown. Peter Riddell, a well-placed journalist, writes that 'officials initially found it hard to penetrate the frequent Blair/Brown relationship and it was only after the arrival of Jeremy Heywood [private secretary] that a record was kept of their discussions'. More broadly, 'the idea that officials at Number 10 headquarters are smoothly pulling strings and levers, effortlessly controlling events, is ridiculous'.[49]

Knowledge of the existence of informal groups at cabinet level, though less often of their methods and meeting-places, entered the textbooks in the middle of the twentieth century. Lloyd George had a 'kitchen cabinet' of favoured ministers; Churchill had 'cronies'. Wilson had a varying group of intimates. Thatcher relied on a succession of fixers, including Willie Whitelaw and John Wakeham. Analysts (not excluding a prime minister's own colleagues) generally start looking for an 'inner cabinet' of some kind whenever a prime minister has settled into office. The recent demystification of the system has enabled academics to plot their incidence more elaborately than before, in the kind of literature discussed earlier.

Secretiveness is a common feature of these informal processes. Because they are likely to be seen as the 'real' ways in which policies and issues are settled, they are of great interest to journalists. The prime minister, both personally and through the agency of the press office – and, no doubt, of other intermediaries – will be active in managing the flow of information about them, as one method of getting his way.

The prime minister's *informal parliamentary tasks* are aimed principally at sustaining his reputation in the party among backbenchers. Neglect and isolation are dangerous risks. Eden lost touch during the build-up to the Anglo-French invasion of Suez in 1956. Thatcher did so in 1990, at a time of domestic difficulty with the unpopular 'poll tax'

---

[49]   Peter Riddell in Anthony Seldon (ed.), *The Blair Effect*, pp. 37, 38.

intended to replace the local authority rates. During the Conservative leadership contest forced upon her by backbenchers, she attached a higher priority to attending a European summit in Paris than to staying at home in order to bolster her support. The tea room, smoking room and bars at Westminster are the traditional haunts which from time to time a prime minister should visit. For instance both Wilson and Callaghan, the former aide Bernard Donoughue writes, 'spent a fair amount of time in the House of Commons both before and after Question Time, meeting with ministers and MPs who sought a brief word with them'.[50] Even the lengthy process of trooping through the voting lobbies in a division gives opportunities for chat, and John Major voted on many occasions, nursing his small majority after 1992, on days when he did not otherwise take part in proceedings.

The usual intermediary in these encounters is the prime minister's principal private secretary, who is chosen for his or her suitability to interpret the prime minister and the party to each other. His job will include attending party meetings on the prime minister's behalf, as well as dealing with individuals. Major's PPS 'would meet individual MPs for meals, and arrange for groups of them to take tea with Major'.[51] Such meetings do not necessarily take place at the Commons. Blair was keen on entertaining at Downing Street, for instance. Wherever they happen, they need more organizing than in the past, because MPs now have offices of their own – and these may be several minutes away from the Commons facilities. (See chapter 4.) Much of the casual contact in the public rooms of the Commons is a thing of the past.

Conclusion

That is a summary survey, and it takes no account of party activities carried out by the prime minister not strictly in that capacity. But it is enough to indicate that some of the prime minister's tasks *must* involve him in public communication, and others *may*. Only a few, concerned with security, positively ought not. The flexibility of both the formal and informal parts of the job give him great range as a performer and as a news source. A leitmotiv of the job can thus be the claim, a truism since Blair came to power but not so long ago a novelty, that presentation is part of substance. Whether a prime minister is wise to try and

[50] Thompson and Donoughue, *On the Treadmill: Presidents and Prime Ministers at Work*, p. 20.
[51] Burnham and Jones, 'Accounting to Parliament by British Prime Ministers', p. 15.

do something at all and, if so, what and how, are all matters affected, in this era of electronic glut, by whether the decision can be sold. The ultimate buyers are the electorate. Typically the prime minister uses public communication in conjunction with his formal powers. The formal powers, it was suggested at the start of the chapter, give him authority; public communication turns it into power. This process will be explored further in chapters 2 and 3.

2

Public Communication as a Prime Ministerial Resource

The prime minister can carry out some of his tasks to at least a minimum level of satisfaction, but not more than that, chapter 1 has suggested, without assistance from public communication. This chapter first illustrates the kind of powers enabling him to do that, and secondly discusses the nature of his public communication as a power resource.

The Prime Minister's Powers Independent of Public Communication

The prime minister's formal tasks of appointment and organization are carried out by powers derived from royal prerogative, convention and statute. When he was principally First Lord of the Treasury (as he still is formally), the basis of the prime minister's power was financial: command of the public purse, used in conjunction with patronage. Although it is based now in his position as party leader and is subject to more rules about 'standards in public life' than existed before the 1990s, the power of appointment remains largely untrammelled by formal restrictions.[1] Even the convention that a minister must sit in parliament is commonly fulfilled by putting an outside appointee in the Lords or, very rarely, in a specially vacated Commons constituency. When Tony Blair's friend and colleague Charles Falconer, to whom Blair wanted to give a ministerial job, failed to impress the Labour constituency selection committee towards which he was steered, he was made Lord Falconer instead.[2] Informally, however, the power of

---

[1] John Major established a committee in October 1994, initially under the chairmanship of Lord Nolan, on 'standards in public life', in response to cases of 'sleaze' during his premiership. The committee made a considerable impact on codes and procedures in public bodies.
[2] The leading trade unionist Frank Cousins was found a constituency in 1965 *after* appointment to Wilson's first cabinet.

appointment is modified by a variety of considerations, of which public presentation is one.

The power to appoint ministers is typical of the prime minister's 'command powers'. The authority of his decisions is firmly grounded – but the informal influences affecting them (and their eventual success) can be a big constraint. Such powers apply generally to the institutional prime minister's management of the civil and armed services. They include historic but influential relics like the Privy Council oath sworn by ministers, which formally underpins cabinet secrecy and informally is often disregarded. The Official Secrets Acts provide a comparable statutory underpinning of secrecy.

The tension between formal power and informal constraint is perhaps best illustrated in the convention of collective cabinet responsibility. Even what this term *should* mean constitutionally, let alone what it does mean, is endlessly disputed. In simple terms, it is summed up in the saying, 'If we don't hang together, we shall all hang separately'.[3] Its essence is a point of public communication: ministers (not only the score or so in the cabinet) must publicly support and share responsibility for the government's policies, or else resign. Regardless of whether the principle means ministers ought to (or realistically could) be involved in making 'cabinet' decisions, the principle is undoubtedly a powerful prime ministerial instrument of coordination and discipline. As *The Ministerial Code* illustrates, it justifies the prime minister requiring ministers to clear their speeches in advance with the Downing Street press office. More importantly, the principle entitles the prime minister to interfere in a ministerial colleague's departmental business. In particular, as Mrs Thatcher's powerful Chancellor, Nigel Lawson, wryly commented, it gives the prime minister a *de facto* power of veto over specific policies.[4] (Forcing a policy upon a reluctant colleague, by contrast, is more difficult and requires more elaborate efforts by the prime minister.)

The equally contested principle of individual ministerial responsibility (that is, for actions done in the minister's name in a department) gives the prime minister, in the same way, the formal authority to dismiss a minister who has become a liability. The sensitive judgement whether it is wise to do so generally involves issues of news management and estimates of public perception. This is especially true when

---

[3]   This remark was made by Benjamin Franklin to John Hancock, when they signed the Declaration of Independence in Philadelphia on 4 July 1776. It is often quoted as applicable to the cabinet.

[4]   Quoted by Martin Smith in *The Core Executive in Britain*, London: Macmillan, 1999, p. 90.

a minister has been hounded by the media and there is a large gap between actual incompetence and the volume of media complaint – as happened to Transport and Local Government Secretary Stephen Byers in 2002.

A number of powers which strictly are informal also help the prime minister accomplish his tasks successfully, without resort to public communication. One is the culture of *the Whitehall bureaucracy*. This broad term includes the traditions of civil service anonymity, loyalty and non-partisanship. All of them were under stress at the start of the new millennium. It will be interesting to see how far their decline weakens the authority of the institutional premiership, and how far the reforms proposed in the Blair administration (such as opening top jobs to candidates who have not worked their way up through an entire Whitehall career) provide an equally efficient alternative.

Second are the powers of *party discipline*. At Westminster the whips can play on MPs' ambitions, loyalty and weaknesses. Party competition supplies the backdrop, especially when the opposition is strong. In general a prime minister gets his way. Beyond Westminster the weapons are different and control is less (patronage, honours, invitations to the inner circles).

Third are the many and various methods by which a prime minister can form *coalitions* within and between the institutions and groups comprising the core executive. These are the stuff of the new wave of literature about the prime minister. To give just one example, Mrs Thatcher, when in an ideological minority in her first cabinet, advanced her monetarist economic goals by the device of sidelining economic policy into key cabinet committees from which her opponents were excluded.[5] Later she operated largely outside the formal cabinet committee system altogether, through informal meetings with ministers and advisers. In the words of Nigel Lawson, she came to believe that 'her colleagues were troublesome and her courtiers loyal', and she turned Downing Street into a bunker.[6] The corollary of a prime minister concerting support for policy in such ways is the attempted construction by powerful colleagues of coalitions to thwart him. Thus Lawson and Douglas Hurd, and then Hurd and John Major, managed to thwart Mrs Thatcher's opposition to British membership of the European exchange

---

[5]   Smith, *The Core Executive in Britain*, p. 89.
[6]   Nigel Lawson, *The View from No. 11*, London: Corgi Books edn, 1993, p. 680. Cf. Peter Hennessy, *The Hidden Wiring*, London: Indigo, 1996, p. 109. The long-term consequence was that Thatcher failed to secure the loyalty of her cabinet colleagues when her leadership was challenged.

rate mechanism.[7] Tony Blair did a lot of business in 'bilaterals' – meetings with individual ministers.

Public Communication as a Power Resource

Reference to coalition-building leads the discussion into the area of public communication, for public communication is an important, if frequently indirect, part of a minister's resources. Martin Smith's list of instruments giving leverage against the prime minister includes a minister's authority, political support, information, policy networks, policy record and available time.[8] The prime minister's own resources have much in common with these. The way in which communication fits into them can be summarized in four related parts. First, in his role as communications manager he oversees a stronger *media management machine* than his rivals. Secondly, the formal position of prime minister gives him unrivalled *direct access to media* in his roles as performer and news source. Thirdly, those two factors enable him to *manage his personal image*, so as to add the influence of informal reputation to that of formal authority. Last, by all or any of those means he can exploit the *flexibility of the prime ministership* to best advantage.

The media management machine

The Downing Street press office is the subject of chapters 6 and 7. For the purposes of an analysis of the nature of prime ministerial power, its chief feature lies in being the institutional expression of the prime minister's control over the flow of information about the core executive. Its purpose is to sustain popular support for the government by winning acceptance for the government's version of events and by defeating other versions.

The interest of prime ministers personally in this process has fluctuated. Mrs Thatcher's long incumbency saw the development of the office to an unprecedented peak of influence inside Downing Street, though without any disproportionate increase of resources.[9] Mrs Thatcher was a willing learner as a public performer. John Major, for all that he was

[7] Britain joined in October 1990. For a case study, see Martin Burch and Ian Holliday, *The British Cabinet System*, London: Prentice Hall/Harvester Wheatsheaf, 1996, pp. 220–6.

[8] Smith, *The Core Executive in Britain*, p. 75.

[9] J. M. Lee, G. W. Jones and June Burnham, *At the Centre of Whitehall*, London: Macmillan, 1998, ch .5.

troubled by the ubiquitous intrusions of television, seemed in comparison to give the management of his communications a lower priority. He left coordination to Michael Heseltine as deputy prime minister. His first two press secretaries were senior civil servants and his third – when the government was at its weakest – was a specialist information officer, whose authority even within Whitehall was less than theirs. Major's own attempts to woo media barons and editors were ineffectual.[10]

The contrast between Major and the incoming Blair administration was stark and immediate. As chapter 1 indicated, Blair gave media management a high priority. His press secretary, Alastair Campbell, a political appointee, was a key member of the prime minister's entourage. Ministerial direction came from another close Blair associate, Peter Mandelson. Downing Street news operations were expanded and given more control across Whitehall. Departmental ministers acquired their own political press advisers. Methods of feedback, including polls, focus groups, media monitoring and rebuttal, brought the techniques of winning office into government itself. The lack of a strong ideology in the New Labour programme made the emphasis on 'style' even more noticeable.

The prime minister's control over the flow of information is increased by his possession of a superior strategic vantage point to that of his colleagues. He is the only minister with an overall view of the main concerns of the government, since most other ministers are blinkered by the problems of their own departments (especially if they run big spending departments like Health and Defence). In particular, the prime minister has a near monopoly, with the Chancellor, of information about the economy and public spending, and, with the Foreign Secretary, of information about foreign affairs. His manipulation of the flow of information within the core executive is a great help in managing his colleagues.

Manipulation of the flow of information out to the news media is also a means of managing colleagues. In this case, it is typically characterized as the management of secrecy, with leaks as the currency of exchange in dealings between the prime minister and ministers. Secrecy/publicity within and outside the core executive is best seen as a continuum. A piece of information will be more or less public according to who knows it, and different groups of people – journalists, civil

---

[10]   The most notorious example of ineffective lobbying was a call after Black Wednesday in 1992 to the editor of the *Sun*, Kelvin Mackenzie, which produced a loud and abusive response. Mackenzie was reported to have said, 'I've got a large bucket of shit lying on my desk and tomorrow morning I'm going to pour it all over your head'. Andrew Neil, *Full Disclosure*, London: Macmillan, 1996, p. 9.

servants, interest groups, party officials and ministers themselves – may learn it at different times. The dynamics of political journalism allow journalists to acquire confidential information long before they publish it openly. The conventions of publication themselves include gradations of disclosure, from the unattributed hint or clear statement, through generalized attributions such as 'government sources', to named but qualified sources ('the minister is said to believe'). Such leaks are not necessarily accurate; indeed they may be deliberate disinformation.

The continuum between total secrecy and total publicity is so long partly because the policy-making process is often not so much secret as secretive. That is, ministers wish publicity to come at a time of their own choosing, not their opponents'. Cabinet secrecy is an obvious example and, within that, the contents of the Budget. These matters are disclosed even to cabinet ministers only a day or so in advance (and introduced, certainly in Wilson's time, by 'a blistering invocation of secrecy').[11] But leaks on any scale annoy prime ministers, and major leaks infuriate them. These latter provoke usually fruitless witch hunts, sometimes consuming the time even of the head of the civil service. They are justifiable because they soothe the *amour propre* of the prime minister and for symbolic rather than practical purposes.

Prime ministers react because leaks are a threat to their personal or institutional control of the news agenda of the core executive. Further, they may damage the prime minister's public reputation, through revealing his government as divided and his leadership, implicitly, as weak. This damage in turn may reduce his ability to direct policy. The cabinet secretary under Major, Robin Butler, was so concerned by ministerial divisions that he warned Major that some ministers were refusing to bring business to cabinet meetings for fear of leaks.[12]

None of these problems applies (or is anticipated, perhaps) when the prime minister himself leaks. But then the prime minister never does leak: he 'gives guidance'. Leaks are unauthorized disclosures by your enemies; guidance is authorized disclosure by yourself or your agents (such as your press secretary). Harold Wilson irritated ministers by leaking, as Richard Crossman grumbled to his diary. But Crossman too, habitually, as he saw it, gave guidance.[13] On one occasion in Edward

---

[11] Harold Wilson, *The Governance of Britain*, London: Weidenfeld and Nicolson and Michael Joseph, 1976, p. 59.

[12] *Guardian*, 6 October 1999, reporting a BBC film about the Major government. See also, for Major's problems with leaks about European policy in early 1995, Anthony Seldon, *Major*, London: Phoenix Books, 1997, pp. 519–24.

[13] Richard Crossman, *The Diaries of a Cabinet Minister*, London: Hamish Hamilton and Jonathan Cape, 3 vols, 1975, 1976, 1977, vol. 1, e.g. pp. 227, 551, 580.

Heath's premiership civil servants had to halt a leak inquiry, when they discovered Heath himself was the leaker.[14] Mrs Thatcher rarely briefed journalists, but some of those briefings of her press secretary, Bernard Ingham, which most provoked her parliamentary colleagues included guidance to journalists, in rich imagery, about the vulnerable position of ministers who were later sacked.[15] Alastair Campbell appeared to give advance warning in a similar way about the departure of ministers Harriet Harman and Frank Field in July 1998.

The purpose of a leak is to try and change people's expected behaviour by introducing new information which may affect their judgement. Leaking is intrinsic to the group dynamics of competitive party politics in a parliamentary and cabinet system. Thus it was predictable that when Tony Blair allowed individual ministers to have their own partisan press secretaries, he would find that they started leaking against each other. It was equally predictable that when Blair found before long that the Chancellor's secretary, Charlie Whelan, was creating bad feeling by prejudicial briefings, he would not tolerate it. Whelan had to resign.[16]

The line between leaking and spinning can be fine. Narrowly defined, leaking means disclosure of facts. But facts acquire significance by being put in context, and spinning involves doing exactly that. The leakers who get caught and punished are typically civil servants. They are pursued relentlessly, for they challenge the political supremacy of the institutional prime minister over the bureaucracy, and especially over the flow of information to ministers and the public. The two notorious cases of the Thatcher era were the successful prosecution of a junior clerk and the unsuccessful prosecution of a senior official, both in the Ministry of Defence.[17] A prime minister, whether personally or institutionally, can never expect fully to control the flow of information – what

[14] *The Times*, 3 January 2003, reporting documents released in the Public Record Office.
[15] The two best examples concerned Francis Pym (Leader of the Commons) in 1982 and John Biffen (also Leader of the Commons) in 1986. For Ingham's own account, see Bernard Ingham, *Kill the Messenger*, London: HarperCollins, 1991, ch. 20.
[16] In particular, Whelan was blamed for the leaks which led to Mandelson's resignation in December 1998. *Guardian*, 14 January 1999.
[17] The clerk, Caroline Tisdall, leaked details about the arrival in Britain of American Cruise missiles; she was sentenced to six months in jail in 1984. Clive Ponting, an Assistant Secretary, was acquitted in 1985 of breaching the Official Secrets Acts by leaking documents about the sinking of an Argentinian battle cruiser in the Falklands War. David Hooper, *Official Secrets*, London: Secker and Warburg, 1988. In the first three years of the Blair government, ministers set up sixty leak investigations. In Major's last two years there were seventy. *Guardian*, 14 February 2000.

is conveyed, when, and with what understanding. But he is in a better position to try than anyone else in the core executive.

The prime minister's media access

Later chapters explore issues about the prime minister's direct relations with media, so this section again is only indicative. One way of visualizing the scale of the prime minister's newsworthiness – and of his predicament in managing it – is to ask how long he could disappear from public (or journalists') view before something was suspected to be wrong. When Winston Churchill suffered a stroke on 23 June 1953, his condition was hushed up. A medical bulletin was changed from referring to a 'disturbance of the cerebral circulation' to saying he was 'in need of a complete rest'. His principal private secretary, John Colville, was able to reflect afterwards that 'Not a word of the prime minister's stroke was published until he himself casually mentioned it in a speech in the House of Commons a year later'.[18] Those days are long past. Now, a period of unexplained disappearance could presumably last only a matter of hours rather than days, except at the weekend or during the summer holidays. Not all explanations might be credible, but an explanation of some sort would have to be given. The challenge, as in the previous section, is for the prime minister to control and manage his media access, both as news source and as performer.

It is difficult to be sure how far the prime minister has become more newsworthy as a source in the electronic age. The fact that he cannot hide from the media does not in itself mean that media actually wish to report him incessantly. It is easier to explore the growth of his role as a public performer. The collective memory is losing its grasp of just how inaccessible television and radio were for politicians until at least the 1960s.[19] Politicians used to broadcast rarely. Access was determined by principles and rules (originally set or agreed by politicians) safeguarding balance, fairness and impartiality. The government had an overriding authority to require that something be broadcast (or not); but this was seen as a power of last resort and was almost never used, except for a few general categories, such as the provision of party political broadcasts and the ban on Irish extremists in the 1980s. Thus Anthony Eden was shocked to discover in 1956 that he could not simply address

---

[18]   *The Times*, 1 February 1984; John Colville, *The Fringes of Power*, vol. 2, London: Sceptre, 1987, p. 329.

[19]   For a summary of stages in the growth of political broadcasting, see Colin Seymour-Ure, *The British Press and Broadcasting since 1945*, Oxford: Blackwell, 2nd edn, 1996, ch. 7.

the nation on radio and TV at will about the Suez crisis. Strictly, he had to be 'invited' to make a 'ministerial broadcast'; and the invitation was likely to involve the offer of a 'right of reply' to the leader of the opposition. Eden even contemplated trying to commandeer the BBC. In the 1982 Falklands War Mrs Thatcher was similarly affronted by broadcasting even-handedness.[20]

In normal times, and regardless of which party was in office, Downing Street and the whips kept control of which politicians broadcast on the narrow range of potentially available programmes. In addition, and as a kind of substitute for paid political advertising, the parties produced their own programmes, the annual series of party political (and election) broadcasts, in meticulously negotiated and measured slots.

By the end of the century the principles of balance and impartiality survived, but with increasing strain. For the prime minister access has become a matter of ensuring that as far as possible he broadcasts on his own terms. (See chapter 8.) At its most comprehensive, he must ideally want control, on any given occasion, over whether he broadcasts or is electronically reported at all, over the location, duration, content and audience, over the purposes of the occasion (for instance a conference), if it is not exclusively for broadcasting, over the conditions of participation by any other persons, and over the recording's subsequent use. Where control is unpractical, he will look for compensating advantages. Phone-ins involve peculiar risks: callers do not always play by the same rules as interviewers, and they have to be treated with the respect due from the elected to the electorate. But the populist rewards make the risks worth taking. A joust with a tough *Newsnight* or *Today* interviewer carries the risk of piercing the prime minister's armour; but its scope and format can be controlled, and a good result can help his reputation and poll ratings.

So when the prime minister lacks control, it should in principle be deliberate and foreseen. It is no accident that prime ministers have made some of their more memorable damaging remarks when caught on the hop. In January 1979 Callaghan's insouciance rightly made his political adviser's heart sink when he descended the aeroplane steps into icy industrial unrest after a summit in the balmy Caribbean and appeared to make light of the national discomfort.[21] John Major's 'bastards' remark to ITN's political editor about the disloyalty of Euro-sceptic

[20] Michael Cockerell, *Live from Number 10*, London: Faber and Faber, 1989, pp. 44–52, 268–75.
[21] The *Sun*'s headline, 'CRISIS – WHAT CRISIS?', accurately conveyed Callaghan's remarks to journalists on his arrival. For a detailed account, quoting the adviser, see Cockerell, *Live from Number 10*, pp. 242–3. See also chapter 8 below.

cabinet colleagues in July 1993, when he thought the microphone was dead, similarly haunted him.[22]

Access to print media has changed much less than that to broadcasting, since the basic structure of the press was comparatively unchanged in the second half of the twentieth century. A prime minister is faced with a small number of rich publishers, often larger than life and rarely owning national papers with the sole aim of maximizing profits. (See chapter 5.) As in the past, it is normal for newspapers to be partisan. A few prime ministers, notably Wilson, have prided themselves on being on the same wavelength as political journalists. Churchill and Macmillan mingled naturally with the longer-established press barons. Successors with less grand backgrounds (Heath, for example) have had to work harder to achieve familiarity and influence. Blair's courting of Rupert Murdoch in the run-up to the 1997 general election was widely remarked in the press. Most modern prime ministers, perhaps all, have given occasional exclusive newspaper interviews; but Tony Blair was the most ready to offer articles over his own signature. After a couple of years the novelty wore off, but he continued to do it and he extended the practice to the internet.[23] In February 2000 he started weekly internet broadcasts on the Number 10 website.

Access to print media is immensely more difficult for the prime minister to manage than access to the broadcast media. Central to the powerful and emotive idea of 'press freedom', after all, is precisely the principle that the government should not be able to control the press. But the point to emphasize in this section is that the prime minister's position gives him unmatched access and the opportunity to try and get himself projected as he would wish.

The prime minister's public personal image

The prime minister's opportunity to design his own image is a modern variant of the truism that he 'writes his own job description'. The aim is to bolster his formal authority through skilful manipulation of his personal reputation by public performance and media management. His reputation is a combination of popular approval, for himself directly and for his government indirectly, as measured in the opinion polls, and of approval by his party, especially at Westminster. Historically his image was both more narrowly based and more indirectly conveyed.

[22] See Anthony Seldon, *Major*, pp. 389–91. The three 'bastards' were understood to be Peter Lilley, Michael Portillo and John Redwood.
[23] Blair published New Year articles to mark the millennium, for example, in the *People*, *Sunday Mirror* and *News of the World*.

The principal places in which the prime minister used to perform were parliament and the public platform, and the audiences observing him were small. Published reports could convey only a very limited image of the prime minister as a person. Few people heard his voice. Once people could see and hear him as often as they read about him, the opportunities multiplied for matching different versions of his image to specific audiences.

The office of prime minister, personal and institutional, brings its own image to the incumbent. Its strongest visual element is probably the front door of 10 Downing Street. In Washington the White House is a similar but much more solid and three-dimensional image of the presidency. The flat, shut, black Number 10 door reflects the historic insubstantiality of the premiership. Nor does the prime minister have a grand seal like that of the president, prominent on lectern or backdrop. The crown is not his; nor is the portcullis – the brand image of parliamentary government. These subtleties can even attract media attention to such trivialities as the prime minister's Christmas card: in 1999 some observers thought the formal pose of the prime minister and his wife more 'regal' than 1998's more informal group with the children.

Ministers themselves respond to the aura surrounding the premiership.[24] It is implicit in the idea of a prime ministerial honeymoon. For the viewing public it is given effect in representative and ceremonial rituals such as memorial services, occasional appearances on the balcony at Buckingham Palace or in the royal box at the opera during state visits, and in attendance at scenes of national disaster and at highly charged sporting occasions. Otherwise lacking tangible form, the prime ministerial image is nonetheless institutionalized and given shape by the precision with which it can be measured in polls and focus groups and the resources spent in doing so.

In managing his personal image the prime minister uses the characteristics and experiences of his informal and non-governing roles to illustrate and symbolize qualities which will give weight to his formal authority. The difficulty of demonstrating that a prime minister possesses the professional skills appropriate to the job has become greater with the rise of the professional politician. What a new prime minister has shown in the process of getting the job is that somehow he has won the confidence of his party elite and activists, and perhaps that he has

[24] Bernard Donoughue, working as an adviser in Downing Street, commented: 'It is very striking to observe how, from the moment Mr Callaghan became Prime Minister, other politicians who had been friends and life-long colleagues began to behave differently towards him. There is a charisma attached to the occupancy of No. 10.' Donoughue, *Prime Minister*, London: Jonathan Cape, 1987, p. 13.

won a general election. But none of that necessarily makes him a good prime minister, let alone a statesman or commander. Given their normally long parliamentary apprenticeship, it is surprising that so many prime ministers, certainly since 1960, have come to the office with little or no cabinet experience. Wilson, Heath and Thatcher had not held senior cabinet positions. Major held the two senior offices of Chancellor and Foreign Secretary – but only for eighteen months in total. Blair had never held ministerial office at all. Only Callaghan came to the premiership (in 1976) with a strong ministerial record as Chancellor, Home Secretary and Foreign Secretary.

How do you carry conviction with interest groups, the City, foreign diplomats, the long-term unemployed? In 1964 Wilson projected himself as a government professional – economist, meritocrat, former civil servant, enthused by and for (in a party conference speech) the 'white heat of the technological revolution'. Leader unexpectedly after Hugh Gaitskell's death in 1963, he competed against an equally unexpected prime minister, Alec Douglas-Home. Douglas-Home disliked television, was a slow learner, made no apparent effort to display political professionalism and talked of matchsticks in an interview about economic policy. It might be said that Douglas-Home was content with an image of what he was, while Wilson sought to convey what he could *do*. The latter practice is typical of the professional politician. Lacking actual experience, aspirant prime ministers present themselves as determined, energetic, intelligent, hardworking, focused, ready to hear advice, well briefed, quick on the uptake. Implicitly, they pray in aid the institutional premiership to back up the personal prime minister. Media profiles may allude to how little they sleep, how fit they keep, how fast they read, how brilliant were their exam results: indices, all, of exceptional capacities.[25]

Prime ministers have to protect themselves, conversely, against images of incompetence. They get old: Churchill, 76 at the start of his post-war premiership in 1951, was stage-managed skilfully by staff and family. They become ill (Churchill again, Eden during Suez, Macmillan with his

---

[25]   Mrs Thatcher, for instance, was said to need only four or five hours' sleep. Burch and Holliday, *The British Cabinet System*, p. 149, citing A. Thomson, *Margaret Thatcher*, London: W. H. Allen, 1989. On Harold Wilson as prodigy, see Leslie Smith, *Harold Wilson*, London: Fontana, 1964, esp. ch. 2. During the 1997 general election which brought New Labour to office, the depiction in the tabloids of the untried Blair's competence to govern was almost entirely in terms of general personality traits – strong, dynamic, purposeful, trustworthy. Colin Seymour-Ure, 'Leaders and leading articles', ch. 10 in I. Crewe, B. Gottschalk and J. Bartle (eds), *Political Communications: Why Labour Won the General Election of 1997*, London: Frank Cass, 1998.

prostate in 1963), tired (Wilson in 1976), out of touch (Macmillan in 1962–3, Thatcher in 1989–90), depressed (Major, after the ERM debacle in 1992). In all such cases, the collective aspects of cabinet government and the resources of the institutional premiership are a boon to the personal prime minister. But even if the public image remains positive (as Churchill's did), reputation at Westminster may slump. Almost as many prime ministers left office from 1945 to 1957 during the course of a parliament (five) as following defeat in a general election (six).[26]

Professional skills shade into images of personality. Eden was known for his charm (his bad temper was less apparent), Macmillan for his languid Edwardian unflappability and 'grouse moor' image, Heath for his awkwardness, except with intimates. Wilson made sure he was much in view as England's football team won the 1966 World Cup, and he was photographed with the Beatles after they collected the MBEs awarded on his recommendation. Mrs Thatcher was dealt an image-maker's ace when President Gorbachev, in the late stages of the Cold War, dubbed her the 'iron lady'. She played up to it, not least with Valkyrie images of tank-riding after the Falklands War. Her sex appeal, though well attested by colleagues, was difficult to convey as part of a public prime ministerial image. In fact, her gender contributed a surprisingly small part to her personal image. Although she was far from being an honorary man, her personal skills, as publicly communicated, involved imagery such as 'handbagging' opponents – female, yes: but feminine, no.

Professional skills and personality define a prime minister's individual style. Even if John Major had not been by temperament a consensus manager, the media would have looked for signs that he was, on the assumption he would wish to distinguish himself from the confrontational, interventionist style of Mrs Thatcher. How far he would have liked to distance himself from her became plain only with the publication of a biography and his memoirs.[27] Harold Wilson the common man relished beer and sandwiches with union leaders at Number 10, in contrast to Douglas-Home's patrician style. Blair projected an informal style through portrayals of his working habits (shirtsleeves and sofa, at first) and his use of first names. When he started to wear reading glasses (which made front-page pictures), the frames were studied for the style message they sent.[28]

[26] Wilson is counted twice in those figures – in 1970 and 1976.
[27] Seldon, *Major*; John Major, *Major: the Autobiography*, London: HarperCollins, 1999.
[28] New frames worn during the 2002 World Cup drew joking questions from journalists about their Swedish look and England's Swedish football manager.

As a prime minister's tenure lengthens, his image will draw more on experience in office. But prime ministers can never altogether escape their backgrounds. Principal among the non-governing features which may influence the governing image are the classic British marks of class. Just as class is a complex factor in voting behaviour, so is it in prime ministers' images. Its effects can be nuanced and turned to advantage, but few prime ministers are likely to disregard them, even in the age of the professional politician. Macmillan could play the Scottish crofter's grandson, the bourgeois publisher, or the toff married to a duke's daughter. Wilson, Heath and Thatcher could play on working class and petit bourgeois roots, or on the professional class attributes acquired through education.

Education is central to class image. Journalists note the number of Old Etonians in a Conservative cabinet and of Oxbridge graduates in any cabinet. Eden, Macmillan and Douglas-Home were all Etonians. But two of Labour's four post-1945 prime ministers were educated at public schools (Attlee and Blair), while the three Conservative prime ministers since 1970 went to state schools (Heath, Thatcher and Major). Oxbridge is the truer gauge of privilege, particularly in a century which ended suspicious of 'elitism'. But Oxbridge elitism strongly reflects meritocracy.

Class background can be modified by self-presentation. The media enjoyed noting that Wilson smoked cigars for pleasure but lugged out his pipe and revived his regional accent on party occasions and TV. Blair was noticed adopting down-market 'estuarine' vowels and glottal stops when talking to down-market audiences or media programmes. Heath, Thatcher and Major, upwardly mobile Conservatives, ignored such artifices. Thatcher, on the other hand, did learn to lower her voice, to make it less shrill. As a woman she had exceptional scope for projecting an image through clothes and hairstyles. Churchill made the boiler suit a personal trademark, Eden had a hat named after him, and Wilson popularized the Gannex mac. (Cf. chapter 10 on political cartoons.)

Prime ministers are more likely than in the past to have spent their entire careers as full-time professional politicians, and their occupational backgrounds send fewer class signals than formerly. Heath never had much of a job at all before entering politics. Thatcher, especially in her early days in office, emphasized her science background. Until Thatcher post-war prime ministers were all within the age range which gave them experience during one of the world wars. Attlee, Eden and Macmillan fought in World War I (Churchill even as a semi-combatant in the Boer War). The war was a common refrain in Macmillan's speeches – for example about European policy. Heath and Callaghan fought in World War II; Wilson was a civil servant. It was a matter of comment during the Falklands crisis in 1982 that ministers without military experience (including Mrs Thatcher) were more hawkish than their colleagues.[29] Major and Blair were not old enough even to have done the compulsory two years' National Service abolished in the late 1950s.

The prime minister's interests and accomplishments can be accommodated to his image. In a phrase coined by Denis Healey, he needs a 'hinterland'. This idea is an echo of the English cult of the amateur: prime ministers should be good at something apart from politics. Again, it is a development brought on by the professionalization of politics, and also by the erosion of privacy in a television era. Churchill was a polymath (and his painting inspired President Eisenhower to have a go). Attlee seemed to lack a hinterland, but in the 1940s it did not matter. Eden presented a very stylish and well-groomed image in public. Macmillan and Douglas-Home were landowners and enjoyed country pursuits. Macmillan talked about literature. Douglas-Home and Major were excellent cricketers. Heath was an organ scholar at Oxford. As prime minister he conducted high-profile orchestras and took a widely publicized Christmas carol service every year in his boyhood church. He deliberately took up competitive ocean sailing in 1966 as a 'hinterland' interest. While in office, remarkably, he captained the victorious British team in the Admiral's Cup.[30]

Hinterland in a different sense may be filled with family and friends. Here the erosion of the prime minister's privacy in the last thirty years of the twentieth century is both threat and opportunity. The prime minister now has no practical alternative but, through media management, to define the private so as to fit a public image. The prime minister's spouse is the most interesting example. In the first half of the century spouses could – and did – remain almost entirely in the background. If a prime minister's marriage was under strain the media regarded it as his own affair. Lloyd George and his secretary could maintain a long-term relationship without threat to his position. As late as the early 1960s the long liaison between Macmillan's wife and the maverick Conservative politician, Bob Boothby, could remain private. Thereafter the mood changed. When journalists thought they sniffed adultery by Wilson in 1963–4, Wilson's solicitors had to threaten writs, to prevent 'the rumour' surfacing in print during the 1964 general election. By the

[29] See, e.g., M. Hastings and S. Jenkins, *The Battle for the Falklands*, London: Michael Joseph, 1983, chs 6 and 8.
[30] See John Campbell, *Edward Heath*, London: Pimlico, 1993, pp. 498–9.

1990s, the prime minister might even have to contemplate going to court. John Major became in 1993 only the fourth prime minister since 1900 to sue for libel while in office, when he acted to protect the reputation of a Downing Street catering manager with whom he was rumoured to have had an affair. In fact he did have an affair, with the exhibitionist Conservative MP Edwina Currie, but it ended shortly before he became prime minister. The affair might certainly have prevented him getting the post, had it been disclosed at the time.[31]

Apart from such problems prime ministers were allowed to let their spouses enjoy remarkable privacy even into the 1990s. Mrs Attlee was known chiefly for her bad driving, which was noticeable since she chauffeured her husband in election campaigns. Mrs Churchill was familiar largely because of her public work in the war. The wives of Eden, Macmillan, Douglas-Home and Callaghan formed almost no part of their husbands' public image. The lack of a Heath spouse worried party managers for a time, and he was encouraged, as a PR stunt, to display a girl on his yacht.[32] Once Heath was in Downing Street, the issue did not matter. Mary Wilson, who greatly valued her privacy, sacrificed some of it by publishing poetry. This was hazardous, for she was mocked in media such as *Private Eye*.

At the time when the potential for image management was developing most strongly, the prime minister's spouse was a man. Denis Thatcher was constantly in view, as Mrs Thatcher travelled around. But he went heroically unheard, a seemingly benign and humanizing presence. His contribution to the prime minister's image was, so to speak, integrated but one-dimensional. Like Mary Wilson, whose fictional 'diary' was published in *Private Eye*, Denis Thatcher's supposed attitudes, derived from his appearance and his CV, were affectionately satirized in that magazine – and on the London stage. Both these spouses, intriguingly, may have contributed to the prime minister's image not by their actual behaviour so much as through sustained literary fantasy.

If Cherie Blair had been in Downing Street in the 1980s, there is no reason to suppose that she could not have become as prominent a part of the prime minister's image as she did in the late 1990s. Her work as a barrister did not in itself put her in the public eye. The difference lay

---

[31]   The catering manager rumours surfaced in a small magazine, *Scallywag*. Major and Latimer acted when they were amplified in the *New Statesman*. The matter was settled out of court. (See also chapter 9 below.) Major's affair with Edwina Currie became public when Currie published her diaries in 2002. Edwina Currie, *Diaries 1987–92*, London: Little, Brown, 2002.

[32]   See, e.g., Andrew Roth, *Heath and the Heathmen*, London: Routledge and Kegan Paul, 1972, pp. 8–9.

in her desire simply to share appropriate parts of her husband's job, especially bearing in mind that she had herself been a parliamentary candidate in 1983. The change was reflected in the unprecedented appointment at Downing Street of an assistant for her – part of whose role was as a press secretary. For the first time, the prime minister's spouse was formally recognized in the institutional premiership. Her image was incorporated into his.[33]

This innovation, arguably, was overdue. In the United States the president's wife has had her own office since Franklin Roosevelt's first administration in 1932. Indeed Eleanor Roosevelt, a formidable public personality in her own right, gave women-only press conferences, in some years once a month or more, right up until the president's death in 1945.[34] In both Canada and Australia, too, prime ministers' spouses obtained offices of their own much earlier. But in both countries, where Governor-Generals have less prominence than the Queen in Britain, the wife has had more of a 'First Lady' role than in Downing Street.[35]

The novelty of Cherie Blair's position showed up at the edges in uncertainties about formal/informal and governing/non-governing distinctions. These had a material side, in addition to the risk of occasionally putting her foot in it with an injudicious remark. The Blairs were said to be fretting after two-and-a-half years in office, for example, about the cost to their private budget of wardrobe items (and hairdressing) necessary to suit the highest standards of prime ministerial image.[36]

Far more important than wardrobes and injudicious remarks, however, was 'Cheriegate', late in 2002. This episode, strictly, was 'private' to Mrs Blair. It involved the purchase of two flats in Bristol, one for investment and the other for Euan, who had started as a student

[33]   This should not be taken to exclude the existence of an entirely distinct image for the spouse in her own non-spouse role. Cherie Booth, QC, had precisely such an image, though it rarely overlapped with Cherie Blair, prime minister's wife. By 2000 the number of assistants working for Mrs Blair, including on public correspondence, was reported as being four. *Guardian*, 10 February 2000.

[34]   Maurine Beasley, *The White House Press Conferences of Eleanor Roosevelt*, New York and London: Garland, 1983; M. B. Grossman and M. J. Kumar, *Portraying the President*, Baltimore, Md.: Johns Hopkins University Press, 1981, pp. 118–19. By 1980 the First Lady's office had a staff of more than thirty.

[35]   Cf. Linda McDougall, Cherie Blair's biographer, who tracked her 'rapidly developing importance as a role model . . . in the absence of any front-line female role models in the Royal Family'. *Independent on Sunday*, 16 December 2001. Linda McDougall, *Cherie: the Perfect Life of Mrs Blair*, London: Politico's, 2001. This development must have been set back by the 'Cheriegate' episode.

[36]   'CHERIE BLAIR BEMOANS COST OF POWER DRESSING', *Guardian*, 16 November 1999.

there. The official rules about ministers' investment management were followed (i.e., via a 'blind trust'), but Mrs Blair accepted help from the partner of a close friend and he turned out to be a convicted fraudster. The response to the resulting media frenzy needed much more than the help of Mrs Blair's own assistant. For days the Downing Street press briefings were dominated by the subject, with Communications Director Alastair Campbell advising in the background – but without always being fully informed. At length Mrs Blair made an emotional televised public statement and shortly afterwards the story faded. How far the facts of the case made it a matter of public interest about the informal and institutional premiership is open to argument. Downing Street's own uncertainty of touch reflects the ambiguities.[37]

The Blairs were the first highly visible family in Downing Street, quite apart from such occasional traumas. Prime ministers have made Number 10 their home to varying degrees. By the time they gain the job, their children are usually grown up, or nearly so; but some have had grandchildren staying (for example the Macmillans). The Blairs needed space for a growing family, and they found it more convenient actually to live in Number 11. Sometimes the prime minister's image may have seemed at risk from the children's doings. Churchill's children had their share of problems. Mark Thatcher was a worry to his mother when she was in office. Blair's eldest son was picked up by the police in Leicester Square, the worse for drink after celebrating the end of exams. More often the children have needed protection and have remained figuratively behind closed doors. In 1999 the Blairs complained to the Press Complaints Commission about press pictures of the same son, then aged 15, kissing at a club disco. They complained also about stories of Euan's university plans and the choice of school for his sister. All three complaints were upheld.[38]

For Labour prime ministers there has been a special reason for downplaying the children – the party's sensitivities about private education. Wilson, in retrospect, looks fortunate not to have been bludgeoned for

[37] For Cherie Blair's statement see the press of 11 December 2002. The story dominated the media for the first two weeks of December. The ambiguity of Mrs Blair's 'official' position, in matters of public propriety, was pointed out by Sir Gordon Downey, former Parliamentary Commissioner for Standards, in a letter to *The Times* (17 December 2002): she had involved herself in 'government affairs' and 'policy meetings' – yet being neither minister, MP nor civil servant, she was 'not governed by any official code'.

[38] The disco pictures were published in the *Daily Sport*, 21 December 1999. Other papers, including the *Sun*, had felt they infringed the Press Complaints Commission's privacy code. When it was on their own terms, the Blairs were happy to use their children in the media. See, e.g., 'Euan's snog wasn't in the PR Plan', *Independent on Sunday*, 26 December 1999. For the other complaints, see *The Times*, 22 March 2002.

educating his sons at a public school. Callaghan, too, educated his daughters privately; but the public school issue never resonated so much about girls. Blair, on the other hand, was immediately in difficulties. 'Education, education, education' was a central priority of New Labour. He could not choose private over state schools for his own children. He therefore fudged by sending his children, as they reached secondary school age, into 'academic' schools outside their local area. He was helped by their mother's Catholicism, for the boys were put into a Catholic school.

Some of the strongest visual images of Blair as prime minister in the aftermath of the 1997 general election showed him with his family. Commentaries drew attention not only to the obvious factors of youthfulness, but also to the lifestyle features – shell clothing, trainers – which signified a new image and a new regime. Novelty reached a stunning pitch when Cherie Blair's pregnancy, at the age of 45, was announced in November 1999. This excitement would pose unprecedented questions of image management in due course. At this stage, and unusually, press comment was tinged with mild embarrassment – perhaps at what was in one sense an unplanned piece of image management.[39]

The prime minister's image may be affected too by extended families and friends. They can have a disconcerting impact. In the context of the prime minister's high office, their own lives may look incongruous. Knowledge of them will anyway be imperfect or skewed. John Major's brother Terry came into the incongruous category. Blair's brother Bill, like him a barrister, went almost entirely unremarked for two-and-a-half years until the *Spectator* published a profile of him in January 2000.[40] Cherie Blair's father had once been well known as an actor; but his personal and family life was turbulent and hardly what image-makers might have chosen. Of family and friends in general, it seems particularly true that the private must be managed so as to fit the public image (one of the failures of 'Cheriegate'). Holidays and friendships make the point. Prime ministers in the new millennium must holiday more or less literally in a fortress, to safeguard privacy. At the same time, the books they read, the games they play, the guests they entertain, are noised beyond the walls and tuned to the public ear.

[39] See, e.g., *Independent on Sunday*, 21 November 1999: 'OMIGOD! THE PRIME MINISTER HAS SEX! WITH HIS WIFE! WHAT A WEIRD CONCEPT FOR A POLITICIAN'. When Cherie Blair had a miscarriage in the summer of 2002, her privacy was fully respected.

[40] Jasper Gerard, 'The nice Mr Blair', *Spectator*, 15 January 2000. Gerard had found only two newspaper references to him from 1997 until then.

Other aspects of private life such as health and religion can be played up or down. Early in his premiership journalists noticed Blair privately attending mass by himself in Roman Catholic Westminster Cathedral. Did he intend to be noticed? The prime minister must be constantly self-conscious about his behaviour and how it is likely to be reported. Everything private is potentially public. The full range of contributory elements to his image is exhaustive. But as far as he can, he must nurture it.

Conclusion

These examples show that the prime minister's formal powers give him the authority and the potential to achieve his goals. They enable a minimum performance of such tasks as the appointment of ministers and the implementation of statutes. But they do not guarantee that ministers will be effective or that statutes will pass the informal test of popular approval. Even a strong formal power, such as political command of the armed services, will be unhesitatingly obeyed – but may not be greeted with enthusiasm, nor enjoy a successful outcome. The Suez invasion of 1956 divided the nation and ended in humiliation. The bombing of Kosovo in 1999 and Blair's support for George W. Bush's Iraq policy in 2002 were controversial (and likely to become more so, if and when war broke out). In contrast the Falklands War of 1982 gave Mrs Thatcher a big electoral victory. The role of public communication is to help the prime minister get beyond the minimum, using the resources available in his office, in his media access and in his reputation, to win his battles – both figuratively and literally.

3

Public Communication: Turning Authority into Power

The essential quality and purpose of the prime minister's public communication is its potential to convert his authority into power. In particular he can use it, both personally and through the institutional premiership, in conjunction with the flexibility of the job. His aim will be to manage as effectively as possible his administration (including appointments) and his programme (including legislation, income and expenditure, and foreign affairs). He will of course want his programme to succeed (whatever that may mean in particular cases); but his ultimate aim will be to protect his reputation, in order to maximize the chances of staying party leader and winning the next election. His general strategy will be to attach himself publicly to, or detach himself from, events, persons and policies in such a way as to prevail over colleagues and competitors. His tactics will be defensive as well as offensive, since he will wish to avoid personal unpopularity for failures.[1]

Managing Events

This process has many variations. For instance the prime minister can attach himself to something just to cash in on its success, even if this actually owed nothing to his support. He can attach himself to help

---

[1] The question whether a prime minister is actually his party's main electoral asset is complicated. But even if he runs behind his party in the opinion polls during the course of the preceding parliament, he may still be the chief asset in the campaign, since media campaign coverage is so heavily concentrated on the party leaders. For Gallup polls matching prime ministers and parties since 1945, see D. Butler and G. Butler, *British Political Facts*, London: Macmillan, 2001. The studies by David Butler and co-authors, titled in the form *The British General Election of [date]*, London: Macmillan, various years, provide a record of the growing prominence of prime ministers in broadcast coverage.

make something successful – and withdraw if failure looms: a struggling minister may be backed, for example, but then dumped. Or the prime minister may be involved but choose to keep his involvement quiet. This last variation is particularly easy in a system where individual ministerial responsibility operates alongside general cabinet responsibility. Again, the prime minister's attachment may be advertised as personal but effected through the offices of the institutional premiership. When research showed Blair's government was regarded as 'out of touch', the prime minister told senior advisers that he wanted 'eye-catching initiatives'. 'I personally should be associated with this as much as possible.'[2] How much he could truly be associated in detail is open to question.

One must emphasize again that the prime minister is not obliged to use his public communication in such ways. Or he may not be good at it. But not to try is to risk losing the initiative to others, within and outside the core executive, who will also be using media to influence the same things. So there will be competing public versions of the prime minister's involvement and effectiveness – some of which may be damaging to him. These will include the constantly renewed versions offered by media commentators themselves.

A prime minister's reputation is likely to be highest, and his scope for exercising influence greatest, when he has just secured a mandate in a general election. Once his reputation slides, experience suggests it is extremely difficult for it to be retrieved. Eden never recovered from the Suez debacle. Macmillan was badly damaged by a botched cabinet reshuffle in 1962 ('the night of the long knives') and by the Profumo scandal of 1963, Wilson by the forced devaluation of sterling in 1967, Thatcher by the poll tax, and Major by the ejection from the European exchange rate mechanism on 17 September 1992 ('Black Wednesday').

Major's experience can serve as a general illustration of prime ministerial attachments. Major's reputation was enhanced by somewhat unexpectedly winning the general election of May 1992. He now had his own popular mandate and had cut Mrs Thatcher's apron strings. But over the next five years he lost control of the flow of information, his media access was poorly managed, his public performance was indifferent, his personal and professional image made his reputation plummet, and his incumbency ended in electoral disaster. Ejection from the ERM, following a catastrophic run on sterling, provoked an immediate collapse of public confidence in the government's economic management. At the cabinet meeting confirming the decision to leave, Major

[2]   *Guardian*, 22 March 2002.

bound his colleagues into collective responsibility by going round the table and making each minister explicitly give his agreement. Major had been too closely involved to be able to distance himself personally from the policy failure, and he did not sack the Chancellor, Norman Lamont, until the following May. Rival versions of the precise roles of the two men, including claims that Major had come close to nervous collapse, were still being replayed seven years later, when each published his memoirs. Lamont's most damaging criticism, in his Commons resignation speech, was that 'we' – the government, not the prime minister, which he easily might have said – 'give the impression of being in office but not in power'. So telling was the remark that Lamont used it as the title of his memoirs.[3]

Major's personal reputation never recovered. His authority was then repeatedly challenged by the Conservative party's divisions over Europe. Dissent within the Cabinet was exposed by leaks and highlighted in such incidents as Major's unwitting complaint to camera about the 'bastards' among his cabinet colleagues (mentioned in chapter 2). After three years, in a bold effort to reassert authority (and giving, in the process, a nice illustration of the difference between the prime minister's formal and informal roles), he took the unprecedented step on 22 June 1995 of resigning the party leadership – but not the premiership. Re-election as leader made little difference. To improve the media management of the institutional premiership, he set up the formal Cabinet presentation subcommittee, EDCP. But he did not signal its importance by chairing it himself: he put Michael Heseltine, his rival, in charge.

Some of the policies to which Major attached his name, such as the Citizen's Charter, were electorally trivial. Others were public relations disasters and misfired, like the 'family values' policy of 'back to basics'. The latter coincided with an outbreak of 'sleaze' – a rash of sexual and financial indiscretions by Conservative backbenchers. Major successfully dissociated himself from them (although his career might have ended abruptly, if his affair with Edwina Currie had been exposed). But such incidents were easily construed as yet more evidence of weak leadership. Major ended his term of office with the lowest-ever opinion poll approval ratings for a prime minister.[4] Better public communication doubtless would not have saved him. But it surely would not have made things worse.

---

[3] Norman Lamont, *In Office*, London: Little Brown, 1999. The resignation speech was on 9 June 1993. H. C. Debates 6th series, vol. 226, c.285–6.

[4] From mid-1993 Major's standing dropped frequently to 18 per cent. For monthly Gallup figures from 1945 onwards, see D. Butler and G. Butler, *British Political Facts*.

Managing Persons

The working of these processes of attachment and detachment, when applied to the management of persons, is well illustrated by the prime minister's use of his formal powers of appointment and dismissal. The appointment of specific ministers is influenced by a large number of constraints. Simon James distinguishes no fewer than nine types, some of which have nothing even indirectly to do with public communication (for instance, the need for capable committee chairmen, and the specific requirements of posts such as Lord Chancellor). But others do – notably 'the balance of party factions' and 'cultivating younger talent', to use James's terms. A prime minister's first cabinet will certainly include several ministers whose appointment is intended to send a strong symbolic message about such factors. They may or may not turn out to be good administrator–ministers – no one will yet know, unless they are old hands. That does not matter, for they are chosen principally on political grounds. In 1964 Wilson put Frank Cousins into the cabinet to symbolize Labour's commitment to its industrial base. He turned out to be uncomfortable in the Chamber and he did not adapt well to cabinet conventions. He left the government after less than two years. Heath, in 1970, played a symmetrical game by giving a cabinet job to John Davies, the Director-General of the employers' organization, the CBI. Davies (who found a seat in time for the election) adapted more happily than Cousins.

Those appointments, and their symbolism, attracted special attention because they took the media by surprise. Blair achieved the same result in a minor key by appointing the populist Cockney Tony Banks minister for Sport in 1997. More substantially, Blair sent a strong symbolic message about the importance of 'Old Labour's' traditional roots by giving the deputy leader, John Prescott, the formal status of deputy prime minister, with a large and unwieldy departmental portfolio in addition – and keeping him as deputy prime minister after the 2001 general election, despite his poor policy record and occasional incomprehensibility.

Most appointments are not part of the formation of an entirely new cabinet but of the partial reconstruction of an old one. Mrs Thatcher made sixteen major reshuffles of her cabinet; nearly sixty people served in it, and when she resigned in 1990 she was the sole survivor from the team appointed in 1979. One-quarter of Blair's first cabinet had changed after eighteen months; he made seven reshuffles between 1997 and 2001. The replacement by Macmillan of as many as one-third of his cabinet in 1962 was extremely unusual – and its scale contributed much to the media's opinion that it constituted a crisis. But however large or limited the changes, and whatever the circumstances, the prime minister has actively to sell them. Sacked, aggrieved ministers, such as Norman Lamont in 1993 or Mo Mowlam after losing the Northern Ireland Office in 1999, can at the least make work for the prime minister's news managers, who have to counter their complaints.[5]

The best case for the prime minister is the reconstruction planned to his own timetable. The summer recess is a preferred time, to such an extent that media speculation tends to happen then, even when changes are not planned. If changes are not trailed at all, their suddenness may make them look unplanned and journalists may smart at not appearing to be in the know. Yet if changes are trailed and speculation becomes too fevered, the prime minister may be forced into rushing the final stages, thereby creating an impression of confusion and bad management.[6] The process of trailing can itself cause resentment, including when press secretaries seem to be briefing against ministers. Ministers who are sacked, even (perhaps especially) if they know it is coming, are sensitive to the way it is done. It is not surprising that the standard image about cabinet changes is whether a prime minister is 'a good butcher'.

The timing of cabinet changes is thus an important factor in their public reception, and one over which the prime minister cannot always keep control. Control is especially hard when changes are forced on him by resignations. These happen quite often, for either personal or political reasons. Almost all prime ministers find themselves having to replace colleagues who have become mired in personal difficulties. Mrs Thatcher had to find a new party chairman soon after the 1983 general election, when Cecil Parkinson resigned following public exposure of the pregnancy of his mistress. David Mellor's colourful adultery forced his resignation from John Major's cabinet. Tony Blair's close adviser Peter Mandelson, a rising ministerial star, resigned in December 1998 only months after joining the cabinet in July: he had failed to declare a £373,000 loan from another minister, Geoffrey Robinson, whose financial affairs led him also to resign at the same time. In October 1998 Blair's Welsh Secretary, Ron Davies, resigned too over indiscretions in his personal life.

---

[5] See Lamont, *In Office*, and Mo Mowlam, *Momentum*, London: Hodder and Stoughton, 2002.

[6] This is exactly what happened with Macmillan's 1962 reconstruction, which was immediately dubbed 'the night of the long knives'. What was intended as an act of rejuvenation seemed like an old man losing his grip. See Colin Seymour-Ure, *The Press, Politics and the Public*, London: Methuen, 1968, ch. 8.

In all those examples media were the catalyst. Five of Blair's seven reshuffles in the 1997 parliament were provoked in some way by media. So were the resignations in 2002 of Estelle Morris (Education Secretary), who admitted to wilting under media pressure and resigned unexpectedly, and Stephen Byers (Transport and Local Government Secretary), who was hounded after a series of policy failures.[7] Despite being caught on the hop, and in circumstances of media whoopee, prime ministers normally have no difficulty in dissociating themselves personally from such embarrassments and tragedies. But the reputation of the institutional premiership and of the government as a whole may be sullied, especially when the prime minister initially backs a minister but is ultimately forced to let the media claim a scalp (as happened with Byers). In two of the examples quoted, however, Thatcher and Blair were able to bring their favourites back into the cabinet. Parkinson waited nearly six years. In the case of Mandelson, Blair implicitly left the possibility open when the resignation took place, and Mandelson's banishment lasted less than a year. It was all the more ironic that he was then obliged to resign a second time in January 2001.

A forced ministerial resignation on political grounds is more likely to implicate the prime minister personally through the overlap between collective and individual responsibility. Mrs Thatcher accepted the resignation of the Foreign Secretary, Lord Carrington, after the Argentinian invasion of the Falklands in 1982. If the campaign to regain the islands had not been so successful, her own position would have been in danger. But such resignations are rare – one might say notoriously so.

Far more serious are the unforced ministerial resignations. These take a prime minister unawares. They are often hostile in intent. By definition they involve rival versions of events. They can make major demands on the communication resources of the premiership. Although the prime minister's media operation will have bigger guns, the resigning minister starts with the initiative. On his own ground he may well prove a better performer than the prime minister, either in parliament (where a resignation statement is a major event) or in the broadcasting studio. Resignations of this kind generally transcend the significance of the issue which provokes them, for their purpose is political. They destabilize the government and threaten the prime minister's authority. Until the media assess the support for the resigning minister, the scale of the crisis (and whether it deserves that name) remains unclear.

Among the best examples of this type since 1945 are the resignation in 1951 of Attlee's Labour minister, Aneurin Bevan, on the issue of NHS

---

[7] Byers resigned on 28 May and Morris on 24 October 2002.

charges for teeth and spectacles, and of Macmillan's Chancellor, Peter Thorneycroft, with two junior Treasury ministers, in 1958.[8] Later, a classic hostile resignation was that of Michael Heseltine as Defence minister in 1986. The substantive issue was comparatively trivial – the future of the small Westland helicopter company. Heseltine's challenge was to Mrs Thatcher's authoritarian decision-making style. His first publicity coup was to resign by walking out of a cabinet meeting, an unprecedented and powerfully symbolic act. Because journalists were not warned, the first pictures were of his back view, striding along Downing Street. Within the next twenty-four hours he held a press conference to explain his behaviour and gave seventeen broadcasts, which in 1986 was a somewhat larger blitz than it would be in the 2000s. Downing Street's riposte, and Mrs Thatcher's personal performances, were barely adequate to save her skin. In particular, her performance in a key Commons debate was judged inadequate, but the opposition leader Neil Kinnock failed to exploit his opportunity. Other hostile resignations were to follow. Mrs Thatcher lost her Chancellor, Nigel Lawson, in 1989, and her deputy prime minister, Geoffrey Howe, in 1990. The mild-mannered but lethal resignation speech of the latter provoked the formal leadership challenge that ended in her defeat.

A prime minister needs to sell cabinet changes, in sum, through effective presentation about their timeliness (if within his control), about the dispensability of the persons he is sacking or who have resigned (past sell-by date, incompetent, unfortunate, misguided), and about the suitability of new appointees, especially if they are unexpected (through youth, inexperience or previous career).

Managing Policy

The prime minister's use of his public image and reputation to manage policy can be illustrated, in principle, through a few simple distinctions. On a general level, first, the prime minister's media access enables him increasingly to play the American president's role as an opinion leader or mobilizer. Wilson sought to lead the country into the European Community, and he prevented the circulation to the cabinet of counterarguments by his Trade minister, Douglas Jay. Mrs Thatcher (more as institutional premier, perhaps, than personally) reversed conventional

---

[8] Bevan took with him Harold Wilson, President of the Board of Trade, and John Freeman, a junior minister. Thorneycroft took Enoch Powell and Nigel Birch, junior Treasury ministers.

post-war wisdom about public ownership of utilities. Major evangelized (but in vain) about a return to 'family values'. Blair spent much rhetoric expounding the 'Third Way' (given a measure of credibility by the Director of the LSE).[9] He brought a new focus on constitutional structures, including the monarchy. He made 'education, education, education' a mantra. He seemed at times obsessed with 'newness': his millennial message to the nation used the word 'new' twenty-three times (and 'old' once, pejoratively).[10]

Where nothing so radical as a major change of attitude is intended, this opinion-leading can be seen as a simpler process of prioritizing particular policy goals. Blair was reported to be 'personally taking charge' of a government review of adoption law in February 2000, following a child abuse scandal in care homes. A month later he was 'personally leading a dialogue' with NHS professionals about faster delivery of health care. At the height of a scare about the MMR vaccine for children in 2001–2 he took pains to signal his support for the vaccine, intimating that baby Leo had been vaccinated (but without explicitly breaking his self-imposed rule of not disclosing details of his children's private lives).[11]

At the other end of the scale the prime minister is in a unique position very occasionally to make specific policy decisions on the hoof, through a public commitment which his colleagues cannot without disproportionate effort overturn. For example, in 1999 Tony Blair announced on BBC's *Question Time* (8 July), in answer to a surprise question, his intention to legislate a ban on foxhunting before the next election. While clearly on the record, however, this promise was not quickly turned into law. Much more dramatically Blair 'pledged' on BBC's *Breakfast with Frost* in January 2000 that the government would raise British healthcare spending to the EU average by 2006. This commitment was provoked, in a winter when health services were under exceptional stress and making headlines, by the outspoken criticisms of one of Britain's well-known hospital consultants, the Labour peer and TV personality, Lord Winston. It was a sweeping commitment in a notoriously imprecise field, potentially capable of being spun almost into

---

[9] Anthony Giddens, *The Third Way*, Cambridge: Polity, 1998; *The Third Way and its Critics*, Cambridge: Polity, 2000. Blair's contribution was a pamphlet, *The Third Way: New Politics for the New Century*, London: Fabian Society, 1998.
[10] John Sutherland, *Guardian*, 3 January 2000. Sutherland counted from the *Guardian*'s 'edited text'.
[11] *Guardian*, 18 February 2000, 22 March 2000; *Independent on Sunday*, 23 December 2001; *Guardian*, 9 February 2002. The triple vaccine against measles, mumps and rubella was alleged by some researchers to be linked to the development of autism.

meaninglessness – and likely to be sniped at privately by other spending ministers. It was a commitment, none the less – and was taken up in the March 2000 Budget.

Between these poles lie the complex possibilities involving a prime minister's relations with other people in the core executive and his preferences for particular policies. Blair routinely signalled his attachment to projects from which he could easily have kept clear, such as the controversial Millennium Dome and the arrangements for the new London mayor. He stepped into the trivial if symbolically fraught Anglo-Greek issue of ownership of the Elgin marbles.[12] He lent his authority at key moments to the Northern Irish peace process. When he replaced his popular Northern Ireland minister Mo Mowlam with Peter Mandelson and moved Mowlam to a non-departmental cabinet role, which she disliked, he was quick to indicate publicly that she was not being sidelined.[13] He used John Prescott to sell policy to 'old' Labour supporters at the grass roots and in the trade unions. He even made critical remarks which helped force the England football manager, Glenn Hoddle, to resign. He took a high-profile role in the Kosovo crisis and the NATO bombing campaign, and after the New York and Washington attacks on 11 September 2001 he so dominated the government's publicity that the Foreign Office and the Ministry of Defence were said to feel he was 'grandstanding'.[14]

Foreign policy deserves special mention. Several features make the prime minister's role here distinctive; and, by its nature, foreign policy is unusually susceptible to spinning. If not on his own, the prime minister works often with only one or two ministerial colleagues, and when overseas he is unusually sheltered from opponents. The policy process itself tends to be tortuous and incremental. Its products are typically intangible (at the level of pounds in the voter's pocket) and their evaluation depends on how they are perceived. Progress, especially in the increasingly numerous multilateral engagements, is punctuated by summits. These both lend themselves to, and are substantially directed at, carefully controlled publicity events. Even in bilateral dealings, such as visits to Washington and Commonwealth countries, the prime minister, personally and institutionally, can schmooze with journalists on the plane and enjoy a normally comfortable press conference platform in the host country. (See chapter 8.)

---

[12] *The Guardian*, 13 December 1999. At the time, the Greek government was pressing its case for returning the Parthenon marbles to Athens.

[13] For a full analysis, see the *New Statesman*, 10 January 2000.

[14] Michael White, *Guardian*, 7 January 2002.

A second area to emphasise is crisis. It is a commonplace to say that crises are defined by the reaction to events, not by events themselves. (The definition of an 'event' too is artificial, insofar as its beginning and end may be open to arbitrary definition, which may vary with the context in which it is considered.) The prime minister is in an exceptional position to influence definitions of political crisis through his media access. One sure sign that a crisis has erupted is the broadcast of an unscheduled head-and-shoulders address to the nation by the prime minister. Eden pumped up Nasser's decision to nationalize the Suez Canal into a major international crisis in 1956 (including through a rare broadcast to the nation). Heath turned the 1974 miners' strike into a national crisis, calling an election (and broadcasting to the nation) on the issue of 'Who governs?', and losing it. Wilson made a kind of torpid crisis out of the terms of British membership of the European Community in 1974–5, choosing to launch a national referendum upon a largely indifferent public. The purpose had most to do with internal Labour party politics. Thatcher could have finessed the Argentinian invasion of the Falkland Islands in 1982, since most voters probably did not know where they were and the economic and strategic threat was negligible. Blair, when still new in office, involved himself closely in the aftermath of the death of Princess Diana in 1997, which was widely portrayed in the media as a crisis for the Royal Family.[15] In the foot-and-mouth crisis of 2001 Blair donned a protective yellow suit to visit an infected farm and show, in the words of Alastair Campbell, that it was 'a crisis management issue being led from the top'. Photos went round the world – and frightened off tens of thousands of tourists.[16] Blair's close cooperation with President George W. Bush over the 'war against terrorism' after 11 September 2001, and subsequently the existence of an Iraqi threat, inevitably played up the sense of crisis in 2001–2.

The less direct the impact of events upon people (loss of food, electricity, petrol), the more a communication from the prime minister will provide the evidence of crisis. Conversely the experience of Callaghan showed that in the presence of direct evidence of that kind (uncollected

[15]   Did Blair's behaviour make the death and funeral more of a crisis for the monarchy, or less? He called Diana 'the people's princess' – a phrase (of Alastair Campbell's) which instantly stuck and which contrasted her with her traditionalist in-laws. He then took a prominent role in the funeral service by reading one of the lessons – which there was no constitutional reason for him to do. One could argue that simultaneously he both increased the sense of crisis and assisted in the catharsis which resolved it.
[16]   Campbell admitted later that the domestic and overseas messages of the visit clashed, with costly consequences to the tourist industry. *Independent*, 28 August, 2002.

garbage and industrial stoppages in the 1978 'winter of discontent'), a mere prime ministerial reassurance was insufficient to define a crisis away. Callaghan had the right prime ministerial instinct – seek to impose your own definition on events – but he made the wrong choice. Similarly Blair's televised commitment to NHS improvement in January 2000 could be construed as the panicky response to (at least) a mini-crisis over whose definition he had lost control and for which he could expect to be blamed. While a rally-round-the-flag effect can be expected in popular reaction to an international crisis (the Falklands being a prime example), there is no such reliability about a domestic crisis. Blair's response shows, however, that the existence of a crisis can empower a prime minister to initiate correspondingly exceptional measures. A crisis breaks the rules; the response may do so too – in the NHS case, the rules about public expenditure allocation.

Conclusion

This chapter has taken further the analyses of the previous two. It has argued through examples that the prime minister can use his resources of public communication – his media management offices, his media access and his public reputation – to turn authority into power, over events, people and policies. Some of the broader implications can be briefly explored in conclusion.

The chances of the prime minister's public communication *succeeding* in turning authority into power, firstly, have been immeasurably increased by what these chapters have called, for brevity, electronic glut. Performances which used to be given to a fairly small audience, notably in the House of Commons, now provide the prospect of triumphs or disasters witnessed by potential TV, radio and internet audiences of millions. Party conferences, visits to schools and hospitals, and even non-governing occasions such as holidays, are fitted with the same tripwire. The opportunities for broadcast public performance are limitless. They extend far beyond overtly political programmes to include such features as gardening and children's programmes.

The effect of these developments on the inherently flexible nature of the premiership has been to *highlight informal elements as opposed to formal*, to *personalize hitherto impersonal, institutional and mysterious elements*, and to *bring the formerly private, non-governing parts of the prime minister's life to the aid of his governing objectives*. The scope and scale of the prime minister's public communication, the opportunity of using it as an instrument, and the potential consequences of doing it badly, lead inexorably to communications management being a top Downing Street priority.

Public communication therefore takes up more of the prime minister's resources of time, staff and energy. Deployment of the time and staff of the institutional premiership is nowadays fairly easy to trace, in the form of the Downing Street offices responsible for media management. What is less clear is how far the personal prime minister spends more time than did, say, Harold Macmillan in the early 1960s actually being involved in communication. A fiasco at the despatch box during Question Time may reverberate more than it would have done before television. But once the techniques of performance are learnt and the immediate preparations are streamlined, the overall time taken up by Question Time need not be much greater than formerly. To that extent it may be that the prime minister simply has to spend more time thinking, and perhaps worrying, about communication, and that he need not spend more time doing it. (He has the option, moreover, of leaving the thinking and some of the worrying to an aide or a minister.) On the other hand electronic media have stimulated the creation of new forums altogether. Tony Blair started to give televised press conferences after the 2001 general election (see chapter 8). These must have stolen their time from something else. They too would reverberate if unsuccessful, and they too made demands on the skills of performance.

The omnipresence of media justifies the claim – which is at the heart of these three chapters – that *public communication cannot avoid being relevant to, and thus an influence on, almost any of a contemporary prime minister's tasks*. The problem (and frustration) for the student of prime ministerial power is that because the extent of this influence is neither fully visible nor measurable, it cannot easily be incorporated into the models developed in core executive studies. Public communication must be seen, none the less, not as one distinct, self-contained and limited resource available to the prime minister, but rather as a factor helping to determine how successfully his other resources can be used.

Another consequence of the (claimed) pervasive influence of communication is the argument, mentioned earlier, that presentation is part of the substance of policy. Another again is the idea that government is carried on within a 'permanent campaign' (i.e., for office). This is linked to the further observation that, more than its predecessors, the Blair government brought the techniques of winning office into the conduct of office itself. All those propositions imply a strong emphasis on process and style. Election campaigns give overwhelming priority to the party leader/prime minister. It follows that a permanent campaign requires the prime minister's public image and reputation to be in good order at all times; and this reputation provides much of his leverage within the core executive.

The more accurate the arguments in the previous paragraphs, the more apt are questions about their effects on the broader nature of the prime minister's job. One of the most obvious is the suggestion that the prime minister's power is becoming relatively more of a 'power to persuade' (in Neustadt's classic phrase about presidential power in the United States).[17] One can argue too that, like the American president, the prime minister has a growing role (if he wishes to play it) as an opinion leader or mobilizer. A third argument, similarly, sees increasing potential for the symbolic premiership. Presidents have symbolic roles as heads of state built into their job description. Prime ministers formally do not. They have always communicated *in* symbols, and electronic glut gives scope for the kinds of visual symbol discussed in the section about prime ministerial images. The prime minister who began routinely to communicate *as* a symbol in the electronic age was Mrs Thatcher – the 'iron lady'. Visual symbols have inherently ambiguous meanings, so their use requires effective management.

Each of those three tendencies is consistent with the emergence of a populist premiership. They do not make it inevitable, but if other conditions are right it becomes more likely. A prime minister may well be tempted to sell people what research suggests they want or what can readily be sold. The 1990s were a decade without 'isms'. Old Labour had failed to sell the electorate socialism in the 1980s. Thatcherism (which anyway had populist elements) had run its course. Major and Blair both groped without success for a big idea. It was small wonder that New Labour in particular (because its communications were so good), seemed obsessed by spin and driven by considerations of style. In Blair's second term, when the sheen wore off, they were increasingly criticized for it, and in his first appearance before the Commons select committee chairmen he admitted there had been an over-reliance on spin.[18]

All those tendencies – and populism too – raise also a question about an informal head-of-state role for the prime minister. This question is less shadowy than before the domestic troubles of the Windsors in the 1990s. After Blair eulogized the dead Diana as 'the people's princess', we should perhaps, by implication, have begun aspiring to a 'people's monarchy'. The Blairs were a comparatively young, glamorous and

[17]   Richard E. Neustadt, *Presidential Power*, rev. edn, New York: John Wiley, 1976, p. 78.
[18]   *Guardian*, 17 July 2002.

modern 'first family', at a time when the front-rank royals were none of those things. (Critics pointed out that the Blairs' lives were populist more in style than in substance.) The fuss about who should pay for Cherie Blair's wardrobe, and small things such as their 'regal' Christmas card in 1999, fed a drip of comment. Even the slight cringe about Mrs Blair's pregnancy ('the people's pregnancy', as a *Times* columnist called it) can fit into this argument.[19] The British monarchy, in Bagehot's famous Victorian phrase, is part of the 'dignified' branch of the constitution. If a prime minister was sleeping with somebody else's wife, the tabloid press would scrabble for details – as it did with Prince Charles. Sleeping with his own wife, on the other hand, was his own business. The cringe was a nod of deference to the mystery that cloaks majesty. ('THAT'S A LITTLE TOO MUCH INFORMATION FOR ME, THANK YOU.')

How far might a resurgence of ideology put any of those tendencies in reverse? The question can be put in terms of alternative models of the premiership. Martin Smith describes Thatcher and Blair respectively as 'interventionist' and 'directive' prime ministers. Their methods differed, but they kept the high ground, and they contrasted strongly with Major. Major was a 'collectivist', seeking consensus in his cabinet and delaying decisions until he was sure of support.[20] All sorts of external difficulties undermined Major, including a paper-thin parliamentary majority, divisions on Europe and the collapse of key economic policies. But would he have seemed such a weak prime minister, granted those problems, in a pre-electronic age? In our present era, when the scope for using public communication virtually creates expectations of interventionist or directive leadership, it may be that, regardless of majority, a prime minister who sets out to be a consensus-managing collectivist will in that very process undermine his own reputation.

One can return finally to the problem of getting beyond a tentative description and evaluation of the part played by public communication in the prime minister's job. A further cause of frustration about the difficulty of measuring it is that communication is a two-edged weapon. Poor communication can positively weaken a prime minister. This disadvantage reinforces the fundamental importance to the prime minister of managing to *keep control* of his public communication. He has stronger weapons than any of his competitors and colleagues, but they can never guarantee success: communications management remains obstinately different from manipulation. Information or arguments may

[19]   Mary Ann Sieghart, *The Times*, 26 November 1999.
[20]   Martin Smith, *The Core Executive in Britain*, London: Macmillan, 1999, p. 88.

not be understood as the prime minister intends, because of poor institutional management or personal performance, or better communication by a competitor. Or they may get across, but without having the
intended effect on the recipients' opinions and behaviour. Or the prime
minister may have made an unwise choice about what to try and communicate in the first place. But the prime minister must never let up. To
surrender control over his public communication by default would be
an irrational, irresponsible gamble.

The remaining chapters in this book explore a number of widely dif-
fering factors – spatial, organizational, economic, psychological, graphic
– which challenge or limit the prime minister's ability to control his
public communication.

4

The Capital City as News Environment

Suppose the British prime minister moved to the White House, as prime minister, and the American president moved to 10 Downing Street. How would their patterns of public communication change, even while their jobs remained the same?

Ten Downing Street, part of a speculative cul-de-sac of Georgian townhouses, has no space for press quarters, no lawn for camera stake-outs, no rooms for large press conferences, no helicopter pad to stride towards while fielding (or not) reporters' questions, no tourists to stun with unexpected conversation. A president would have to find ways of literally 'bringing in' the media.[1]

A prime minister in the White House, correspondingly, would have a hard time keeping the press corralled in the galleries and lobbies of Capitol Hill, more than a mile away. Shuttling to and from his parliamentary duties, could he avoid the quick exchange with reporters, while getting in and out of the car? Back home, would his media managers let him ignore the potential of the White-House-as-TV-studio?

Places are not neutral. The spaces within and between them, and the ways of getting from one to another, can all affect how, what and to whom political leaders communicate, and with what results. This chapter explores that claim by looking at capital cities. London and Washington are the main examples, but Ottawa and Canberra, two smaller capitals with 'Westminster' parliamentary systems, provide good illustrations too. First the chapter examines different features of the capital city; and then it considers how these might affect the choices prime ministers and presidents make, when deciding where to communicate.

---

[1] An attractive illustrated guide to the house and its history is Anthony Seldon, *10 Downing Street: an Illustrated History*, London: HarperCollins, 1999.

Features of the Capital City

The capital city as news environment for a prime minister or president (a 'chief executive') has three parts. There is first the city as a whole. The chief executive is touched by its symbolic meanings and will try to exploit them. Within the city, secondly, is a government enclave, of people and buildings. When authors write of 'the Washington community', this, rather than some broader community, is what they mean.[2] There is no 'London community' in that exact sense. But references to 'Westminster' or 'Whitehall' – or increasingly to the 'Westminster (or Whitehall) village' – refer to much the same thing: a fairly compact district containing parliament, Downing Street, the core civil service, party headquarters, political offices of media and lobbyists, and (a key component of news exchange) clubs and 'watering holes'.[3] Within the government community, lastly, lies the chief executive's own enclave. This is limited to a small complex of buildings. For the prime minister it is Downing Street and parts of the Palace of Westminster. For the president it is the White House and nearby buildings.

There are important differences between capitals such as Washington that are purpose-built, and others such as London which have evolved. Each by definition contains the seat of government. But the former is more likely to be dominated by government, to be self-conscious as a capital, and to have a clear relation between its governing functions and its layout and buildings.[4] The evolved capital is more likely to be a

---

[2]   See, e.g., Nelson Polsby's caustic and entertaining essay 'The Washington community, 1960–1980', in Thomas E. Mann and Norman J. Ornstein, *The New Congress*, Washington, D. C.: A. E. I., 1981, pp. 7–31.

[3]   Strictly, the 'Whitehall village' would include only civil servants and ministers. In another variation, a Downing Street press secretary talked to me in 1994 about 'maintaining the purity of the Downing Street island'. (The context was security.) Tony Blair talked of 'a sort of Westminster village' at his first monthly press conference on 20 June 2002. I know no definition of a media 'watering hole', but its connotations are obvious.

[4]   The District of Columbia, occupying about seventy square miles of land ceded by Virginia and Maryland, became the seat of government of the United States of America on 1 December 1800. The city of Washington was planned by Major Pierre Charles L'Enfant, a French engineer. By 2001 the population was 572,000, and that of Greater Washington was more than four million. In Australia, the city of Canberra covers twenty square miles within the 910 square miles of the Australian Capital Territory, established in 1909. The international competition for a design was won by a Chicago architect, Walter Burley Griffin. By 2000 the population of the ACT was 312,000. The city of Ottawa grew out of the settlement of Bytown, on the river boundary between Ontario and Quebec. It was selected by Queen Victoria in 1857, on the advice of the Colonial Office, as the capital for those two provinces. It became capital of Canada as a whole when the nation was created in 1867. Its population by 1996 was 323,000, and the Ottawa region as a whole included more than one million.

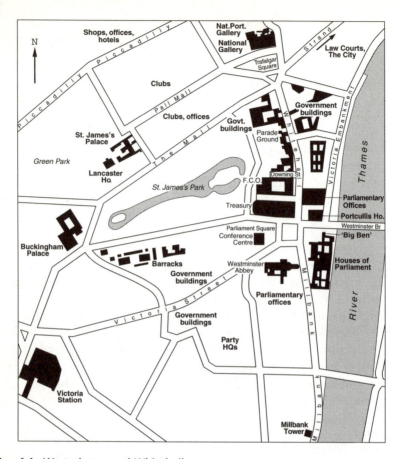

Map 4.1: *Westminster and Whitehall*

The Westminster/Whitehall 'village' extends east from Victoria Station and Buckingham Palace to the Thames. It is home to government buildings, clubs, political consultancies, interest groups, military barracks, the metropolitan police, Church of England offices and royalty, in addition to 10 Downing Street and the Houses of Parliament. Parliament, squeezed between the Thames and Millbank, has made extra space both by acquiring and constructing offices along Millbank and at the end of Whitehall. Downing Street is flanked on its south and east sides by government buildings and on the other two sides by Horse Guards Parade and St James's Park.

metropolis, the seat of major financial, economic, cultural and media institutions in addition to government. Government institutions are one enclave among many, and they may be partly dispersed. In London the major financial institutions are in 'the City', which, as foreigners discover, is not the same place as 'London' at all and is nowhere near Westminster. National newspaper offices, now scattered from Fleet

Street, remain distant from Westminster, and Westminster, not the office, is the base for their political staffs – who, partly as a result, enjoy exceptional autonomy.[5] The Law Courts too are more than a short walk from Westminster.

The purpose-built capital is a symbol. The American president works in a city where everything from legislature to litter bins is a conscious expression of values of national origin and identity. The symbolism starts with the city's very location. This needs to take account of regional sensitivities, and in federated states (USA, Canada and Australia, for instance) the principles of selection mean the capital may be inconvenient for physical communications – or even climatically.[6] Washington's position on the eastern seaboard, logical in the late eighteenth century, makes less sense now. President Nixon used his San Clemente estate as a 'Western White House' in the 1970s, so that he could work at home in California. But there are nuances about how much the president can or should stray from Washington without incurring political costs.[7] George W. Bush was in Florida during the attacks on the Pentagon and the World Trade Center on 11 September 2001. There were good security reasons for not flying directly back to Washington (he went to Nebraska). But he was criticized for not communicating more quickly that he was 'in charge', though in a remote location, in the way that the president's presence in Washington normally signifies 'being in charge'.

The symbolism continues in a capital's design. The city celebrates the nation. Grand avenues traverse swards of public space, much of it better for looking at than doing things in. Some of Canberra's avenues radiate from a central point along compass bearings of the national cities after which they are named (a pleasing touch which does little to help the navigation of the geographically challenged). Washington's heroic monuments – notably to Lincoln, Washington and Jefferson – provide

[5] See Jeremy Tunstall, *The Westminster Lobby Correspondents*, London: Routledge, 1970, esp. pp. 68–71, 89–97; and the same author's *Newspaper Power*, Oxford: Clarendon Press, 1996, ch. 16.

[6] In South Africa the government actually moves every six months between Pretoria and Cape Town. As to climate, Polsby quotes a veteran Congressman suggesting in 1960 that 'the installation of air conditioning in the 1930s did more . . . than cool the Capitol: it prolonged the sessions. The members were no longer in such a hurry to flee Washington in July'. Polsby, 'The Washington community, 1960–1980', p. 30.

[7] When Nixon held regional press briefings at San Clemente, for instance, they were seen as a deliberate means of bypassing the Washington press. Jeb Stuart Magruder, *An American Life*, New York: Pocket Book edn, 1975, pp. 112–13. Contrast Australia, where prime minister John Howard (appointed in 1996) was able to indulge his preference for living in an official residence in Sydney, rather than in the prime minister's house in Canberra.

focal and axial points, with Capitol Hill paramount.[8] In Ottawa the Victorian government buildings rise above the bluffs over the Ottawa river at its confluence with the Gatineau, with the proudly named Peace Tower (contrast London's jokey 'Big Ben') rearing from their centre. Australia's savage losses in World War I made the national war memorial the dominant building of 1930s Canberra, a position superseded by its 1980s Parliament House. Street names – whole suburbs in Canberra – memorialize past leaders.

Evolved capitals such as London obviously have similar features (the Mall, Nelson's Column), and Paris provided the inspiration for the architect L'Enfant's Washington. But in London and Paris such symbols are, comparatively speaking, an overlay.[9] An evolved capital, too, may be defined by its centre: the purpose-built capital is defined rather by its boundary. Washington, Ottawa and Canberra all have distinct administrative and legal status within their country's government. The boundary instantly creates an ambivalence about inside and outside. By the 1950s Washington could easily be seen as arrogant and self-absorbed, and not just by people who anyway saw government as wasteful. After the corruption of the Nixon era, Jimmy Carter could run for president 'against' Washington. Ottawa and Canberra too are the butt of resentful jokes. 'Ottawans treat [Ottawa] as though they own it and most other Canadians treat it as if they don't,' wrote the journalist George Bain in 1964.[10]

Capital city media are not exempt from such criticisms. Purpose-built capitals spawn insider magazines, newsletters and media cliques and clubs. The *Washington Post* conceals within sections focused on national affairs a thoroughly parochial core. This seems less strange than it would if the USA had a national daily press, since the same could be said of the *New York Times* or the *Los Angeles Times*. In London, the *Evening Standard* has a touch of the same character.

The media with which the American president lives are the high-prestige bureaux of the big groups, papers and broadcast networks (including the comparatively recent and increasingly important CNN

---

[8]   Washington is designed as a system of avenues punctuated by circles, diagonally overlaying a grid lined up with the points of a compass. The whole system radiates out from the Capitol building.

[9]   An example of what might have been: Sir John Soane amused himself in 1817 with the design for 'an elevation of a National Monument, forming part of a general design, for the improvement of the two Houses of Parliament, the Courts of Judicature, the buildings appertaining thereto, and to commemorate the victories of Waterloo and Trafalgar'. Trustees of Sir John Soane's Museum.

[10]   George Bain, *I've Been Around*, Toronto: Clarke, Irwin, 1964, p. 28.

continuous news network). But he will also want to get beyond these to the media based all across the country, especially if he feels the Washington media are against him, as presidents not infrequently do. (It can be a case of blaming the messenger for bad news.) Developments in electronic technology have made this much simpler.

The symbolic meaning of the purpose-built capital may include, thirdly, a deliberate expression of the nation's principles of government. (If this happens in an evolved capital it will, again, be an overlay.) Washington is plainly a republican city. There is no palace for the head of state: the palatial residences are embassies and hotels, and the Capitol is a palace in all but name (it has 533 rooms, a central rotunda and a statuary hall). The constitution has a fine home in the national archive building. The White House is small because the president's role was supposed to be small. It has few large areas for public display and it was built, obviously, without facilities for the press. Both houses of Congress, in contrast, soon let reporters onto the floor and later set aside space for them in the galleries.[11] The USA is a secular state, so there is no privileged site for a cathedral. The judiciary, on the other hand, has a key constitutional role, so the Supreme Court sits in a prominent building (but only since 1932).[12]

Most striking of all, L'Enfant placed the White House one-and-a-half miles from Congress, in physical confirmation of the separation of powers. There can be no casual (even if contrived) mingling of president, legislators and press, as would be possible if the president had an office on Capitol Hill. 'No message to nor from the President', observed L'Enfant, 'is to be made without a sort of decorum.'[13]

Comparable observations could be made about the design of Ottawa and Canberra (and that of Babar the Elephant's capital city

[11] For details of a quite complex story, see Donald A. Ritchie, *Press Gallery: Congress and the Washington Correspondents*, Cambridge, Mass.: Harvard University Press, 1992.

[12] Former President Taft, later Chief Justice, persuaded Congress to provide the Supreme Court with its own premises, completed in 1935. Previously it had met in the Capitol Building.

[13] S. Kernell, *Going Public*, Washington, D.C.: CQ Press, 1986, p. 53, quoting James Sterling Young, *The Washington Community: 1800–1828*, New York: Columbia University Press, 1966, p. 6. 'Despite continuous interaction today', Kernell comments (pp. 53–4), 'the institutional distance created between Congress and the presidency . . . has not been greatly shortened. Even as informal face-to-face negotiation occurs, it is commonly preceded and facilitated by the preparatory public activities institutional distance encourages.' Kernell also cites Douglass Cater, who noted that unofficial communication between the legislative and executive branches goes on regularly through the press in advance of official communications. Cater, *Power in Washington*, New York: Vintage Books, 1964, p. 224.

Celesteville[14]). The contrasts with London are strong. The functions and symbolism of buildings have changed with shifts in the system of government. The monarch's residence, Buckingham Palace, is a 600-room pile fronting the ceremonial Mall. It became the regular royal residence only with Queen Victoria. To suggest it should be open to the public would have been like shouting in church, until the 1990s.[15] The House of Commons met in the former St Stephen's Chapel at Westminster, till it was burnt down in 1834. Barry's new Houses of Parliament in 1850 still incorporated the galleries, robing rooms and ante-chambers of a royal palace, especially on the Lords side. The whole complex was known, strictly, as the Palace of Westminster, until it slipped imperceptibly into 'the Houses of Parliament'.[16] Westminster Abbey, site of the monarch's enthronement, is over the road. Ten Downing Street is round the corner, an inconvenient combination of residence and workplace. Dwarfed by the massive government offices of the imperial age across the road, it perfectly represents the informal, evolutionary nature of the British constitution and the prime minister's developing role within it.

Having said all that, purpose-built capitals evolve like others. From the chrysalid company town grows a butterfly capital city. The towns acquire heightened grandeur and self-consciousness, and more symbols of national pre-eminence. The completion of the Beltway round Washington in the 1960s gave the city a new symbol of inside/outside status well beyond the District's historic rectangle, with mushrooming suburbs either side. The governing enclave was less and less synonymous with 'the Washington Community'. The city acquired a decent international airport and a stylish metro, carpeted and uncharacteristically devoid of adverts. A string of new museums and memorials along the Mall interpreted American history, air and space, the Jewish holocaust, the Vietnam war. The national art galleries expanded; the Kennedy Centre for the Performing Arts was opened. Universities and research

---

[14]　The layout of Celesteville, named after the paternalist King Babar's wife, is illustrated in *Babar the King*, New York: Random House, 1976, one of the classic children's books by the Belgian Jean de Brunhof. Palaces of industry and pleasure flank the royal residence at the top of the hill. The elephants' identical houses are in regimented lines beneath. At the foot is a recreational lake. Written in the early 1930s, de Brunhof's books epitomize for children an idealized colonial regime.

[15]　On 20 November 1992 Windsor Castle was badly damaged by fire. The repairs were partly paid for by opening Buckingham Palace to the public.

[16]　See the excellent essays edited by Christine and Jacqueline Riding, *The Houses of Parliament*, London: Merrell, 2000. Note that it is still at 'Parliament as Palace of Westminster' that kings and queens lie in state before their funeral – most recently Queen Elizabeth the Queen Mother in 2002.

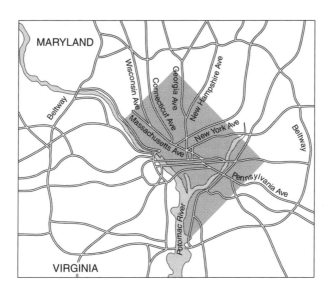

Map 4.2: *Washington, D.C.*

The District of Columbia was originally a square, ten miles by ten, on land ceded by Maryland and Virginia. In 1846 the land south of the Potomac River was returned to Virginia, leaving an area of some seventy square miles. The real and symbolic modern-day boundary is the motorway – the Beltway. The District's political neutrality as the nation's capital since 1800 is reflected in the fact that until the 1970s it neither elected members to Congress nor had an elected self-government.

institutes thrived. Convention hotels and exhibition centres proliferated (what to do with that old railway terminus).

The same development happened in Ottawa (even down to the converted railway station) and in Canberra. Ottawa, given the country's gnawing concern with national identity, built a particularly spectacular Museum of Civilization. The old military Rideau Canal, curving through the city, was prettified. Above all, in a symbol of Canada's bicultural Anglo-French co-partnership, the squat French-Canadian city of Hull, straight across the river from the parliament buildings, took delivery of a bulk supply of government offices.[17] In the 1980s and 1990s, Canberra too built a variety of museums and galleries. In 1999 the

---

[17]   Cf. John Turner, later briefly prime minister, speaking in 1970: 'We are Canada in microcosm. The National Capital Area is a national symbol. The struggle for a bicultural nation is concentrated here. . . . No unity, no Canada. No Canada, no capital.' Quoted by Frederick W. Boal in 'Integration or division: Canada and Ottawa into the twenty-first century', paper to the London Conference of Canadian Studies, 30 November 1990.

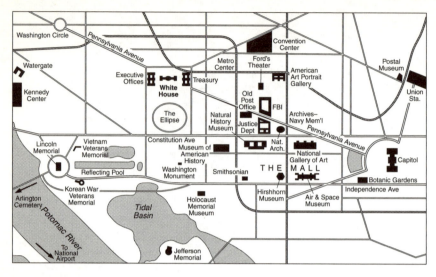

Map 4.3: *Central Washington*
The architect L'Enfant's grand design echoes the constitution in distancing the legislature (in the Capitol) from the executive (in the White House). Monuments and memorials form focal points for the city's avenues and for its broad, central Mall. On the Mall
they have been joined by an increasing number of modern museums – which are both
cultural symbols and tourist attractions.

redundant old Parliament House found a new use as the national portrait gallery, neatly summing up the shift from company town to self-
aware capital city.

Many of these changes stimulated or reflected the capital city as a
tourist attraction, exemplifying the axiom that objects observed are
changed by the act of observation. Tourists have never gone to London
or Paris just to see the government sights. But in company towns that
was all there was to see. The growth of tourism required that people be
given something else worthwhile to do – especially after a possibly
transcontinental journey getting there. People want to 'bond' with their
capital – to edify and enjoy themselves, educate the kids, touch the hem
of history, feel a sense of pride. They may want to 'possess' a bit of it
too, and what better way than by being photographed outside the White
House beside a life-sized cut-out of the president himself?

On the Washington, Ottawa and Canberra governing communities,
then, is superimposed a slow-motion, over-eating tourist community,
insulated from deprived and dangerous districts such as Washington's
Anacostia, riding fake trams and other dinky forms of archaic public
transport, taking over the Washington Mall from jogging civil servants
in high season, swamping the Supreme Court cafeteria in Canberra,

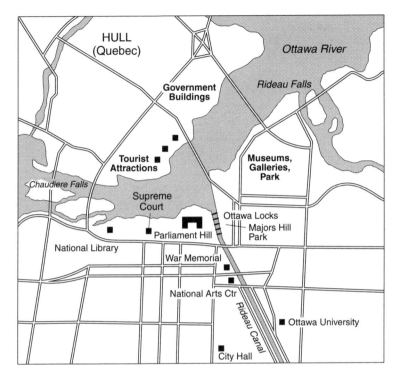

Map 4.4: *Ottawa*

Canada's federal parliament stands high above the Ottawa River, looking across to the Quebec city of Hull. Government buildings cluster on both sides, jostled since the 1960s by a growing range of museums and tourist attractions. These include the beautiful Rideau Canal (originally dug for military purposes), with a long staircase of locks dropping sharply to the river.

watching the changing of the guard on Parliament Hill in Ottawa. (What are they guarding? The ceremony was introduced for tourists.) In the same spirit, Sussex Street, home to the Canadian prime minister, was renamed Sussex Drive. Tourist and security pressure forced the closure of the Australian prime minister's gardens (1951) and those of the Canadian Governor-General (1986).[18]

[18] In 1951 Robert Menzies installed a 'guard room' at the gates of The Lodge, the prime minister's house in Canberra, as tourists (including at least one coach party) had started going into the grounds. Stewart Cockburn, *The Bulletin*, 7 April 1954. Another group which seems to enjoy protected capital city status is cats. In the late 1980s the author met a colony of feral cats occupying bushes just behind the Ottawa parliament. Well-wishers brought Kentucky Fried Chicken and comfy cardboard boxes lined with black polythene. Security staff looked on them benignly. In other cities, would the cats have been cleared out as vermin? Six months later the author found a colony protected in the same way in the parliamentary shrubbery of Canberra. A Commonwealth of Cats . . .

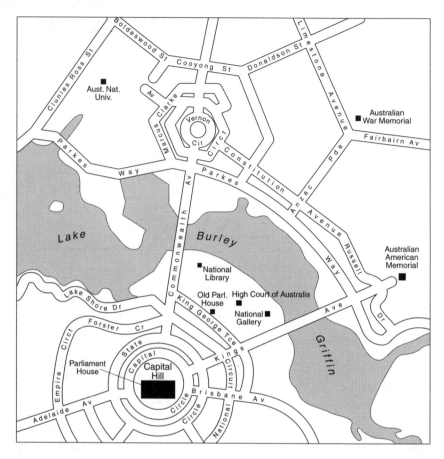

Map 4.5: *Canberra*

Canberra's Parliament House, on the summit of Capital Hill, is the main hub of the city. One-and-a-half miles away on the far side of man-made Lake Burley Griffin (named for the city's American architect) is the 'City' hub, Canberra's original commercial centre. Different radii link Capital Hill with the monumental Australian War Memorial and the Australian American Memorial. Along the lake lie capital city cultural institutions – National Library, National Gallery, National Portrait Gallery (the former Parliament House) – and the High Court of Australia.

Such snapshots should not be overdone. The claim here is simply that by making a difference to the character of the city in which the chief executive carries out so much of his public communication, they make some difference to how he does it and perhaps to how people react. At the very least, the city is a stage backcloth and an opportunity for propaganda.

Before looking at the third part of the city, the chief executive's own territory, three specific cases of the changing relations between physical places and political functions on the broader scale can be singled out. First is the fluctuating historical role of mass public assembly and display. This can range from spectatorship to 'direct action', from the mob to the disciplined demonstration, from the affirmation of government power (as in a Soviet Red Square parade), to a protest against it (as in Beijing's Tiananmen Square). Hordes of people have converged on the Washington Mall, to pressure the president or the legislature.[19] Television gives such demonstrations supercharged potential. Even when they are comparatively small, they are likely to get more national publicity because of being in the capital. Can a president remain unaffected? In a dramatic spontaneous gesture Richard Nixon, brooding about Vietnam in the White House in May 1970, famously went out at dawn one day to engage anti-war protesters at the Lincoln memorial literally at Lincoln's feet. Much of the gesture's significance came from the contrast between the location and the protesters on the one hand, and the beleaguered president – reaching out to ordinary people from his isolation at the apex of power – on the other.[20]

The area outside the White House itself is the wrong size for public assembly and is crossed by a major road. The president has always been inaugurated, for example, at the Capitol. The simple outdoor rite, in an often freezing January, spills out from the steps of the Capitol for a crowd which can watch or walk on as it pleases. The inauguration is followed by a mile-and-a-half ceremonial ride down Pennsylvania Avenue to the White House. The populist Jimmy Carter scored by leaving his car and walking part of the way, hand in hand with his wife.

A British prime minister has no such inauguration. Nor is there an obviously attractive place for the celebration of a general election victory: hence cramped pictures of (say) Mrs Thatcher leaning from the upper windows of Conservative Central Office. The victorious party leader will at first be in his constituency, in a town hall or modest party headquarters. He quickly makes a beeline for the capital. In 1966

---

[19]   Haussmann, designer of the Parisian boulevards, which were a model for other planners, was fully aware of their suitability for firing on the mob. The Melbourne parliament house, in which the first Australian parliament met, stands at the end of Bourke Street, a traditional gathering-spot for demonstrators. Its classical façade incorporates discreet gun slits, wide enough to accommodate machine guns.

[20]   Being spontaneous, the gesture was not managed by the White House press staff, and so its potential for sympathetic news coverage was largely wasted. The episode is described in detail in William Safire, *Before the Fall*, New York: Belmont Tower, 1975, ch. 8.

Wilson travelled by train. This enabled him incidentally to punish the BBC for 'unfair' campaign coverage, by refusing to be interviewed live in his compartment, even though the BBC had installed expensive equipment and fixed up the interview three weeks in advance.[21] In 1997 Blair created a sense of 'inauguration' by walking into Downing Street past lines of seemingly spontaneous flag-waving crowds (mostly party supporters and their families).

The immediate vicinity of parliament is inconvenient for very large assembly, not least because it is bounded on one side by the Thames. Trafalgar Square and (much farther off) Hyde Park are better spaces. Downing Street itself is tucked away and inaccessible, though much is visible from Horse Guards Parade at the back. Arguably, then, the governing enclave in London is not as well suited to political assembly as Washington.[22] London is perhaps more impressive for mass display in motion. The classic cases remain the Aldermaston marches organized annually at Easter by the Campaign for Nuclear Disarmament, at the height of the Cold War. Routed in 1958 from London to the Atomic Weapons Research Establishment at Aldermaston, the obvious publicity advantages meant that from 1959 the marches went from Aldermaston to London, gathering numbers for a climax in Trafalgar Square. The 'countryside march' attracted 400,000 people to London in September 2002. The focus of endeavour was to march *through* one of two arches, not to an assembly point; so 'display in motion' was indeed the purpose.

A second change to which London in particular has had to adjust is the growth of modern political parties. In a broad historical sweep, one can trace a shift in the location of many of their activities from the great patrician houses of the eighteenth century (Devonshire House, Holland House) to the Victorian clubs in and around Pall Mall, ten minutes' walk from Westminster, and then to the party offices on the other side of Victoria Street. The all-male Carlton Club was still a significant enough forum for the Conservative leader for Mrs Thatcher to agree to become an honorary member; and John Major's biographer describes him making a 'keynote speech' there, as his troubles mounted in 1993.[23]

---

[21]   For details, see Michael Cockerell, *Live from Number 10*, London: Faber, 1989, pp. 129–30.

[22]   When the prime minister has appeared before very large crowds in London, it has probably most often been in the company of the royal family on the balcony at Buckingham Palace for some great national occasion.

[23]   Seldon, *Major: a Political Life*, p. 361. Mrs Thatcher gave a lecture at the Carlton club in November 1984, not long after her escape in the IRA Brighton bombing. Hugo Young says her honorary membership was offered 'after considerable grumbling among the baffled clubmen'. H. Young, *One of Us*, London: Macmillan, 1989, p. 304.

The Labour party benefited from the TUC having headquarters in Smith Square, like the Conservative party. The distance from parliament was undoubtedly an inconvenience when the party moved its offices across the river to Walworth Road in 1980. Part of the modernization of New Labour, in preparation for the 1997 election, was a move back across to Millbank Tower, right next to the local premises of the broadcasting organizations and ten minutes' walk from parliament. (In 2002 the party moved to cheaper offices even closer.)

More of an impact on Washington was made by the growth of interest-group politics. Lobbyists and lawyers multiplied like rabbits in the late twentieth century. Registered lobbying firms grew from 365 to 23,011 between 1961 and 1987, lawyers from 12,564 to 46,000.[24] The developments came later in London, but by 2000 there were many lobbyists around Westminster – and their insinuation into the Palace of Westminster itself was an increasingly controversial issue, not least, initially, because of the space 'researchers' took up.

The third change to note has been the periodic adjustment of the government enclave to the needs of media. Typically this has involved the informal colonization of space and its subsequent institutionalization. In the United States the press won control over credentials for access to the congressional press galleries back in the 1860s. When reporters went to the White House, certainly by McKinley's time (1897–1901), they used to loiter under the east portico of the entrance, where they could collar people going in and out – including sometimes the president himself (see chapter 8). Teddy Roosevelt (1901–9) invited the reporters in out of the cold and enforced, by a simple process of excluding offenders, a set of rules about confidentiality and how they used the information he gave them. Under successive presidents, the rules became firmer. Eventually – and most important – the press corps was given responsibility for policing them. In the 1920s the White House Correspondents Association was founded. By the inauguration of Franklin Roosevelt in 1933, the Washington press corps had evolved from 'an amorphous collection of visiting editors, reporters on temporary assignment and disguised job seekers, to a stable community of professional journalists'.[25]

Already by 1900 there had occasionally been more than 150 reporters crowding into the Oval Office. By the Nixon era some 1700 were registered, including 600 broadcasters. In a further step of institutional-

---

[24] Hedrick Smith, *The Power Game*, London: Fontana, 1989, p. 39.
[25] Kernell, *Going Public*, p. 55. Chapter 3 of *Going Public* includes a good summary of relations between the president and the press up to the 1980s.

ization, after a period using adapted accommodation, media premises were constructed in the White House west wing, with a briefing room and offices for the press secretary's staff. A subsequent development (again initially informal) allowed reporters to broadcast from 'stake-outs' on the lawn. These patches of grass became literally 'media turf', the nearest thing at the White House to private studios. Broadcasters used them at their own initiative and controlled the proceedings within them.[26]

Presidents of course have talked with journalists in numbers varying from one-to-one to the large theatrical televised press conferences dating from the Kennedy era. On the whole, the huge size of the press corps has reduced and routinized the contact of its members with the president, increasing their reliance on intermediaries such as the press secretary.

In London the prime minister's roots in parliament, for public communication as for most other purposes, rooted the press there too. Parliament was never everything, obviously (for instance at weekends and for party work). But right up until the spread of political broadcasting, most of what mattered to news media went on in or near the chamber of the House of Commons and formerly the Lords. The result was a kind of physical duality at Westminster. Facilities for parliamentarians were matched, on a plebeian scale, by facilities for the media. Certain places were (and still are) common ground. Most were places of transience and informality, such as corridors, lobbies, lavatories, lifts and bars. All became subject to rules of exchange, reflecting the tension between parliamentarians' ownership of the buildings and their desire for publicity.

The first illustration of this tension came at a trial sitting in Barry's new House of Commons in 1850. No one in the press gallery could hear a word. 'What's to be done?' asked the prime minister, Lord John Russell, having been up to hear for himself; 'The House has been built.' The windows were blocked up and a false roof was put in – a remarkable triumph of function over design.[27] The opening was delayed until 1852.

Everywhere in parliament space has been a scarce resource. This has often been treated as an advantage by people who see milling and inter-

[26] Competitors in neighbouring spaces were not supposed to eavesdrop – a convention causing occasional rows. There were also arguments about dress codes, after one broadcaster was filmed from the waist up, wearing a formal jacket over tennis shorts. Robert Pierpoint, *At the White House*, New York: G. P. Putnam, 1981, pp. 20–4.

[27] Memorandum by T. T. Clarkson (*Daily News*), 1889, in Press Gallery archives, Westminster.

mingling as essential to effective parliamentary government. For the press it meant inconvenience in the office space behind the gallery, heroic rows about separate press catering facilities, and the privileging for decades of *The Times*, which had an office big enough to accommodate a double-digit reporting staff.[28] The advantage was ease of contact with MPs, since 'bumping into them' was more than a figure of speech.

The supreme example of the effect of space on parliamentary news-gathering was the use of the lobby outside the Commons chamber. Indeed this space gave its name to a system. MPs – including ministers and the prime minister if they wished – crossed the lobby to get to the chamber. At first, access for non-Members was unrestricted. From 1884, on security grounds, it was strictly limited to reporters on daily papers. Journalists too became 'members' – of the lobby group. Ever after, space limitations were used, often by journalists themselves, as the reason for preventing expansion of membership. Sunday and weekly papers, the foreign press, broadcasters: all had to struggle for access. Eventual success did in fact do much to devalue the system by making it too big (see the discussion in chapters 6 and 7).

The danger for parliament in restricting access was that parliamentarians themselves would be driven outside, to spaces where publicity was available, and the Commons would thereby be diminished as a forum. By 2000 this was widely believed to have happened. The causes were complex, but an unimaginative response to media was probably one of them. The Commons dithered for nearly thirty years before allowing its proceedings to be televised. Meanwhile, the broadcasters took over an adjacent block on Millbank. Rather like the White House lawn, the lawn on College Green, opposite the public entrance to the Palace, became an open-air broadcasting studio. On busy days, up to a dozen interviews might be going on simultaneously. Only in spring 2000 did the Commons agree to permit broadcast interviewing inside the building and to allow journalists to use mobile phones. Tape recording in the press gallery and filming in MPs' offices were other permitted innovations.[29]

---

[28] *The Times* took a full note of the Commons proceedings, rather than rely on Hansard. It still had a reporting staff of about ten in the early 1960s. In the nineteenth century several London papers had parliamentary staffs of fifteen or more. See Colin Seymour-Ure, 'Parliament and mass communications in the twentieth century', ch. 10 in S. A. Walkland (ed.), *The House of Commons in the Twentieth Century*, Oxford: Clarendon Press, 1979, pp. 527–95; Arthur Baker, *The House is Sitting*, London: Blandford Press, 1958.

[29] *Guardian*, 25 March 2000, 11 April 2000. As a three-months experiment, a glassed-in alcove off the central lobby was provided.

During the same period MPs and staff were for the first time routinely provided with offices in refurbished buildings outside the Palace of Westminster. Some of these became part of an integrated complex, described as a 'parliamentary campus', when a major new building across the street from the Palace opened in 2000. In addition to offices, committee rooms and TV studios, the facilities included a suitably stately feature – a glass-covered internal courtyard, with a tantalizingly visible private restaurant and mature fig trees costing a stately £150,000. The building's name – Portcullis House – reflected increasing use of the portcullis symbol as a parliamentary brand image.[30]

Taken together, all these developments amounted to a progressive loss of control by parliament over the communication outside of goings-on inside the precincts – and an unprecedented expansion of 'parliamentary space' beyond the limits of Barry's walls. The private meetings, chance encounters, chats over a drink, phone conversations – many such contacts which used to be carried on by journalists within, and conditioned by, Barry's design – were now dispersed. 'It is often more productive for journalists', wrote one of them, Jackie Ashley, 'to loiter around the television and radio studios of Number Four Millbank, than the often-deserted Members' Lobby of the House of Commons'. The *Guardian*'s political editor saw the same advantage in Portcullis House.[31]

It is difficult to be sure of the implications for the prime minister. The Chamber remains the physical heart of Westminster – the place where public performance and reputation are potentially most exposed. But writing about the prime minister, as distinct from reporting him, has become a physically less concentrated process, certainly in the stages of gathering information and ideas. At the very least, the emphasis has moved from the Palace to Downing Street. Looking at it from a prime minister's perspective, the idea of 'going down to the House', with the club-like connotations familiar in memoirs, must mean something less intense than in the past.

The prime minister's place, more than ever, is Downing Street. The scope to accommodate media there is extremely limited. The prime minister did not acquire a press secretary until the 1930s. The first modern secretary, Francis Williams in 1945, had virtually no staff. (See chapter 6.) The lobby correspondents crowded into the secretary's office in the mornings, until a briefing room was constructed in the basement at the end of John Major's premiership. For their afternoon meetings the lobby still use a turret room of their own at the Commons.

[30]   For details of Portcullis House, see www.portcullis-house.com.
[31]   Jackie Ashley, *I Spy Strangers: Improving Access to Parliament*, London: Hansard Society, 2000; Michael White, *Guardian*, 6 January 2003.

Figure 4.1: *A 'doorstep' press conference.*
Tony Blair gives a 'doorstep' press conference outside Number 10 during the 2001 general election campaign. The setting is simple but contrived – a rather formal version of the 'real' prime minister. 18 June 2001.
Photograph: Adam Butler/Associated Press.

John Major started to use the Downing Street garden for occasional formal meetings between the lobby and himself, as opposed to his press secretary. More substantially, as chapter 8 relates, he developed the use of the road outside the Number 10 front door – another political image with very high recognition – for important televised announcements or mini-conferences, especially with overseas visitors. By 2000 these encounters, initiated by Mrs Thatcher, were routinely described as 'doorsteps'. They institutionalized a hitherto informal practice, whereby journalists tried to quiz ministers as they came in and out. The doorsteps became practicable only after the entrance to Downing Street was gated in 1990, excluding casual bystanders and creating a secure enclave.[32]

---

[32] See also chapter 8. The practice of 'doorstepping' is international, and it should be contrasted with the type of intrusive journalism which bothers people at home. The enclosure of Downing Street, sadly, prevents aspirant prime ministers from posing for their photographs, as did the eight-year-old Harold Wilson, outside the Number 10 front door. The photo is widely reproduced, including by Anthony Seldon in *10 Downing Street: an Illustrated History*, p. 154.

From Mrs Thatcher's time onwards prime ministers increasingly let the television cameras into Downing Street for interviews and documentaries. The house was increasingly used too as a location for ceremonies, receptions and awards. Overall, however, Downing Street has not lent itself so well as the White House to accommodating the media. When Edward Heath decided to experiment with televised press conferences in 1971, he chose to hold them in the grand surroundings of Lancaster House, an aristocratic mansion on the Mall now run as a government conference centre.

That account of the adaptation of government enclaves to the needs of media has taken us well into the chief executive's own territory. In all the capitals discussed here, the main problem during the second half of the twentieth century was to adapt buildings to a chief executive's hugely expanded workload, for which they were never intended. Downing Street did so by colonizing adjoining houses and parts of Whitehall. The American president did so by incorporating adjacent offices – notably the Old Executive Office Building immediately next door – into an enlarged White House precinct.[33] Canberra did so by building large executive offices in its new Parliament House.

The British prime minister seems rather well sheltered in Number 10. He is sheltered even from the Cabinet Office by the famous internal door to which only a select group have the key (or swipe card). As we saw in chapter 1, he need not go to the Commons very often. He rarely meets journalists personally in Downing Street, and wherever he communicates publicly he does so very largely on his own terms.

The American president starts from a different constitutional position. Because he has no place in the legislature, he has to make an unending series of decisions about where to communicate, since every place will have a different significance. The White House itself is much more flexible than Downing Street. Clinton used twenty-one separate White House locations for 251 public occasions covered by media during 1993, for example. More than one in four was in the Oval Office (many of them brief photo opportunities). Other venues included the Rose Garden, the state dining room, the cabinet room and the library. Almost as often (235 times), Clinton left the White House and put on his performance somewhere else, either in Washington or beyond. Wherever he went, we may be sure, the locations were carefully researched and chosen for their appropriateness to what he wished to convey.[34]

[33] In a typical piece of capital city dignification, the building (which dates from the 1870s) was renamed in 2002 the Eisenhower Executive Office Building.
[34] For further analysis of Clinton's public performances in 1993, see Colin Seymour-Ure, 'Location, location, location', *Harvard International Journal of Press/Politics*, 2.2, 1997, pp. 27–46.

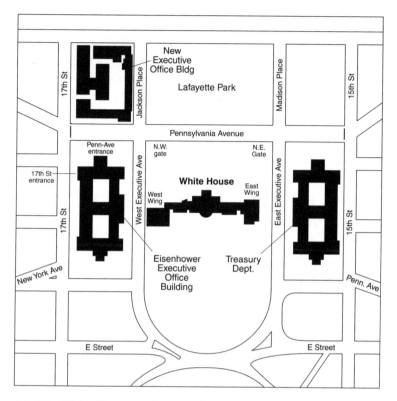

Map 4.6: *The White House Precinct, Washington*

The White House was not designed for 'big government' and strong presidential leadership. So presidential staffs have progressively taken over the House's west wing, the Executive Office building next door, and most recently the new offices on the northwest side of Pennsylvania Avenue. In effect, there is now a sizeable White House Precinct.

Matching Places to Communications

The question of choice introduces the second theme of this chapter – that of control. Chief executives will wish to control the places in which they perform publicly, or where their private activities are reported. This means control over *access* to a location (the number and type of people, the presence of media), the *terms of communication* (the time, duration, subject matter; the nature of any exchanges), and the *use by media* of the material they get. Control will rarely be complete, so the prime minister or president will have to make trade-offs. The less he controls the terms, for instance, the more his control over access will matter. When he speaks privately to a trusted journalist, he will talk more freely than in public to an open press conference. The president has no control over the huge indiscriminate audience for his inaugural speech, so he can do little but deliver 'noise' – inspirational but vapid rhetoric.

The factors which a chief executive might consider when making these choices about places would certainly include the following: the *purpose of a place*; its *ownership*; its *symbolic meaning*; the *needs of his job*; the *needs of media*; *convenience*; and *working routines*.

Places can have at least three types of purpose which might affect a chief executive's decision. The first lies on a public/private dimension. When a president goes jogging or a prime minister goes walkabout, they probably use public spaces; for security reasons, 'private zones' then have to be established around them. The floor of the Commons chamber is a semi-public space – open to observation by media and the public gallery, but private at floor-level. Many spaces have ambiguous public/private uses. The White House and Downing Street are the obvious examples. Media locations have their private sides too. More than one prime minister has found that remarks made in a broadcasting studio, but not actually in the recording area, have made their way into the press.

The second dimension of purpose is political/non-political. The Commons chamber is unambiguously political, but the American president has no counterpart. The non-political purpose of a place is very likely to affect the way in which it can be used for public communication – its suitability for partisanship, for instance. Churches and schools are clear examples.

The third dimension concerns whether a place exists for the explicit purpose of public communication. At one extreme are broadcasting studios and public halls; at the other come, say, hospitals. Communication from the hospital bed, such as President Reagan's one-liners after being shot in 1981, is highly charged.[35] The majority of places come between those extremes, including again the Commons and the offices and sitting rooms of Downing Street and the White House.

The next factor for a chief executive to bear in mind is the ownership of a location. Ten Downing Street and his personal home (if any) are the only places the prime minister 'owns' in London, with Chequers a rural retreat.[36] The president, as single chief executive, 'owns' much

[35] 'Honey, I forgot to duck,' Reagan told his wife when she rushed to his bedside. 'Please tell me you're Republicans,' he said to doctors preparing him for surgery. White House spokesmen released a reassuring trickle of such quips. L. Cannon, *Reagan*, New York: Perigree Books, 1982, p. 404.
[36] Chequers, a Tudor mansion in large grounds west of London, was donated to the nation in 1917 by Lord Lee of Fareham, so that modern prime ministers, often without estates of their own, could live and entertain at weekends like country gentlemen.

more, but with large quotation marks round most of it. President Johnson once retorted, when told his airforce helicopter was waiting, 'Son, they're *all* my helicopters' – a remark significant in itself and also for being reported.[37] Other places are owned by media. Others again belong to a third party: convention hotels (much used in Washington), university campuses (good for visionary speeches), airport lounges. Yet others, such as pavements, the location for many an unguarded remark to journalists, do not really belong to anybody.

The point about ownership is that it tends to go with control over access and the terms of communication. Two times out of three during 1993 President Clinton's public communication took place on his own territory. When he left it, he almost never went onto media ground, and generally he went to non-political places. It is very difficult to force a prime minister too onto media ground. The early years of political television included several incidents of prime ministerial annoyance and embarrassment on broadcasting premises.[38] From this point of view, the ability to broadcast in their own places, as a result of modern technology, has removed a disadvantage.

Taking purpose and ownership together, two examples can illustrate the kind of proposition which could be pursued more systematically. It is reasonable to suppose, firstly, that chief executives are most likely to be able to control access to, behaviour in, and subsequent use of what they have communicated, in places that are private, non-political, owned by them and without a public communication purpose. These are the family homes, gardens, holiday locations, private apartments – even bedrooms.[39] The president's country retreat outside Washington, Camp David, comes into this category, like Chequers for the prime minister. Use of such places is exceptional and therefore involves *ad hoc* rules. The chief executive can make these an implicit condition of access, such as when people are rewarded for some reason by tea at Number 10 or a weekend visit to Chequers, or when presidents chat with tourists

---

[37] I cannot trace the source of Johnson's remark but I know I did not make it up. The remark reflected both Johnson's personality and the constitutional authority of the president as commander-in-chief.

[38] A good example was a TV address to the nation by Anthony Eden on 8 August 1956, during the earlier stages of the Suez crisis. Eden had to broadcast in an overheated studio with lights shining in his eyes. Michael Cockerell, *Live from Number 10*, pp. 44ff.

[39] It is worth noting that the origin of the political usage of the word 'cabinet' in the early seventeenth century is the antechamber to the king's private apartments. Winston Churchill used to give dictation sitting up in bed. Lyndon Johnson (more than once?) gave an interview to a TV journalist while in the lavatory off his White House bedroom. Robert Pierpoint, *At the White House*, pp. 134–6.

in the White House garden. Access may contain elements of hospitality and privilege: hence a soft interview for John Major, for instance, when he gave the interviewer a televised tour of Downing Street.[40] Or it will evoke sympathy (Reagan's hospital jokes), or place journalists on unfamiliar ground.

When a chief executive does lose control over the use of information conveyed in those places, the result is a 'leak' (and possibly a scoop, from the media point of view).[41] On each side, the information gains importance precisely because of the way in which it was made public and regardless of its intrinsic worth. John Major's opinion of dissenting cabinet colleagues as 'bastards' was news mainly because it was accidentally recorded when he thought the microphone was off. But would he have been quite so unguarded if the interview had been in a studio, not at Number 10? Again, the rumpus over a publication planned by the Blairs' nanny in 2000 was essentially trivial. She evidently broke a legal agreement, but the Blairs reacted with extreme firmness – and then had to protest their sympathy for her.

The second illustration is at the opposite extreme. Chief executives are least likely to be able to control their public communication in public, political places that have a communication purpose and are not owned by them. The obvious example is an open-air public meeting or its broadcast equivalent, a discussion with a participating audience. In rather the same way, leaders give more information in private briefings during international summits, at locations they 'own' (embassies and delegates' hotels), than in the often huge open briefings.[42]

The symbolic meaning of various aspects of capital cities has already been discussed. The way in which 'the location as message' can be incorporated into public performance is self-evident. In principle, every chief executive could be presented with a gazetteer classifying places in the city according to their 'meaning' if he or she personally were to use them for communication. The president has a wide choice of symbolic places in Washington. If the place itself is neutral, like a hotel or conference centre, then the audience within it may be chosen to symbolize the message.

The symbolic meaning of a place partly acts as a measure of the weight the chief executive attaches to the subject being communicated. In this sense the inside/outside significance of the capital is important:

[40]   *The Prime Minister and Mrs Wilson at Home* (ITV, 25 July 1969) was the first such unchallenging televised tour. See Cockerell, *Live from Number 10*, pp. 145–6.
[41]   Cf. chapter 2.
[42]   Nearly 2000 American journalists applied for accreditation to the 1988 Moscow summit between Reagan and Gorbachev, for example.

it is a place sometimes to go to and sometimes to leave. Presidents have returned from holiday to the White House during crises, or have been criticized for not doing so, purely to symbolize their involvement – even if they did not need to be there. In one of the landmark episodes of desegregation, Eisenhower flew home to broadcast his decision to send federal troops to Little Rock, Arkansas, to enforce desegregation in 1957. He could easily have broadcast from his New England holiday retreat.[43]

Equally, it is routine to leave the capital to make a point. For example, when sensitive measures of national wealth (house prices, unemployment rates) showed the south of England continuing to prosper more than the north under New Labour, Tony Blair predictably made a prominent visit, with keynote speeches, to northern locations.[44]

A special case of leaving the city is to visit the scene of accidents and emergencies – an activity which blurs the president's roles as political leader and head of state, and which a prime minister has to judge whether to do himself or leave to a colleague – or to the Queen. Often words cannot match the trauma and emotions of the occasion, but the visual symbolism is potent.[45]

The symbolism of the White House is much more powerful than that of Downing Street, because of its size, specific position and occupier. The president has to strike a balance between the symbolism of going out to the people and that of bringing the people into the White House. An unusual illustration is provided by the tragic bombing of a government building in Oklahoma City in 1995, in which 168 people died, including nineteen children. President Clinton flew to Oklahoma to share the people's grief in a memorial service. But he brought the victims symbolically to the White House too, by planting, with Mrs Clinton, a dogwood tree in the garden before he went. At the service he explained that this was the idea of one of the government employees' children. Photographs brought both events together in the same newspaper

---

[43] Sherman Adams, *Firsthand Report*, New York: Popular Library edn, 1962, p. 350.

[44] *Guardian*, 6 December 1999.

[45] 'I have been now to the Midwest four times since this flood began,' President Clinton took care to point out at a flood relief bill-signing ceremony in St Louis, Missouri, on 12 August 1993, after disastrous floods. (*White House Information: Speeches and Town Halls, 1993*, White House internet site, 1995.) Peggy Noonan, President Reagan's speechwriter, writes eloquently of her anxiety about drafting President Reagan's televised remarks following the explosion of the Challenger space shuttle on 28 January 1986, and of her relief and that of her colleagues when the remarks were judged a success. (Peggy Noonan, *What I Saw at the Revolution*, New York: Ivy Books, 1990, ch. 13.)

pages.[46] Numerous Rose Garden and South Lawn ceremonies at the White House, as a matter of routine, assemble symbolic groups, brought in to receive recognition of awards, achievements, courage, service. But these groups serve too as set decoration for presidential announcements about policy initiatives, performance targets, legislative proposals – all the stuff of executive leadership.

The city can be used also to project the chief executive's ordinariness. John Major used to be photographed watching cricket at Lords and the Oval. Blair went to football matches. Such appearances are controlled without difficulty. Clinton's jogging seems to have been more difficult. Variation of route coped with the security problem. But in a public thoroughfare watchers feel entitled to throw questions. To the extent that Clinton answered them (especially if he stopped), the ostensible purpose of the (literal) exercise was lost.[47]

Tony Blair gave a neat example of the unpredictabilities which can arise when the chief executive deliberately gives up control of the terms of exchange in a public place. Late in 1999 he took the underground to see the new Millennium Dome: an ordinary guy, travelling the ordinary way. Journalists appear to have shrunk back in the carriage, to avoid spoiling the unself-consciousness of it all. But normality crumbled: the prime minister said 'Hello' to someone. He thereby broke a basic rule of tube behaviour – that you do not talk to other passengers. The passenger, on the other hand, kept to the rules: she ignored him. If the prime minister had not tried to behave like an ordinary person, she could have accosted him ('Aren't you the prime minister?'). He, by pretending to be an ordinary person yet speaking to her, behaved eccentrically. She, by cutting him dead as prime minister, behaved eccentrically too. He, in the photographs, seemed mildly embarrassed. She, the centre of a surreal scene, avoided eye contact and concentrated on listening to her personal stereo. The journalists got a funny story and the cartoonists a good cartoon.

All this was the outcome of uncertainty. Who 'owned' the tube at that moment? Was it a public or private space? What message did Downing Street intend it to convey? How far did the prime minister wish to

---

[46]   For the photographs, see *Washington Post*, 23 April 1995. The bombing, for which Timothy McVeigh and Terry Nichols were convicted, was the worst such act of terrorism in United States history, up to 11 September 2001. It did not appear to be part of a larger conspiracy or campaign.

[47]   'We've worked out our accommodations [with the security services] so that I can at least jog every day,' Clinton explained to a TV interviewer. 'I run different routes and we do different things. And I try to get out and see the people when I can.' *Larry King Live*, 20 July 1993.

Figure 4.2: *Tony Blair, commuter.*
Tony Blair takes the tube to the Millennium Dome. He succeeds so well at pretending
to be ordinary that he is cut dead. 14 December 1999.
Photograph: Jeremy Selwyn/*Evening Standard.*

dictate the rules of communication and exchange? The episode was
tidied up by getting the woman identified (her employers recognized the
photo), inviting her to tea and a photo-call with the prime minister at
Number 10, and telling the press that she said she had not meant to be
rude to him. Certainty was restored, eye contact made. The rules of
exchange were clear, the hand on the teacup steady.[48]

The formal requirements of the job to some extent constrain the
chief executive's choice of places in which to communicate. The prime
minister's job description has been discussed in earlier chapters.

---

[48] *Guardian*, 15 December 1999, 22 December 1999, 23 December 1999 (cartoon by
Steve Bell). The 29-year-old secretary explained that she had just wanted to concentrate
on listening to the latest Whitney Houston album on her Walkman. Other passengers
also ignored the prime minister.

Figure 4.3: *Steve Bell cartoon.*
Steve Bell's cartoon has fun with the resulting embarrassment.

Different places, for the president as for the prime minister, fit different versions – the officeholder, the human being, the family man, the party leader, the lover of sport or the arts. The president's role as head of state gives him, of course, a special affinity with the capital. A little bit of the prime minister, on the other hand, is always anchored in his constituency.

The chief executive's need to accommodate media is a constraint too, and it is closely linked to considerations of convenience and routine. We have already seen how parliament, Downing Street and the White House have been physically adapted to suit the convenience of the media – and so to suit the chief executive. Routinely used places naturally develop routine rules of access and behaviour. In the House of Commons, Prime Minister's Question Time follows a strict pattern, affecting permissible language, turn-taking among participants and the ways listeners may react. At the White House, transcripts of the daily briefings by the press secretary clearly reflect rules born of routine in an idiosyncratic language peculiar to the briefing room.

Figure 4.4: *Passenger and prime minister.*
A week later, passenger and prime minister are united in Downing Street over the teacups: Tony Blair at Number 10 with Georgina Liketi-Solomon, 22 December 1999. Photograph Peter Jordan/PA Photos.

The best comprehensive example with which to finish this discussion is the contrast between the prime minister's relations with parliament and the president's with Congress. The House of Commons is a public political place, where seeking media attention is an important purpose. The chamber has a strong symbolic meaning. This extends to obscure details, such as the lines in the carpet which speakers must not cross, so as to keep them beyond reach of each other's sword. Even if the prime minister's performance at Question Time is ritualistic and often criticized as a game, it symbolizes the ideal of accountability. His appearance there is a requirement of the job. As head of the government, he 'owns' the chamber – but only in a weak, custodial sense. He has almost no control over access, terms of exchange and the use made of the proceedings by media. The chamber has adapted physically to the needs of publicity. Its procedures and practices are dominated by routine and govern behaviour, manners and dress, in addition to the sophistications of the legislative process itself.

In other parts of the Palace of Westminster the prime minister has more discretion and control over what he does, and he can be private.

But the crucial significance of his appearances in the chamber is that they provide a reliable measure of the 'real' prime minister. There, his looks, language, mannerisms, personality and reputation become familiar, albeit largely through the interpretations of the media. The reality is artificial, like that of any public person, but it is consistent through time, and it is linked clearly to the political institutions in which he plays a leading role – a regular part in the same soap opera.

There is no consistent measure, by contrast, of the 'real president'. This may help explain the American fascination with presidential election debates. Candidates generally are not familiar to the public through a long-running performance on the congressional stage. The debates are a better-than-nothing substitute. But once he is in office, commentators are forever asking who is the 'real' president, in a way they do not about the prime minister. For the constitution does not link the president to any single or consistent type of reality that is measurable in public performance and in a specific place. The White House, as we have seen, is a private residence as well as a public office. 'Taking care that the laws be faithfully executed' does not have to be done in the Oval Office, in the sense that Congress has to meet on Capitol Hill in order to be Congress. The White House has immense symbolic meaning; it is regularly adapted to the needs and routines of the media; and the president is more in control of it than the prime minister is of parliament. But it is not a stage like Congress or the Commons. Therefore the president seeks stages beyond; and the capital supplies him a variety.

Conclusions

When they were constructed, purpose-built capitals such as Washington, Ottawa and Canberra, and the Westminster enclave within London, linked buildings to specific governing functions. The buildings helped influence how the functions were carried out. Since then, at the start of the twenty-first century, one of the effects of new technology has been to weaken this link. Almost everywhere is accessible to the TV camera and is therefore potentially a place for political communication. Moreover TV makes places suitable not only if they are good for talking in, but also (often particularly) because of what they look like. The symbolic potential of the capital, as a whole or in some small corner, has thereby been enhanced.

Since the office of American president is not restricted to a particular building, these changes were enormously important in Washington. They enabled a president to make a fool of himself on a heroic scale, if mishandled, but they were at least as likely to enable him to strengthen his appeal to the people and his leverage over politicians. In any case, he was bound to use them, since his competitors would, and the style and organization of the presidency have been transformed as a result.

The implications for the prime minister are less clear-cut. In an electronic age, prime ministers obviously want to get beyond Westminster and Downing Street, as we saw in the opening chapters, in order to exploit the communication potential of other suitable places. Downing Street has so little flexibility. Westminster has a very great deal more (sadly under-exploited) but it is not the prime minister's to exploit. Indeed any attempt to treat it as though it were would provoke the collective wrath of the elected legislature, which would see it as interference by the executive. But the prime minister was already being drawn away from parliament even before the electronic age, and the exact contribution of the media to the process is imponderable.

For either chief executive, however, comparable conclusions may be drawn. Both, more than ever (and in contrast to their legislatures), are *mobile* executives. The influence upon them of particular places in the capital has declined. The White House and the Commons remain pre-eminent in their different ways. But the number and range of places used in the capital should, on the argument of this chapter, have gone up. The chief executive has more scope, and more choices to make. The flexibility of modern media positively increases the potential influence of place.

If more places which have no political function (schools, hospitals, factories) are used for political communication, what, finally, is the effect on the chief executive's image? The likelihood is that the office is progressively demystified. Offstage, the actor loses his props. Away from his own enclave, the chief executive will tend to seem more like an ordinary person – unless his entourage sustains the formality of office or the event misfires, like Blair's tube journey. The personal and informal reality of the demystified chief executive may then carry over into attitudes towards the formal officeholder when back on official ground. Would the unprecedentedly explicit exposure of Bill Clinton's behaviour with the White House intern Monica Lewinsky have taken place in an era of greater presidential reticence?

Much of the argument of this chapter applies also to places beyond the capital city. But the capital is home to the chief executive; it is his principal place. Returning to the questions at the start of the chapter, what would happen if the British prime minister moved to the White House and the president to Downing Street? As head of state, the answer for the president is simple: he would take over Buckingham Palace, a secure enclave with lots of space and a suitable distance from Westminster. For a Washington prime minister, the key question is whether the press would stay, as now, in the West Wing. Historical example and the pull of geography suggest they would. The congressional press went along to the White House when they sensed power in the presidency; and later they set up shop there when the president gave them space. Would not the press do the same with the prime minister?

5

Harlots Revisited: Media Barons, Politics and Prime Ministers

Why was the former prime minister Stanley Baldwin so cross in 1931 that he blasted two press barons for seeking 'power without responsibility, the prerogative of the harlot throughout the ages'? One reason he sounded so cross (whether or not he actually was) is that he let rip with the century's most memorable anti-media soundbite, dealt him by a world-class wordsmith, his cousin Rudyard Kipling. That aside, the Conservative leader was cross because Lord Rothermere and Lord Beaverbrook had been threatening to use their newspapers against him, if he did not change his party's policy. Baldwin called their bluff – and got away with it. The press barons put up several parliamentary candidates, but their campaign fizzled out.[1]

Rothermere had also provoked Baldwin by demanding advance information about the composition of a future Baldwin cabinet, as the price of electoral support. Rupert Murdoch, the leading baron at the end of the century, never did anything so crass (at least publicly). But successive prime ministers clearly treated him with respect. No one has managed actually to prove that newspapers can deliver votes to order; but it is common sense for a leader to work, to some extent, on that assumption. Murdoch never became a Baron with a capital B and he spurned, as a good republican, the company of the upper cases. But how far should a prime minister today treat him and his contemporaries as 'press barons' like their predecessors?

[1] Baldwin's speech was on 17 March 1931. The barons' campaign, which was for free trade within the British Empire, protected by a tariff wall, is covered in standard histories of the inter-war period, such as A. J. P. Taylor, *English History, 1914–1945*, reprinted with revised bibliography, Oxford: Clarendon Press, 1976; John Ramsden, *The Age of Balfour and Baldwin, 1902–40*, London: Longman, 1978.

Barons and Baronies

What counts as a press baron – more accurately, now, a media baron – and how do people get to be one? Part of the charm of the term may be its lack of precision. In essence it means someone who controls a media property, who takes entrepreneurial risks, who is not motivated just by profit, and who runs it with a distinctive personal style.[2] But not all barons have all those characteristics. Some control without owning, or own their business without running it. Some are not empire-builders. Some do not have a cause to champion. Some do not have personalities that ricochet around in public life.

Until the 1950s there was at least no doubt what counted as 'media'. From a politician's viewpoint, newspapers effectively had no competitors. Lord Northcliffe, Rothermere's brother and the founder of the *Daily Mail* in 1896, controlled before World War I a larger share of national morning sales (nearly forty per cent) than Murdoch in the 1990s. When Northcliffe died in 1922, cinema and radio were already taking off. But cinema developed only a marginal interest in news; and while radio news had great potential, it was held back until World War II, because party leaders feared its propagandist potential and the press feared competition. The spread of the mass-circulation popular papers across the country, driving provincial papers out of business or into chains controlled from London, brought their owners a prominence both unprecedented and unchallenged by other media. Hence the arrogance with which Rothermere made his demands of Baldwin.

This expansion made the scope of the press barons national, rather than simply metropolitan. But by 1945 it had not yet produced much concentration of ownership among the national titles. In the early 1920s the twelve dailies were divided among eleven owners (see table 1). By the end of the war, each of the nine surviving papers was in a different ownership. (So were the *Financial Times* and the *Manchester Guardian*, which did not yet quite meet the definition of 'national'.) Concentration began from about 1955, when the end of paper rationing effectively reintroduced competition.

[2]   A good comparative analysis of the barons is Jeremy Tunstall and Michael Palmer, *Media Moguls*, London: Routledge, 1991. Tunstall updates his analysis succinctly in Jeremy Tunstall, *Newspaper Power*, Oxford: Clarendon Press, 1996, esp. part II. The Northcliffe–Beaverbrook–Rothermere era is usefully discussed in D. G. Boyce, 'Crusaders without chains: power and the press barons 1896–1951', ch. 4 in James Curran, Anthony Smith and Pauline Wingate (eds), *Impacts and Influences*, London: Methuen, 1987.

Table 5.1   *National daily newspaper ownership: 1920, 1945*

Paper	Owner 1920	Owner 1945
Daily Chronicle	D. Lloyd George	(amalg. *D. News*, 1930)
Daily Express	Lord Beaverbrook	Lord Beaverbrook
Daily Graphic	H. Baines	(amalg. *D. Sketch*, 1926)
Daily Herald	TUC/Labour Party	TUC/Odhams press
Daily Mail	Lord Northcliffe	(2nd) Lord Rothermere
Daily Mirror	Lord Rothermere	Various
Daily News (*News Chronicle* from 1930)	Cadbury family	Cadbury family
Daily Sketch	Sir E. Hulton	Lord Kemsley
Daily Telegraph	Lord Burnham	Lord Camrose
Daily Worker (1930)	–	D. Worker Co-op. Society
Morning Post	Lady Bathurst	(amalg. *D. Telegraph* 1937)
The Times	Lord Northcliffe	Col. J. Astor (Lord Astor of Hever)
Westminster Gazette (closed 1928)	Lord Cowdray	–
Total papers:	12	9
Total ownership groups:	11	9

Note: The *Financial Times* and the *(Manchester) Guardian* did not yet count fully as national newspapers in 1920 and 1945.
Sources: Various.

Titles and owners came and went, but at any one time there were usually one or two barons owning two or occasionally three national dailies. For example in the late 1960s Rothermere owned the *Daily Mail* and the tabloid *Daily Sketch*, and Cecil King's IPC the *Daily Mirror* and the pre-tabloid *Sun*. In the late 1980s the *Daily Sketch* had gone, but Lord Stevens's United Newspapers owned the *Daily Express* and the *Daily Star* (founded in 1978), and Murdoch owned *The Times*, the *Sun* and *Today*.

Comparable changes happened with the Sunday papers. In 1947 one-quarter stood by themselves. By 1995 all were linked to national dailies. Putting dailies and Sundays together further dramatizes the reach of the barons. In 1947 the three largest barons (in circulation terms) controlled only five titles out of a score or so, accounting for just half total circulation. By 1970 the three largest (a different three) controlled seven titles and nearly eighty per cent of circulation. By the mid-1990s a different three again controlled the same proportion of circulation, but spread across no fewer than thirteen titles.

Long before such end-of-century permutations, however, the definition of a media baron had been complicated by the growth of

commercial broadcasting and other electronic media, and by diversification. The Conservative government which introduced ITV in 1955
expected the press barons would join in. But the barons were chary, and
Kemsley, who was initially keen, withdrew at the last minute. Much of
the money came instead from the cinema and show business. Here the
key baronial figures, suitably bulky, were the Grade brothers (especially
Lew, of ATV) and Sidney Bernstein of Granada. When it was clear, after
a rocky start, that ITV was immensely profitable, the press barons came
on board. The outstanding early example was Roy Thomson, the Canadian owner of a string of papers back home and of the *Scotsman*, who
snapped up Scottish Television and famously described the franchise as
a licence to print money.

The moving spirits behind ITV reinforced its momentum as an entertainment medium. ITV's financial base – advertising – meant that it was
bound to stress entertainment anyway, to maximize its audiences. BBC
television, too, had an entertainment bias, since TV news-gathering was
still constrained by technical limitations. Without much exaggeration,
one can say that even in the later 1950s 'newspapers were for news;
television was for entertainment'. The increasing cross-ownership of
ITV and newspapers over the rest of the century therefore involved more
than just the cooperation of different technologies. Northcliffe and his
imitators had won huge circulations largely by making their papers
more than bald conveyors of hard news, stuffing them instead with
gossip and the scantily clad sides of life and leisure. But almost in defi-
ance, politicians persisted in thinking of newspapers as somehow 'for'
politics in ways in which radio, television and cinema were not. Apart
from a few cringe-making attempts to engage pop musicians in election
campaigns, this mindset did not change until the proliferation of broadcast news outlets in the 1980s and 1990s.

The rules setting limits to the accumulation of ITV franchises and to
press/ITV cross-ownership forced the ITV companies, from the start, to
reinvest profits outside the industry. Granada, for example, diversified
into motorway services, theme parks, bowling and leisure centres, contract catering, TV and video equipment sales and rental, and eventually
computer services and mobile phones. Granada began the new millennium by merging with the hugely successful Compass catering group –
a move which turned out to benefit neither.

The logic of such diversification often had a sort of 'media' thread.
Thomson, for instance, became a major travel operator – and in the
1970s you could have read the ads and features in your Thomson
Sunday Times or searched for the local office in the Yellow Pages, which
Thomson introduced from North America. More recent businesses fol-

lowed comparable paths. Michael Green's Carlton began life as a photo-processing company. It expanded into video production and distribution, hire of TV studios and facilities, and a variety of digital and other technical services. Then in the late 1980s Green, barely into his forties, moved into ITV, and within ten years he became a major force in Channel 3 and the (costly and unsuccessful) development of digital terrestrial television.

Diversification could also have a different logic. In hard newspaper times Thomson's papers floated on the profits of North Sea oil. The connection owed nothing directly to media but resulted from the shrewd exploitation of an investment opportunity. In some cases a conglomerate might include properties with no apparent logical connections at all. Until the 1990s, Pearson, owners of the *Financial Times* and *The Economist*, also owned Royal Doulton China and the prestige Château Latour claret vineyard. Long before the link-up between football and TV, Robert Maxwell owned (or part-owned) at least three football clubs.

Diversification made media businesses more international. In 1945, every press group was predominantly British, even if it had overseas interests such as the Rothermere lumber mills in Canada. In the new century, there is none of any size which does not have overseas interests or part-ownership by such interests. In 1945, again, all British broadcasting was owned by a public corporation – by definition, nationally owned. The legislation introducing ITV banned overseas control of the franchises – and even put limits on the amount of time given to imported programmes. By 2000, the franchise companies and the BBC itself were heavily involved in joint enterprises with foreign partners. The new technologies, such as satellite, are no respecters of national boundaries. Alike in ownership, technology and supply of content, therefore, big media businesses tend to be international in scope and scale. Government legislation in 2003 aimed to make ownership by foreign companies largely unrestricted.

An associated feature is the level of concentration. If the media marketplace is increasingly international, British-based companies must be large enough to compete with American and European giants, themselves in constant flux, such as AOL Time Warner and Bertelsmann. A historic concern for 'regionalism' underpinned the division of ITV into local franchises, to ensure a pungent supply of morris dancing and traffic jam stories. By 2000 this had virtually disappeared, and the path to a single, national, Channel 3 company was being smoothed. Local programming would be safeguarded by regulations about content rather than ownership. Special interests of most kinds, in the coming digital world, would be represented in niche channels.

The baron in the new century also controls a much more fluid enterprise than his predecessors. Barons move more freely in and out of media altogether; and within media, they chop and change. Groups commonly have shareholdings in each other, bought and sold in a continuous minuet, as they position themselves for takeovers and advance into new markets. (Nicholas Coleridge, researching his book *Paper Tigers* in the early 1990s, found the major barons keenly informed about, and watchful of, each other's whereabouts and goings on.[3]) Major groups change shape all the time. Charts and lists of who owns what change between the drafting and the publication of a book like this.

A final consequence of these developments is that barons typically own rather less of their organizations than they used to, even where an empire has been inherited. Colonel J. J. Astor (Lord Astor of Hever) owned ninety per cent of *The Times*, when he bought it after Northcliffe's death. Beaverbrook at first owned nearly all the voting shares in Express Newspapers and three-quarters of the non-voting shares. The *Telegraph* titles were a private company owned by the Berry family until Conrad Black bought them. Dominant owner–proprietors indeed survive – Black among them. But many of their fellows, as Lord Stevens of United Newspapers (the *Express* titles and the *Daily Star* in the 1990s) modestly admitted of himself in a House of Lords debate, are 'mere employees'.[4] Even the mighty Murdoch owned less of his empire than did his banks. Borrowing from banks enabled him to keep control better than financing expansion through share issues – although at the risk of finding himself overexposed in economic downturns.

How far one stretches the term 'media' in order to define what counts as a baron depends, lastly, on why one wants to know. Thus prime ministers – who are our present concern – might be interested in all or any of the technical, economic, social and political aspects of a medium. Some of the empires, for example, such as Granada or Thomson, have had a strong element of 'leisure', which makes them relevant to social and economic issues. Others, such as Black and Murdoch, have not strayed so far from traditional newspapers and TV – which puts them at the heart of political communication and partisanship. So when a prime minister focuses, say, on media policy, the barons who concern him may overlap with, but will not be identical to, those who exercise his mind about election campaigns or invasion of privacy. The media barons therefore vary not only with the scope of their own businesses, but also, in particular cases, with the purposes of politicians.

---

[3]   Nicholas Coleridge, *Paper Tigers*, London: Mandarin, 1994, p. 7.
[4]   1 July 1992, 538 H. L. Debates. c.779.

Certain types of person should also be mentioned, lastly, because they may not strictly meet the definition of a baron but nevertheless have the potential to be tiresome. The prime minister may therefore need to treat them much the same as barons. One such is the Chairman of the BBC Governors. The Chairman cannot follow a personal baronial agenda, but he is responsible for nurturing a long-established set of public service values, which repeatedly bring clashes with politicians. Harold Wilson made Lord Hill Chairman in 1967, as a deliberate slap in the face of the BBC: he had previously been in charge of the rival ITV network. In 1980 Mrs Thatcher put in George Howard, a safe Tory blueblood, and then found he went native during the Falklands War. He stoutly defended the BBC's measured coverage of the conflict. Howard was later followed by the more reliable Marmaduke Hussey, who had been Lord Thomson's key manager at *The Times*. In the BBC example, the Chairman becomes a quasi-baron because the prime minister appoints him (and then has to hope he behaves himself). Two other types follow the more normal pattern of being involved with media beforehand. The first and less common (and probably the type most easily categorized incorrectly) is the person whose media interests are not in fact his driving force. Lord Derby, for instance, was a first-generation investor in ITV (the Wales and West franchise), and he was very angry when his renewal bid failed in 1967. The victorious bid was headed by Lord Harlech, a former Conservative minister and ambassador to Washington. But neither man really fits the idea of a media baron. In the same way, Lord Gavron, director of a large publishing business, was chairman (unpaid) of the Guardian Media Group. But he had no authority to interfere in editorial policy at the *Guardian*, which is determined by the Scott family trust set up in 1936.

The more common quasi-baron is the editorial elder statesman. At *The Times* under the Astors, the corollary of proprietorial passivity was that the editor had baronial authority instead. Geoffrey Dawson, editor for most of the inter-war period, was a supreme networker among the political establishment. At the *Daily Telegraph* in the 1990s, Lord Deedes's experience made him exceptionally authoritative: he had been a Conservative cabinet minister under Macmillan and a lobby correspondent back in the 1930s. In the Mirror group of papers, similarly, two editorial executives had almost baronial discretion during the Wilson era. These were Lord (Hugh) Cudlipp and Lord (Sidney) Jacobson. At that time those papers were the only mass circulation supporters of Labour. Not surprisingly, Wilson also gave peerages to at least three other journalists in the group.

How to Become a Media Baron

There are three ways to become a media baron: build a business from small beginnings; buy one; or inherit one. When considered from the prime minister's perspective, there is also a fourth way. This is to behave like a baron, using your media property (and perhaps your personality) to promote your favourite political cause.

The greatest twentieth-century example of building a business from scratch was Northcliffe – a feat all the more remarkable because he died before the century was a quarter gone. His brother Harold (Rothermere) did not fully emerge as a baron in his own right until, in the absence of heirs to Northcliffe, he took over the business. Other examples of the type were Sir Arthur Pearson, founder of the *Daily Express* in 1900, Sir Edward Hulton, much of whose empire was based in Manchester, and the Berry brothers, William (Lord Camrose) and Gomer (Lord Kemsley).

By mid-century it had become extremely difficult to build a newspaper empire from nothing. The only successful foundation of a freestanding national daily paper since then has been Andreas Whittam-Smith's *Independent* in November 1986. This was narrowly preceded by Eddie Shah's *Today*, launched in March the same year. Shah built on the success of a regional paper, the *Stockport Messenger*, but he proved ineffective on a national stage. The paper was sold, and Murdoch closed it down in 1995. Whittam-Smith had a more successful formula and better backing. Part of his paper's 'independence' lay in not being dominated by a single proprietor, and initially no investor was permitted more than ten per cent of the shares. Financial difficulties eventually saw him lose control in 1994. The paper passed, from 1998, into the baronial hands of Tony O'Reilly, an Irish businessman (and former rugby international), who had built up an international media organization in addition to running the American Heinz business.

With electronic media, the position is complicated in the same way as the definition of a media baron. For example, the first-generation TV barons could not build up a broadcast business, like press barons, from scratch. They had to compete for a franchise, which meant having the capital beforehand; and anyway the rules permitted only one. But the cinema and show-business money behind the big franchise holders made them logical bidders. Michael Green was a logical bidder in the next generation. If 'TV from scratch' has never been a practical possibility, adding TV to an existing media empire has certainly been an increasingly important development.

Table 5.2 National newspapers: family disposals

Family	Principal paper	Acquisition	Disposal	Seller
Cadbury	News Chronicle (Daily News)	1901	1960	
W. Astor (Lord Astor)	Observer	1911	1976	son David
G. Berry (Lord Kemsley)	Sunday Times	1915	1959	self
M. Aitken (Lord Beaverbrook)	Daily Express	1916	1977	son Max
Col. J. Astor (Lord Astor of Hever)	The Times	1922	1966	son Gavin
W. Berry (Lord Camrose)	Daily Telegraph	1928	1985	son Michael

Note: The Berry brothers had a shared interest in their papers at the time of acquisition.
Sources: Various.

Inheritance of a barony is no guarantee at all of successful continuation. There is a sad remark by one of the last of the Walter family to have shares in *The Times*, founded by his forebears in 1784: 'You cannot perpetuate a dynasty for ever.'[5] The Walters lost theirs to Northcliffe in 1908. In a period of twenty-five years between 1960 and 1985, most of the heirs of the first generation of modern media barons sold up – the ennobled Astors, Aitkens, Berrys and Cadburys. (See table 2.) The reason was usually lack of capital or of management skills. Maxwell's complicated business disintegrated at his death, and it was by no means obvious that Murdoch's empire would long survive his own departure.

The outstanding exception remains the Harmsworth (Northcliffe–Rothermere) family. The *Daily Mail* was the sole national paper in the same family ownership at the end of the twentieth century as at the beginning. The *Guardian* can make the same claim only if qualified by the fact that it was not truly a 'national' paper until the 1960s, and that the Scott family gave it to a trust in which family members are a small minority. Similarly the Pearson family (Weetman, not Arthur) have owned newspapers since before World War I, but not always the same titles (the flagships by 2000 being the *Financial Times* and *The Economist*).[6]

---

[5] I cannot find the source for this remark but I know I did not make it up.
[6] For Pearson's involvement in papers, see J. A. Spender, *Weetman Pearson: First Viscount Cowdray*, London: Cassell, 1930, ch. 21.

Two further examples blur these categories. Rupert Murdoch inherited an Adelaide newspaper from his father, so he had a running start. But of course, from the vantage point of the British market, he 'bought in', starting with the *News of the World* and the *Sun* in 1969. Similarly Conrad Black used his advantages as the son of a wealthy Canadian businessman to build up a group of small-town papers, from which he expanded onto a national scale and eventually into the USA and overseas. In comparison with Murdoch, his empire was much further advanced by the time he bought the *Telegraph* titles in 1985.

The politically motivated men who bought into newspapers, while Northcliffe and his imitators were developing their own, had a variety of motives. Often they did so simply in support of a political party or faction. Weetman Pearson (Lord Cowdray), for instance, made his fortune as a civil engineer (his firm built the Blackwall tunnel), and he got involved with papers on behalf of the Liberals. He underwrote the unsuccessful transformation of the evening *Westminster Gazette* into a morning paper in 1921.

As that example illustrates, this device became less feasible for all except the super-rich, as the costs of the industry grew. The last gasp of the old system was perhaps the purchase of the loss-making diehard *Morning Post* by the Duke of Northumberland and a syndicate of Conservative oligarchs in 1924. (They kept it going until 1937.) For a similar purpose, the Labour party used the instrument of the TUC. The party itself owned the *Daily Herald*, and in 1929, as part of a relaunch, it switched ownership jointly to the TUC and J. S. Elias's Odhams Press. Elias (Lord Southwood) had fifty-one per cent of the shares but ceded control of editorial policy, having no political axe to grind. This arrangement lasted until 1964.[7]

Other purchasers' ambitions were more personal. 'I know the man for you,' said the Conservative politician Bonar Law to the impoverished owner of the *Daily Express* in 1910. 'Max Aitken is enormously rich. He knows nothing about newspapers and is not interested in them. But he wants to have a big political career and will be glad of a paper that will back him.' Thus the future Lord Beaverbrook's entry to the British press.[8] (He became in fact very much a hands-on proprietor.) Waldorf Astor bought his way from New York into British public life by much the same means, purchasing the London evening *Pall Mall Gazette* in 1892 and reversing its politics overnight. Waldorf Astor's

---

[7] Odhams was sold to the Mirror group in 1961, and the group bought the TUC's shareholding too in 1964. The paper was relaunched as the Labour *Sun*, which was sold to Murdoch in 1969.

[8] Quoted by A. J. P. Taylor in *Beaverbrook*, London: Hamish Hamilton, 1972, p. 53.

younger son John was not personally ambitious – but nor did he want to run a party paper. He bought *The Times* deliberately to keep it out of the hands of party politicians and Lord Rothermere. His relatives teased him for not only having nothing to do with it but not actually reading it.[9]

There were echoes of all such motives in some of the purchases towards the end of the century. Robert Maxwell was a Labour MP from 1964 to 1970 (when he got bored), long before he bought the Mirror group in 1984. He relished the role he thought his papers would bring him in Labour politics. Lord Hollick was a Labour sympathizer, but he became involved in media only when encouraged to join the 1991 ITV franchise auction. He had made his fortune by building up a major European financial services company, MAI. After his ITV successes (the Meridian and Anglia companies), he soon stepped into newspapers by merging his company with Lord Stevens's United Newspapers and taking control of the *Express* titles and the *Daily Star*. By 2001 he had had enough of their losses and sold them to Richard Desmond, who had built a magazine empire (including many 'top shelf' titles) from nothing and was reported to 'crave respectability'.[10]

The motives of other entrants were less clear. The Texan Robert Anderson, of the Atlantic Richfield oil company, bought the *Observer* in 1976 out of self-indulgent curiosity, having been headhunted by one of the paper's senior staff. Five years later, tired of the losses, he sold it to 'Tiny' Rowland of the African trading conglomerate Lonrho, who used it to pursue his own foibles and sold it to the *Guardian* in 1993.[11] Victor Matthews of the Trafalgar House construction business enjoyed owning the *Express* titles and *Evening Standard* but bought them, apparently, as a result of refurbishing the building next door. Then what moved the reclusive Barclay twins, who made their money in property and lived in Monaco and the Channel Islands, to buy the loss-making *European* from Maxwell's estate, and later the *Scotsman*?

The three categories of empire-building, inheritance and buying-in elide. Each seems to find new recruits in the changing media world. But before trying to see how a prime minister might view them, some other distinctive features need bringing out. For instance the amount and variety of turnover are striking. This ranges from selling up by heirs (a long-run cycle), to the whims or tactics of 'in-and-outers', like Matthews and Hollick (short-run cycle), and the loss of control by worthy inno-

---

[9]   Michael Astor, *Tribal Feeling*, London: John Murray, 1963, p. 146.
[10] *Guardian*, 22 December 2000.
[11] Tom Bower, *Tiny Rowland: a Rebel Tycoon*, London: Mandarin, 1994, pp. 393ff.

vators such as Shah and Whittam-Smith (short of cash). Well over half the changes in the ownership of the national press during the last fifty years of the twentieth century took place in the 1980s and 1990s. The TV landscape increasingly erupted, with the spread of satellite and the expansion of channels. Compared with predecessors up to the time of Mrs Thatcher, prime ministers face a media industry which seethes.

Another intriguing feature is the long tradition of the media baron as outsider. Many have been foreign by birth or have spent formative years abroad. This may give them a view of Britain tempered by detachment and suiting the business of journalism. Murdoch and Black were good late twentieth-century examples. The plaque in St Paul's Cathedral commemorating Roy Thomson describes him as 'a strange and adventurous man from nowhere'. Even the Lord Rothermere who died in 1998 was at school in the USA and lived much abroad, in France and later in Japan. The list in table 3 includes examples going back to Waldorf Astor.

The difference between Astor and Beaverbrook on the one hand, and most of the post-1945 examples on the other, is that the former immersed themselves in British life and politics. But Roy Thomson kept clear of politics and maintained his international business, even though he had to give up his Canadian citizenship for a peerage. Black's empire remained international, though he too had to give up his citizenship, after a fight with the Canadian government, in order to enter the Lords. Maxwell was to a great extent assimilated after serving in the British army during World War II. But his ultimate corporate home proved to be Liechtenstein; his business links were strong with eastern Europe and latterly North America; and he was at pains to be buried in Israel. (Beaverbrook, similarly, insisted in his will that he be buried in his birthplace, in New Brunswick.) The extreme case, perhaps, is Murdoch. Despite his impact on the British media, he spent only 1969–73 actually living in London, and he was content to exchange his Australian citizenship for American in furtherance of expansion in the United States. These shifts in emphasis reflect both the internationalization of the media industry (and of the technology) and Britain's diminished world role.

The last and most entertaining feature of the media barons, and the most tantalizing (can they really behave like this?), is their typically mercurial and autocratic management style. This, indeed, is the classic baronial hallmark. Northcliffe, for one, died mad (and threatened to shoot his dressing gown as an intruder).[12] Robert Maxwell, drowning off his yacht near the Azores in 1991, his empire foundering with him, may well have ended up too, in plain man's terms, somewhat unhinged.

---

[12]   R. Pound and G. Harmsworth, *Northcliffe*, London: Cassell, 1959, p. 870.

Table 5.3 *Media barons born overseas and/or buying-in from overseas*

'Baron'	Country of birth/business	First British acquisition/date
Waldorf Astor (Lord Astor) (1848–1919)	United States	*Pall Mall Gazette*, 1892
Max Aitken (Lord Beaverbrook) (1879–1964)	Canada	*Daily Express*, 1916
Brendan Bracken (Lord Bracken) (1901–58)	Ireland (grew up in Australia)	*Financial News*, 1928
Roy Thomson (Lord Thomson of Fleet) (1894–1976)	In UK from 1920 Canada	*Scotsman*, 1954
Lew Grade (Lord Grade) (1906–98; b. Leo Winogradsky)	Russia. In UK from childhood	ATV, 1955; also impresario and agent
Bernard Delfont (Lord Delfont) (1909–94; b. Boris Winogradsky)	Russia. In UK from childhood	Theatre and cinemas from 1941; impresario and agent
Rupert Murdoch (1931–)	Australia	*News of the World, Sun*, 1969
Robert Maxwell (b. Jan Hoch) (1923–91)	Ruthenia. In UK from 1940	*Daily Mirror*, 1984
'Tiny' Rowland (b. Roland Fuhrhop) (1917–98)	India (Anglo-German). In UK from 1934; also Africa	*Observer*, 1981–93
Conrad Black (Lord Black of Crossharbour) (1944–)	Canada	*Telegraph* titles, 1985
Tony O'Reilly (1936–)	Ireland. Business also USA and international	*Independent*, 1998

Note: This is not a complete list.
Sources: Various.

Northcliffe organized a priest to give thanks for his 'guiding aright the destinies of this great Empire', at a twenty-fifth anniversary lunch for 7000 *Daily Mail* employees. He liked being referred to as 'Chief', and he signed himself so with a big flourish. It can be seen on the frontispiece of Tom Clarke's *My Northcliffe Diary*, below a chilling letter which reads simply: 'My Dear Tom Clarke, Fire —' (the name is excised).[13] In similar style, Beaverbrook looked a new recruit up and down and pronounced: 'Small head. Big feet. Won't do.' The man made

---

[13] Tom Clarke, *My Northcliffe Diary*, London: Victor Gollancz, 1931. See also Colin Seymour-Ure and Jean Chalaby, chs 1 and 2 in Peter Catterall, Colin Seymour-Ure and Adrian Smith (eds), *Northcliffe's Legacy*, London: Macmillan, 2000.

a new life in Canada.[14] Beaverbrook, indeed, was famously autocratic, with a redeeming charm lost on the printed page. Those charmed come across in memoirs as fawning. As an old man after World War II, he still dominated his papers by telephone and dictating machine. When he came into the office, 'the whole building shook'.[15]

Lord Kemsley's self-importance extended to inserting under the title block of his numerous newspapers (all sold in 1959) the words 'A Kemsley Newspaper'; and he styled himself Editor-in-Chief of the *Sunday Times*. Vere Rothermere (the one who died in 1998) evidently described himself as a 'nobleman' – a fine irony, since King George V initially rebelled when invited to make his grandfather a viscount. Brendan Bracken's butler, when the editor of Bracken's *Financial Times* rang him late at night, replied: 'You may wish to speak to Mr Bracken, sir, but what makes you think that Mr Bracken wishes to speak to you?'[16] Conrad Black reportedly named Margaret Thatcher as his Honorary Senior International Adviser, and he loaded international statesmen onto his boards as non-executive directors.[17] Tiny Rowland lumbered readers of the *Observer* with pages of copy about his battle with Mohammed al-Fayed for control of Harrods department store. Lord Hartwell kept things in proportion at the *Daily Telegraph* by nurturing his rooftop lawn.

It is tempting to dwell too long on such random and trivial examples, so often droll. They are paralleled on a large scale by idiosyncratic business decision-making of make-or-break potential, at the boundary between 'flair' and recklessness. But barons can afford to be mercurial – not only because they may be their own boss but because they can literally afford the consequences. In this sense, they are pure, risk-taking capitalists. In another sense, however, they are not. For few owner– barons have been profit maximizers, rather than loss avoiders; and sometimes they are happy not even to be that, unless they are employee– barons such as Lord Stevens.

[14] Charles Wintour, *Pressures on the Press*, London: Andre Deutsch, 1972, p. 182. I happened to tell this story to a journalist in Ottawa. 'That was me,' he replied. The episode evidently was not uncharacteristic. Wintour writes: 'In assessing character, [Beaverbrook] had one weakness: he placed too much reliance on the size of people's heads.'

[15] Anne Chisholm and Michael Davie, *Beaverbrook: a Life*, London: Hutchinson, 1992, p. 474, quoting Beaverbrook's personal assistant, Mrs Ince.

[16] Obituary of Sir Gordon Newton, editor of the *Financial Times* 1979–92, *Daily Telegraph*, 3 September 1998.

[17] *Independent on Sunday*, 28 January 1996, quoting Richard Siklos, *Shades of Black*, London: Heinemann, 1996.

Those judgements would not originally have applied to TV barons. After ITV's shaky start in the 1950s, profits came easily anyway. But ITV regulations laid down quite strict content requirements, including about matters such as political balance and impartiality. Barons with a non-commercial agenda would have been cramped by TV. The last decades of the twentieth century in principle reduced this problem, however, for multi-media barons could indulge their temperaments at their newspapers and their accountants at their TV and radio stations.

Colour is added to the media barons, moreover, by the fascination of media people with personalities and by their tendency to hype their own kind. 'Great man' theories are preferred over economic or other abstract explanations of the successes of their bosses. Unlike many other super-rich, such as showbiz, pop or sporting stars and royalty, media barons are not by trade public performers. But they are ideally placed to get publicity, if they wish it – and even, in some cases, if they do not. Other types of industrialist seem less likely to court publicity in the first place or to achieve it if they do. The overall result arguably creates a larger-than-life image. Media barons continue often to appear as idiosyncratic, one-dimensional personalities – victims of stereotype and caricature, which are the typical product of random or imperfect knowledge.

The media baron in the new millennium, in summary, has got his barony by purchase, by rags-to-riches empire-building, or by inheritance. Mercurial and autocratic management styles survive, though less in broadcast media than in the press, and perhaps exaggerated by the barons' public depiction as larger than life. Droll this last characteristic may be. But in combination with the potential to use a barony for political purposes, it has a darker side.

Barons, Politics and Prime Ministers

Compared with Baldwin, a prime minister today has to deal with media barons whose involvement with politics is more indirect than Beaverbrook's and Rothermere's but extends more widely. The most obvious reason is the growth of broadcasting as the principal political arena. From its small beginnings as an unobtrusive observer, broadcasting has grown to bend institutions and behaviour to its shape. But the principles of non-partisan public-service broadcasting, though precarious in a multi-channel world, still limit outright political advocacy.

Newspapers of course remain a political arena too: they report and interpret the political elite and the mass public to each other, and they often take sides. There is no reason in principle why barons should not use their newspapers now like Beaverbrook and Rothermere, and a prime minister needs to bear that in mind. But the nature of press partisanship has changed. Baldwin's complaint came towards the end of an era when the links between the ownership of newspapers, party policy, party leadership and the partisan expectations of readers, were all much closer than they became in the second half of the century. The change is epitomized in the award of peerages. The barons used to be clients of parties, buying their peerages with cash or the promise of editorial support. Now party leaders are the clients of the barons, pressing peerages upon them. Beaverbrook and Rothermere, in fact, behaved as a modern baron might – using their papers as embryo party organizations against the established parties. When Baldwin grumbled, he was simply whining that they were not playing fair.

While barons' relation to the party system has changed, so have parties themselves. Mass membership has gone: embarrassingly herbivorous groups like the Royal Society for the Protection of Birds are bigger. The two major parties' share of the vote went from 96.8 per cent in 1951 to 74.7 per cent at the 2001 general election. Popular support has been volatile since the 1960s. The party machines are chronically in debt. Parties' capacity to generate solidly researched policies has declined. Fundraising is a risky ethical mess. The chief functions of party are the generational renewal of a pool of parliamentarians and ministers-in-waiting, and the organization of election campaigns.

The ground parties have lost, interest groups have made up. Many of the things parties used to do, interest groups do as well or better, across a wide range of fields – economic, educational, overseas, environmental, consumer, industrial, social and cultural. They have active members, assured resources, policy expertise, Whitehall and Brussels know-how, media and public relations skills. This politics of plurality is tailor-made for a conception of public-service broadcasting which, increasingly since the 1960s, has cocked its ear to a wider variety of voices. Interest groups fit the new patterns of media politics, just as political parties fitted the heyday of print. In many of the fields referred to above, indeed, groups generate much of the stuff of broadcast discussion and analysis. The growth of niche channels – for sport, music, movies – gives those subjects a place in the endless jostle for advantage in competing for society's resources. One by-product of this development is that a prime minister might well now regard not only the Chairman of the BBC Governors but also the Director-General himself as a media baron – and one over whose appointment some informal influence may be exerted.[18]

---

[18] Tony Blair made the retiring Director-General of the BBC, John Birt, a life peer in 2001 and gave him a job as a Downing Street policy adviser.

The press too has adapted. The broadsheet papers have supplemented (and arguably diminished) the anonymous editorial voice, by playing up a range of columnists and opinionated feature writers. The trend is less noticeable in the tabloids, which anyway give politics a lower priority. But in either case, press partisanship in the new millennium is both less categorical and less deeply committed. John Major suffered a more critical press from 1992 to 1997 than any Conservative predecessor – from papers whose interests and instincts were traditionally conservative. In 1997 Tony Blair enjoyed the support of six out of ten national dailies – twice the previous highest number for Labour.[19] Yet in his first term he could not rely on the consistent support even of traditional backers such as the *Daily Mirror* and the *Guardian*. Although the number of supporters rose to seven in 2001, they all had clear reservations.

The experiences of both those prime ministers reflect the extent to which, arguably, barons commit themselves nowadays more to leaders or to causes than to parties. This could be because parties are less ideological and leaders more 'presidential', or because the barons themselves are less locked on to the system which kept them, in Baldwin's word, 'responsible'. Thus Murdoch was an enthusiast for Mrs Thatcher rather than the Conservative party – and not at all enthusiastic about her predecessor Ted Heath or her successor John Major. Again, the Euro-scepticism of Murdoch and Black cut across tidy support for either major party. Euro-scepticism, indeed, drove Sir James Goldsmith, a media baron *manqué*, to launch the Referendum Party in the 1997 campaign. Lacking a newspaper, he distributed an amazing five million party videos through the nation's letterboxes.[20]

In one political field today's media baron does have an interest which is direct and fundamental: media policy. Until about the 1980s this was an invisible field. The legacy of late nineteenth-century liberal thought meant that governments of every colour pretended not to have a media policy. 'Freedom of the press' was construed as freedom from government intervention, while broadcasting was kept uncontroversially under public regulation because of channel scarcity. Policy relevant to media, of which there was a great deal (trade, competition, official secrets, fiscal, industrial relations) did not count as 'media policy', because it applied to other bodies too.

[19] See Colin Seymour-Ure, 'Newspapers: editorial opinion in the national press', in Pippa Norris and Neil T. Gavin (eds), *Britain Votes*, Oxford: Oxford University Press, 1997, pp. 78–100.
[20] The pollster MORI found 22 per cent of households claiming to have received the video. David Butler and Dennis Kavanagh, *The British General Election of 1997*, London: Macmillan, 1997, p. 219. Goldsmith owned the French magazine *L'Express*. In the 1970s he started the short-lived news magazine, *Now!*.

This convenient fiction became untenable with the arrival of cable and satellite TV, telecoms deregulation, and the national and international ramifications of further electronic innovation. The option of leaving media barons in peace is no longer available. Governments have to have media policies. When prime ministers make media policy, moreover, they know – which must inevitably give them pause – that they legislate for organizations which are an instrument of the government's own accountability and which do not care to be treated roughly.

In a media baron, then, the prime minister greets a man with a crunching handshake. The baron can commit his papers to a party, if he wishes; or, changeably, to whatever batty or sinister cause may tickle him, in addition to providing a marketplace for interest groups in general. He need not suffer the consequences of his actions, for he quite likely spends much of the year overseas.

Above all, what cannot be stressed too highly in the new century is the combination of newspapers with TV and radio. This gives the millennial baron a large share of control over the weapons of political combat (the flow of news and argument), the arenas in which the battle is fought, the prioritization of issues being fought over, and the vantage points from which the citizen/spectator observes them. Small wonder if people are inclined to believe he can sway the outcome; for this all adds up to an awesome potential, none the smaller for being difficult to measure, and all the more for being open to unpredictable and eccentric application.

How much leverage does a prime minister have when treating with such persons? The question is specifically about the prime minister's own leverage over the barons personally – not the daily grind of Downing Street news operations carried out on his behalf and directed at the barons' employees. (For these, see later chapters.) The prime minister's tools are formal and informal, but in either case rather limited. For instance, he has a certain power of patronage. Acquisition of a media empire remains one of the quickest ways of parachuting into the House of Lords. Despite its diminished status (even before the 1999 reform of its composition), barons still seem pleased to become Barons. The list in table 5.4, which attempts to track all who might qualify as media Barons since 1900, includes about as many who were created in the last quarter of the century as in the first.

Once there, however, the barons have generally taken no great part in proceedings (and less, one has the impression, than ennobled journalists). Much was made of Lord Rothermere's announcement that he would sit on the Labour benches after the 1997 general election; but the question how often he would actually go there was not pressed, and

Table 5.4 *A century of media barons in the House of Lords*

Created	Inherited	Age	Family name	Title	Prime minister	Media interests
1895		65	A. Borthwick (1830–1908)	Ld Glenesk	Salisbury	*Morning Post*
1903		70	E. Lawson (1833–1916)	Ld Burnham	Balfour	*D. Telegraph*
1905		40	A. Harmsworth (1865–1922)	Ld Northcliffe Viscount (1917)	Balfour Lloyd George	*D. Mail, The Times*, etc.
1910		54	W. Pearson (1856–1927)	Ld Cowdray Viscount (1916)	Asquith Lloyd George	*Westminster Gazette*, provincials
1914		46	H. Harmsworth (1868–1940)	Ld Rothermere Viscount (1919)	Asquith Lloyd George	*D. Mail, D. Mirror*, etc.
	1916	54	H. Lawson (1862–1933)	2nd Ld Burnham Viscount (1919)	Lloyd George	Sold *D. Telegraph* in 1928
1916		68	W. Astor (1848–1919)	Ld Astor Viscount (1917)	Asquith Lloyd George	*Pall Mall Gazette, Observer*
1917		38	M. Aitken (1879–1964)	Ld Beaverbrook	Lloyd George	*D. and S. Express, E. Standard*
	1919	40	W. Astor (1879–1952)	2nd Vis. Astor		*Observer*
1920		55	G. Riddell (1865–1934)	Ld Riddell	Lloyd George	*News of the World*
1927		73	D. Dalziel (1854–1928)	Ld Dalziel	Baldwin	*Morning Standard*
	1927	45	W. Pearson (1882–1933)	2nd Vis. Cowdray		Westminster Press, provincials
1929		50	W. Berry (1879–1954)	Ld Camrose Viscount (1941)	Baldwin Churchill	*D. Telegraph*
1933		56	E. Iliffe (1877–1960)	Ld Iliffe	MacDonald	*D. Telegraph*, provincials
	1933	69	W. Burnham (1864–1943)	3rd Ld Burnham		Periodicals
	1933	23	W. Pearson (1910–95)	3rd Vis. Cowdray		*Economist*, provincials
1936		53	G. Berry (1883–1968)	Ld Kemsley Viscount (1945)	Baldwin Churchill	Nat. and provincial; sold up in 1959
1937		64	J. Elias (1873–1946)	Ld Southwood Viscount (1946)	Baldwin Attlee	*D. Herald*, periodicals
	1940	42	E. Harmsworth (1898–1978)	2nd Vis. Rothermere		*D. Mail*, etc.
	1943	53	E. Lawson (1890–1963)	4th Ld Burnham		Periodicals, *D. Telegraph*
1947		63	W. Layton (1884–1966)	Ld Layton	Attlee	*News Chronicle, Economist*
	1948	30	E. Stanley (1918–94)	18th E. of Derby		TWW (ITV), 1955–67
1952		51	B. Bracken (1901–58)	Ld Bracken	Churchill	*F. News & F. Times*
	1954	45	J. Berry (1909–96)	2nd Vis. Camrose		*D. Telegraph*, periodicals
1956		70	J. Astor (1886–1971)	Ld Astor of Hever	Eden	*The Times*
	1960	52	E. Iliffe (1908–96)	2nd Ld Iliffe		Provincials
	1964	54	M. Aitken (1910–85)	Disclaimed Beaverbrook barony 1964		Sold *Express* papers 1977
1964		69	R. Thomson (1894–1976)	Ld Thomson of Fleet	Douglas-Home	*Times, S. Times*, STV (ITV)
	1964	46	D. Ormsby-Gore (1918–85)	5th Ld Harlech		HTV (ITV), 1968
1964		60	H. Renwick (1904–73)	Ld Renwick	Douglas-Home	ATV (ITV)

Table 5.4 (*Continued*)

Date Created	Date Inherited	Age	Family name	Title	Prime minister	Media interests
1968		56	M. Berry (1911–2001)	Ld Hartwell (disclaimed Vty of Camrose, 1995)	Wilson	Sold *Telegraph* titles 1985
1969		70	S. Bernstein (1899–1993)	Ld Bernstein	Wilson	Granada (ITV)
	1971	53	G. Astor (1918–84)	2nd Ld Astor of Hever		Sold *The Times* 1966
1974		61	H. Cudlipp (1913–98)	Ld Cudlipp	Wilson	*Mirror* group, ATV (ITV)
1975		58	D. Ryder (1916–2003)	Ld Ryder	Wilson	*Mirror* group, magazines, etc.
1975		58	W. Barnetson (1917–81)	Ld Barnetson	Wilson	Provincials, Thames (ITV)
1975		66	S. Jacobson (1908–88)	Ld Jacobson	Wilson	*Mirror* group
	1976	53	K. Thomson (1923–)	2nd Ld Thomson of Fleet		Relocated to Canada
1976		69	L. Grade (1906–98)	Ld Grade	Wilson	ATV, etc.
1976		66	B. Delfont (1909–94)	Ld Delfont	Wilson	Impresario
	1978	53	V. Harmsworth (1925–98)	3rd Vis. Rothermere		*D. Mail*, etc.
1980		62	V. Matthews (1918–94)	Ld Matthews	Thatcher	*D.* and *S. Express*
	1982	44	M. Hare (1938–)	2nd Vis. Blakenham		Pearson, *Fin. Times*, etc.
1987		50	D. Stevens (1936–)	Ld Stevens of Ludgate	Thatcher	*D.* and *S. Express*, *D. Star*
1991		45	C. Hollick (1945–)	Ld Hollick	Major	Meridian (ITV), *Express*, etc.
	1995	51	M. Pearson (1944–)	4th Vis. Cowdray		Pearson, *Financial Times*, etc.
1996		72	M. Hussey (1923–)	Ld Hussey	Major	Thomson group, BBC
1998		71	P. Hamlyn (1926–2001)	Ld Hamlyn	Blair	Reed (magazines, books)
	1998	31	J. Harmsworth (1967–)	4th Vis. Rothermere		*D. Mail*, etc.
1999		68	R. Gavron (1930–)	Ld Gavron	Blair	*Guardian*, Octopus
2001		57	C. Black (1944–)	Ld Black of Crossharbour	Blair	*D.* and *S. Telegraph*

Total peers of first creation: 33
Total 'media barons': 51

Notes
See text for definition of 'media baron'. Among peers excluded are book publishers (e.g. Lord Weidenfeld, 1976) and public relations/advertising people (e.g., Lord Saatchi, 1996; Lord Chadlington, 1996; Lord Bell, 1998). Persons may have been wrongly excluded or included – especially in the second and subsequent generations, when a Baron's media properties may have been dispersed or become secondary.

Media baronets and knights (many of them publishers of provincial papers) are excluded. The majority of the 'barons' received those honours on their way to becoming barons and viscounts. 'Advancement' within the peerage (e.g. from baron to viscount) was a regular part of the system before the Life Peerages Act of 1958. Since then the majority of media barons have been life peers. Lord Thomson of Fleet and Lord Astor of Hever, for example, were exceptions.

The Life Peerages Act also made possible the disclaimer of succession to a peerage. Media examples are Max Aitken (1964) and Michael Berry. Berry accepted a life peerage in 1968 and disclaimed his late brother's viscountcy (Camrose) in 1995.

Peerages are recommended by the prime minister, but several in this list have effectively been nominees of the leader of the opposition – for example Lord Southwood, Lord Layton, Lord Hartwell, Lord Hollick and Lord Black.

Sources: Various, but particularly *Debrett's Illustrated Peerage* (London: Macmillan, 2000), David Butler and Gareth Butler, *British Political Facts* (London: Macmillan, 1994), *Who's Who* (various editions), Viscount Camrose, *British Newspaper and their Controllers* (London: Cassell, 1947); House of Lords Library.

he died before it could be properly put to the test. The point is, however, that barons can be wheeled in to make speeches at critical moments, if required. Otherwise their peerage has a purely social cachet.

A more substantial kind of leverage used to derive from the barons' interest in formal political office. Several were MPs. C. P. Scott, owner–editor of the *Manchester Guardian*, was a Liberal MP between 1895 and 1906, and Weetman Pearson between 1895 and 1910. Colonel J. J. Astor was MP for Dover from 1922 to 1945, while owning (and reading or not) *The Times*. Esmond Harmsworth, heir to Lord Rothermere, was in the Commons from 1919 to 1929, Edward Iliffe between 1923 and 1929, and Brendan Bracken between 1929 and 1951.

As to government office, Lloyd George offered Northcliffe a non-cabinet post as Secretary of State for Air in 1917. Northcliffe did not want his hands tied, and his brother Rothermere was given it instead (1917–19). Northcliffe went off to head a government mission to the USA, and in 1918, to keep him quiet, Lloyd George made him Director of Propaganda in Enemy Countries. Edward Iliffe worked in the Ministry of Munitions during the war. The younger Waldorf Astor (the *Observer*) held two Parliamentary Secretaryships between 1918 and 1921. Lord Burnham (*Daily Telegraph*) declined ministerial office, as he did not want to risk compromising his paper's independence.[21]

More significantly, Beaverbrook was a cabinet minister in both world wars: in 1918 (strictly, of cabinet rank but not in the war cabinet); in 1940–42; and outside the war cabinet again from 1943 to 1945. He even seems to have believed he could become prime minister if Churchill failed.[22] Sir John (later Lord) Reith was in Chamberlain's last cabinet in 1940, within a few years of leaving the BBC. There, as Director-General, his management style had been fiercely baronial. Under Churchill, despite their mutual antipathy, Reith served outside the cabinet as minister of Transport for five months and then as minister of Works until early 1942. Brendan Bracken (*Financial News* and then *Financial Times*) was in Churchill's caretaker government in 1945 and had been minister of Information, outside the cabinet, from 1941.

No baron since 1945, by contrast, has either been an MP or held ministerial office. Cecil King (employee–baron at the Mirror group, and nephew of Northcliffe) was said to be keen for office and to have been snubbed by Harold Wilson with the offer of only insignificant posts. Wilson also offered him a life peerage in 1964, which he turned down

---

[21] *Dictionary of National Biography 1931–40*, Oxford: Oxford University Press, 1961, p. 533.
[22] Chisholm and Davie, *Beaverbrook: a Life*, pp. 439–44.

on the ground that he should have been offered a hereditary one, like his uncles Northcliffe and Rothermere. Robert Maxwell's parliamentary experience, as has been noted, preceded his newspaper experience. Lord Hollick was reported, when the MAI–United Newspapers merger was announced in 1996, to have 'few politicians among his closest cronies' and 'no desire for ministerial office', although he was a Kinnock recommendation for a peerage and a donor to Labour party campaigns.[23] In the Blair government he was given a part-time role as 'adviser' at the Department of Trade and Industry, but it appeared shadowy and insubstantial and lasted about a year.

This decline is not in the least surprising, in view of the changed nature of media baronies and the barons' attitudes to party. That is not to say, however, that the decline is irreversible. In particular, a 'hands-off' baron, in the Colonel Astor sense, could perfectly well decide to accept office. There are comparable examples from other types of business, such as Lord Sainsbury of Turville, who was a junior minister during the 1997–2001 parliament.

The scope for patronage outside the government, on a scale likely to attract a media baron, is small. The obvious example would be ambassadorships – a type of job with which American presidents frequently reward media barons. Top embassies (Washington, Paris) and High Commissions (Canada, Australia) do sometimes go to non-diplomats, but media barons have so far not struck lucky.

The prime minister's informal leverage is much more difficult to evaluate. Until, say, the end of the Macmillan era, there was probably rather more seamless social and political contact between prime ministers and barons than subsequently. (Attlee's lifestyle would have made him an exception.) The veteran lobby correspondent James Margach describes Winston Churchill defending himself in 1953 against complaints by his old Conservative friend, Lord Swinton, of having neglected the press. Churchill reeled off a list of people he regularly met, such as Lord Kemsley. Swinton pointed out that they were all barons not journalists.[24] Schmoozing now, if this argument is right, involves a more engineered kind of contact, which is no doubt why words like schmooze have been popularized to describe it.

The argument can best be explored by immersion in political memoirs and biographies. Quoting them here risks exaggerating the importance of isolated incidents. But take, as a late example, the efforts (more sys-

---

[23]   *Financial Times*, 11 February 1996. Hollick also funded the Labour-inclined Institute for Public Policy Research.

[24]   James Margach, *The Abuse of Power*, London: W. H. Allen, 1978, pp. 68–9.

tematic, rather than unprecedented) made by John Major's press secretary, Chris Meyer, to improve the prime minister's woeful standing after 1992. Meyer set up a routine in which every fortnight a different editor would be invited to Downing Street for a drink at 6.00 p.m. with just the prime minister and Meyer. They were free to use unattributably whatever they heard. None refused to come. Meyer worked on the lobby too.

This was getting at the barons through their underlings. To get at the underlings through the barons, Major was persuaded both to make more use of Chequers for entertainment and to hold dinners at Downing Street. Murdoch came to several of these. Rothermere and Black came to dinner during the visit by President Clinton in November 1995, and Stevens to a dinner for President Chirac.[25]

General contact with barons overlaps with more specific interventions by prime ministers. Rupert Murdoch's career alone provides ample examples. The ambiguously worded monopoly law affecting the purchase of newspapers was interpreted favourably during the Thatcher era, to facilitate the purchase of *The Times* and the *Sunday Times* by Murdoch from Thomson in 1981, and then his purchase of *Today* from Lonrho in 1987.[26] In 1986, Thatcher-inspired industrial relations legislation underpinned Murdoch's successful confrontation with the print unions, when he moved overnight to new plant in Wapping. The Thatcher government made sure too that the 1990 Broadcasting Act's cross-ownership rules did not prevent him from being able to control the Sky satellite channels, in addition to his newspaper empire.

Tony Blair courted Murdoch earnestly in opposition, which may have helped secure the psychologically important victory of *Sun* endorsement in the 1997 general election. In government the courtship continued. Blair seemed ready to help Murdoch's ambitions in continental Europe by intervening with the Italian prime minister, Romano Prodi, about BSkyB buying an interest in the Italian television group Mediaset.[27] In his first administration's broadcast legislation, Blair did nothing at all to threaten Murdoch's interests through adjusting cross-ownership rules, and his proposals in 2003 actually favoured them by entitling papers to buy up ITV Channel 5. Nor did he act against Murdoch's newspaper price cuts, subsidized by his other properties and aimed at dragging down rivals. When the Trade Secretary, Stephen Byers, had to decide whether to permit Murdoch to buy control of Manchester

[25] This account is drawn from Anthony Seldon, *Major: a Political Life*, London: Phoenix, 1998, pp. 708–13.
[26] Jeremy Tunstall and Michael Palmer, *Media Moguls*, p. 108.
[27] *Financial Times*, 13 November 1998.

United, Blair took trouble to make clear it was Byers's decision, not his. (Byers banned it.)[28]

Such activity was not at the expense of other barons. Blair not only attended the memorial service for Lord Rothermere but read a lesson at it – though it stretches credulity to believe that he had been an intimate of the family. Richard Desmond's 'craving for respectability' no doubt began to be satisfied, too, when Blair invited him to tea at Downing Street. In the battle for the Express titles, Blair was reported to have actively backed a bid by the controversial Hinduja brothers.[29]

Even where a prime minister is not involved in the detail of such episodes (and Murdoch is an extreme case) the centrality of media to the political process means that he is almost bound to get drawn in at some level: hence the neatness of the Byers example. Issues which might affect media support in an election touch the prime minister's leadership too closely for him to keep clear; while issues of media policy usually involve several government departments – and, so long as there is no 'minister for communications' transcending the Department of Media, Culture and Sport, the prime minister tends to take the lead.

Media Barons and Accountability

However much prime ministers patronize and schmooze with the barons and give them an occasional helping hand, their formal power is really very limited. They had a far simpler task in the days before the mass circulation barons cut the press free from financial control by parties, and when broadcasting was safely neutered politically by public corporation monopoly ownership.

The exact amount of awesomeness of the media baron's potential depends on your view of media power. Are you interested in conscious or unconscious power, and intentional or unintentional? in impact on knowledge, emotions, attitudes or behaviour? in individuals or in mass audiences? and in the short or the long run? Whatever your interest, however, and whatever power you think the media had in Baldwin's time, their power is unlikely to be less today. It brings with it, as political power always does, corresponding questions of public accountability.

[28]   Andrew Rawnsley, *Servants of the People*, London: Hamish Hamilton, 2000, pp. 293–4.
[29]   Downing Street denied any direct contact between the prime minister and the two brothers, billionaire Indian businessmen who helped sponsor the Millennium Dome and acquired British passports. *Guardian*, 2 February 2001.

The media barons in the new millennium have surely never been less accountable. Certainly their newspapers are accountable to market forces – which is their defence against allegations about the 'dumbing down' of content. But these are lumbering, long-run forces. They are diminished by the readiness of barons to run papers at a loss; and they involve economic more than social or political accountability. The public accountability of broadcast media is more effective in its prohibitions against partiality than in its positive requirements, while economic accountability is infrequent and unpredictable.

What could a prime minister do? Legislation is fraught with familiar difficulties, whether directed at ownership or content. Developments in technology make limitations on cross-ownership even more of a tangle than before (and the Blair government seemed set on weakening them). Besides, legislation runs up against the conundrum about whether prime ministers need to be held accountable by the media more than the media by prime ministers.

As an alternative, why should media barons not be exposed to a Media Register? This could be looked after by whatever the Department of Culture, Media and Sport of the day happened to be called, or as one of the responsibilities of the 'Ofcom' set up by legislation in 2003. Or it could be run independently, like the Press Complaints Commission. What counted as 'media' would have to be reviewed from time to time. The process of review would itself be a spur to the unending debate about how far media should be defined, for policy purposes, by reference to economics, technology, consumer use or social purpose. At least annually, the Register would draw the attention of parliament (for instance through the Culture, Media and Sport select committee) to matters of public interest. These might include changes in foreign ownership, concentration, conglomeration, cross-ownership – anything of significance to public media policy.

Media barons (suitably defined) should have to put on record the nature of their relationship with their media property, and any other information of public interest, such as membership of a political interest group or party. In a world where every matchstick has a mission statement, newspaper barons should also place on the Register, and in their company's annual report, a statement about their papers' political principles and the role of the proprietor in deciding them. (Northcliffe, incidentally, included a mission statement in the first number of the *Daily Mail* on 4 May 1896 – a short paragraph headed 'The Explanation'.) These statements, naturally, would be anodyne. As predictors of behaviour they would have drawbacks similar to those of voluntary codes, such as that established by the Press Complaints Commission.

But those drawbacks do not make such codes entirely useless. They are a benchmark and a hostage to fortune.

The Register, in short, would provide a comprehensive inventory of the changing ownership of Britain's media and of the institutions and individuals which control them. At present such information is too hard to get. Official regulators and trade associations provide it to varying degrees in their own spheres. But no organization maintains oversight as a whole. For the press there has been no regular oversight at all, since the old Press Council was reorganized as the Press Complaints Commission in the early 1990s. Up to then, the Council's annual report was a modestly indispensable source.

Once the scope of media is extended to include film, video, recorded music, book publishing, TV production companies or internet servers, the lack of an authoritative or official source to which an inquirer may routinely go is even more glaring. To personalize the argument, it should have been publicly unacceptable for someone like Lord Hollick to act as part-time adviser to ministers (especially in a department dealing with trade), without formally going on record about his exact role in his media businesses – particularly the newspapers. Maybe Lord Hollick did go on the record. But the lack of a Media Register makes it difficult to find out where.

This idea has met courteous indifference when tried out on audiences (admittedly some of them mainly in the media). Perhaps it is doomed by sounding bureaucratic or feeble. Its underlying objective is 'Light! More light!', its rallying cry 'Oversight, not regulation'. That is hardly the stuff of Henry V on Crispin Crispian's day. But this should make it all the less threatening to the media industry and easier for a government to set up. At present, on top of everything previously outlined, the media baron's role in his media organization is unclear, and by normal standards unresearchable. So are his relations with prime ministers and politicians. He does not submit to scrutiny in the established public forums but sets out his ideas through intermediaries, gossip columns or (the Murdoch way) the big set-piece lecture.

The only plausible defence of such a person lies in the shifting relations of government, media and people. Which, of the former two, is more likely to harm the third? So long as the roles vary, there is at least a sort of defence against the unaccountable baron. But please let the prime minister make the barons come into the light.

6

The Rise of the Downing Street Press Secretary

Harold Wilson's press secretary, Joe Haines, had a rule (jokingly). If anybody in the office, including himself, got their picture in the paper, they forfeited a bottle of wine. That was in the mid-1970s. Ten years later the office would have been chronically tipsy.

The press secretary became more visible through the growth of televised political coverage. But there was more to it than that. Mrs Thatcher's press secretary, Bernard Ingham, held the job for all but the first six months of her long premiership. He was a burly Yorkshireman with a bluff personality and a stock of catchphrases ('bunkum and balderdash'). He was a familiar figure at Mrs Thatcher's side, an item in the diary columns of the press, a target for snipers in parliamentary questions.

Sniping at Ingham became more and more usual. Not only was he visible: increasingly he was controversial. This was difficult for a key member of the prime minister's staff to avoid – as it was later for Tony Blair's press secretary Alastair Campbell, another burly Yorkshireman. But personalities aside, the controversy in each case reflected a growing curiosity among politicians and the media about Downing Street communications management and the precise role of the press secretary – an unelected, unaccountable and apparently very influential official.

Communications management, chapter 2 argued, must be a top priority for any prime minister who does not want to risk losing control of his image, his reputation, his say in the news agenda and his leverage over policies and events. In addition to traditional forums and activities, electronic media have brought into play the informal, personal and non-governing prime ministerial roles and characteristics described in the opening chapters, so that anything the prime minister does and anywhere he does it may hit headlines. More than it used to be, arguably, his power, like the American president's, is the power to persuade.

The prime minister's press secretary tends to be in the thick of all that. By analysing the development of the job since it became firmly established at the end of World War II, we can get a particular perspective on different prime ministers' styles of leadership and their responses to the demands and opportunities provided by the development of media.

Over the years, the press secretary's office has grown and ramified. But much of the growth has been to cope with routines. The press secretaryship itself has fluctuated in the importance prime ministers have attached to it. In this, the job personifies a general conundrum about a prime minister's public communication (touched on at the end of chapter 1). That is, how much effort (time, energy, money, staff) should be spent on the *substance* of government – actual 'governing' – and how much on the *presentation*? Policies (and leaders) are no good unless they are put over successfully. Questions of presentation are therefore intrinsic to decisions about what policies to choose.[1] Whatever the existing level, there is generally a good case for believing that more resources devoted to presentation will increase the chances of success. (Indeed, when things go wrong, governments typically blame the media for misrepresenting them, and they step up their news operations.) But where to strike the balance, and who to put in charge?

It would therefore be wrong to think that the importance of the press secretary has necessarily grown in proportion to the size of the office. A newspaper comment that 'he seemed to have the status almost of a minister', far from referring to Ingham or Campbell, was made in 1947 on the retirement of Attlee's first press secretary, Francis Williams. Not until Ingham, forty years later, were such comments made again.

The Downing Street press secretary, in sum, has often been at the heart of the prime minister's entourage, reflects the prime minister's style of communications management, and has become increasingly controversial. How has the job developed? What are the issues that make it controversial?

The Press Secretary's Development

Until the Attlee government came to power in 1945, the office of press secretary was rudimentary. The word 'office' could refer to a job but

[1] 'The extent to which the Chief Press Secretary influences policy is seldom clear-cut. Sometimes . . . presentational advice can apparently be conclusive in heading off a course of action. On other occasions it may subtly rather than dramatically change the nature, if not necessarily the substance, of an announcement.' Bernard Ingham, *Kill the Messenger*, London: HarperCollins, 1991, p. 326.

hardly to an institution. Thereafter it became in turn *specialized, institutionalized, enlarged* and *diversified*. Existing roles were elaborated and new ones acquired. (The same might be said of the organization of the prime minister's entourage as a whole.[2])

This process was nothing like as cut and dried as the language might suggest. Job descriptions at Downing Street have historically been informal and flexible, symbolized in claims that the house is a home, not an office block. (Ted Heath, for one, was said to refer to the staff as 'the family'.[3]) As late as the 1980s the press secretary had no formal, official job description. But from the start the work included, in varying degrees, tasks as *spokesman, adviser on media relations, agent* (or intermediary) with news media, and *coordinator* of government information. Broadly, these mirror the prime minister's own communication roles (see chapter 1), as a *source of news*, a *public performer* and a *communications manager*. The press secretary also acquired a growing responsibility as office manager. With a few prime ministers (most conspicuously Blair), he has had an important and entirely informal role as a confidant or 'confessor'.

This last role links to one of the press secretary's most distinctive and intriguing features. More than (any?) other members of a prime minister's entourage, the press secretary has a certain 'apartness', occasionally likened to that of a court jester. His primary duty is to the prime minister: yet he cannot fulfil it effectively without a commitment also to the different, and potentially conflicting, goals of his news media clientele. He is a man (never, so far, a woman) in the middle. The tension is constructive, in that the interests of each side are served by taking account of the other. It is best illustrated in the fundamental importance of the secretary's credibility. He is little use to his boss unless he has the confidence of the media, nor to the media without the confidence of his boss. Haines, for instance, though extremely close to Harold Wilson, probably did nothing to help him by falling out with the lobby correspondents and cancelling their traditional twice-daily collective briefings. Anthony Eden's press secretary William Clark, in contrast, soon lost the confidence of the lobby, when it became clear that he was becoming distanced from the prime minister during Eden's secretive and ultimately disastrous Suez policy in 1956. The challenge to Alastair Campbell's survival in office at the height of government clashes with the media in 2002 was, fundamentally, a matter of doubts about his

[2]   J. M. Lee, G. W. Jones and June Burnham, *At the Centre of Whitehall*, London: Macmillan, 1998, pp. 36–40.
[3]   Interview, Sir Donald Maitland, 4 April 1988.

credibility more than about his judgement or veracity.[4] Once lost, the secretary's credibility is difficult to regain; it is better that he leaves.

The development of the press secretary's office can be shown schematically as a circle. (See figure 6.1.) Insofar as it outlines responses to changes in media and in government organization that were similar in parliamentary systems such as Canada and Australia and in the United States, it can be applied more broadly than to Britain alone. Starting from the position in which a prime minister (or president) was his own press secretary, each stage represents a development of function or resources. The path returns to the prime minister, rather than being linear, because the completion of the circle places him or her *personally* (rather than nominally) at the centre of public communication again, as news source, performer, media strategist and manager.

Although the historical tendency has been to move round the circle, movement has not been consistently in one direction. This is because of the argument already set out, which suggests that there is no unique logic for determining the priority for public communication. A prime minister who did not think the effort necessary (such as Churchill, Heath and perhaps Callaghan) can go back to an earlier point on the circle, in some if not all particulars, and making allowance for changes in technology. Equally, some prime ministers, such as Neville Chamberlain and Harold Wilson, took a lot of trouble with public communication before the process of specialization and diversification had gone very far (see chapter 8). In the United States, similarly, one journalist, recalling the Washington of the 1930s, could write of Franklin Roosevelt's press secretary Stephen Early: 'The whole administration was a public relations effort, and Early was right in the middle of it.'[5] This was fifty years before exactly the same kind of comments became commonplace about the Reagan presidency. What changes, in other words, is not the scope for prime ministers and presidents to prioritize public communication but the apparatus and techniques involved.

Press relations were first handled, in London, Washington and comparable capitals, as one of several responsibilities of a general aide or secretary. At the White House the president was anyway permitted only two assistants at the professional level, to cope with all his needs, until the early 1930s. Stephen Early, appointed in 1933, still spread his activ-

---

[4]   The culminating issue (see also Conclusion to the next chapter), was Downing Street's embarrassed withdrawal of its complaint to the Press Complaints Commission about press allegations that the prime minister had sought too prominent a role in the Queen Mother's obsequies. See, e.g., *Guardian*, 13 June 2002.

[5]   Quoted by M. B. Grossman and M. J. Kumar in *Portraying the President*, Baltimore, Md.: Johns Hopkins University Press, 1981, p. 23.

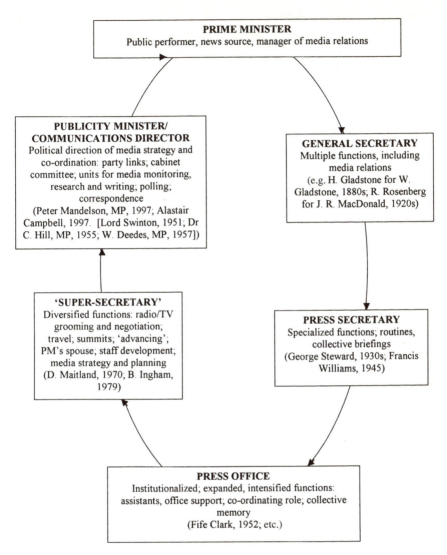

Figure 6.1: *The press office cycle.*

ities beyond press work. In London, if one goes back to the nineteenth century, William Gladstone's son Herbert, for example, who was an MP, used to look after the press for his father in the 1880s. The Downing Street staff remained very small, and it took the financial crash and the formation of an emergency National Government in 1931 to provoke the appointment of an embryo press specialist. This was George

Steward, who was seconded to Downing Street and the Treasury from the Foreign Office, where he had started doing information work in 1915. He prepared press digests for the prime minister, Ramsay MacDonald, and did some briefing and liaison work with the lobby correspondents. But he was a peripheral figure – little more than a functionary, compared with his successors – and most Downing Street news came through parliamentary sources.[6]

The first press secretary whose activities spanned the range indicated earlier was Francis Williams (1945–7). Clement Attlee wanted an authoritative senior figure, well respected in the press and in the Labour party, to interpret the brave new post-war world of a Labour government with a massive first-time majority and a legislative programme to match. Williams was ideal. Pre-war, he had edited the Labour *Daily Herald*, for a time the largest-selling national daily paper. In wartime he had made a success of a senior job in the Ministry of Information, and afterwards he ran British press relations at the San Francisco conference which set up the United Nations. He was offered the candidacy of at least twenty-three parliamentary seats before the 1945 general election. He had known Attlee 'fairly intimately' for fifteen years (and wrote that he never knew anyone less skilled in the arts of political self-presentation). They understood each other well. 'Most of the cabinet were old friends of mine,' say his memoirs, and one minister was even his former employee.[7]

No successor has had such impressive credentials. In keeping with the informality mentioned earlier, Williams did not need briefing about the job; if he had, it would have meant he was not suitable. He stayed for two years. Attlee had hoped he would stay longer. But – consistent with the idea of 'apartness' – Williams was not interested in a parliamentary or ministerial career, nor even in getting back to Fleet Street. 'I wanted to be a private person. Above all I wanted to write.'[8] When he left, in

---

[6]   Richard Cockett suggests Steward's appointment was in 1929, as part of MacDonald's attempt to 'counteract the influence of the all-pervasive Conservative press barons'. But his formal transfer from the Foreign Office certainly did not take place until 1931. Richard Cockett, *Twilight of Truth*, London: Weidenfeld and Nicolson, 1989, pp. 4–6; *Who's Who*, 1945. Until as late as 1965 the prime minister was permitted only three private secretaries paid out of public funds. The number had risen to six when John Major left office. But this simply meant that work was hived off, starting with the creation of the Cabinet Office in 1916. For the last thirty years of the twentieth century, up to 1997, numbers varied between about sixty and eighty, excluding support staff. Lee *et al.*, *At the Centre of Whitehall*, ch. 3; Dennis Kavanagh and Anthony Seldon, *The Powers Behind the Prime Minister*, London: HarperCollins, 1999, esp. ch. 2 and appendix 1.
[7]   Francis Williams, *Press, Parliament and People*, London: Heinemann, 1946, p. 100; Francis Williams, *Nothing So Strange*, London: Cassell, 1970, p. 218.
[8]   Williams, *Nothing So Strange*, p. 208.

a glow of mutual respect, the lobby gave him a tobacco jar made of stone from the bombed House of Commons.

The novelty of a specialist press secretary in the small Downing Street enclave was reflected in an uncertainty of title. 'Neither Attlee nor I could at first decide what to call me,' Williams wrote. 'We finally chose Adviser on Public Relations, which was not very good but served.'[9] To the policy-level civil servants with whom he dealt, the words 'press secretary' at that time would have connoted low status and trivial responsibilities. In 1955 William Clark, Eden's appointee (public school, Oxford and a charming snob) cringed at the very idea of being a 'press secretary'. The Buckingham Palace press people, he noted in his diary, were 'secretaries'. He, of course, was an 'adviser'.[10]

Ten years later again, the status of the job was more secure. The new incumbent in Harold Wilson's 1964 administration was Trevor Lloyd-Hughes, whom Wilson plucked straight from the lobby. Lloyd-Hughes was perfectly happy to be Press Secretary. Wilson's Downing Street was a fluid organization and the title made Lloyd-Hughes's role plain. Joe Haines, his successor, was styled Chief Press Secretary.

'Chief Press Secretary' was the name that stuck. By Thatcher's premiership it was 'public relations' that had the dubious connotations. Bernard Ingham would have disliked being 'Adviser on Public Relations' ('I think a lot of the public relations industry stinks'.[11]) The only subsequent name change was associated not with nuances of language but with the diversification of the job. Alastair Campbell was styled Chief Press Secretary to Tony Blair. But so public did his spokesman role become that he acquired a distinct designation when performing it: he was 'Prime Minister's official spokesman', and he expected to be quoted and sourced as such.[12] When Campbell withdrew from regular briefing and was promoted after the 2001 general election, with the title of 'Director of Communications and Strategy', his joint successors were each named 'Prime Minister's Official Spokesman' (now with capital letters). The 'Chief Press Secretary' title went into abeyance.[13]

[9]   Williams, *Nothing So Strange*, p. 216.
[10]   William Clark, Diary, 21 October 1955. Bodleian Library, Oxford, MS William Clark 7, fols 10–12. Class distinctions meant that, certainly until after World War II, lobby correspondents were seen by many politicians as NCOs, not officers. The famously awkward minister, Sir John Simon, began a lobby briefing, 'Gentlemen! I so address you because I am most anxious to get on the right side of you all.' He thereby managed a double insult, implying both that they were not gentlemen and that he expected to ingratiate himself by pretending they were. Interview, William Deedes, 19 December 1987.
[11]   Interview, Bernard Ingham, 10 February 1988.
[12]   *Report of the Working Group on the Government Information Service*, London: Cabinet Office, November 1997, pp. 9, 27.
[13]   Downing Street press notice, 8 June 2001.

Finding a name was part of the *specialization* of the job. The first steps in its *institutionalization* were the transition to Williams's immediate successors and then the adoption of a similar post by the Churchill government of 1951. The former was complicated by an untimely death, the latter by Churchill's prejudices. The untimely death was that of Philip Jordan, who took over from Williams and died aged forty-eight, about four months before the 1951 general election in which Churchill was returned to office. Jordan was Williams in a minor key: Fleet Street experience, post-war official information work at the embassy in Washington, 'in close sympathy' with the Attlee government, but not so strongly identified with the Labour party as Williams.

For Williams, the choice of Jordan was a halfway stage to making the press secretary 'a normal civil service appointment'.[14] On his death, a permanent civil servant therefore replaced him. The appointee was Reginald Bacon, an information officer since 1939, with previous press experience in the provinces. It was also anticipated – which would have been less likely of Jordan – that he might well continue in the job if there were a change of government.

Because of Churchill's return to office, Bacon barely had time to get his feet under the desk before it was whisked away from him. Churchill felt the idea of a 'press secretary' had a whiff of propaganda. For the same reason he had to be argued out of abolishing the Central Office of Information. This was the entirely peaceable agency dispensing news about road safety and fresh vegetables, but it sounded too much like a Ministry of Truth.[15] When the cabinet considered how to ensure that government policy 'was effectively presented and explained to the public', Churchill's attitude was implicit in the terse minute: 'In discussion the point was made that this was more a matter for the Conservative Party Headquarters than for the Public Relations staffs of Government Departments.'[16]

Ministers, backbenchers and journalists all began to grumble about the new government's poor publicity arrangements. Churchill himself probably missed a press secretary. When he spotted something in the press which he wished to follow up or complain about, he had to do so through someone else in his Private Office instead. The situation was resolved in 1952 through Lord Swinton, one of Churchill's old cronies in the Cabinet and a power in the Conservative party. Swinton took

[14]   Francis Williams, 'The office of Public Relations Adviser to the Prime Minister', *Parliamentary Affairs*, 9.3, 1956, p. 263.
[15]   See Sir Fife Clark, *The Central Office of Information*, London: George Allen and Unwin, 1970.
[16]   Cabinet minute CM (51) 16, 7 December 1951.

soundings in Whitehall and Fleet Street, and the Cabinet Secretary consulted the lobby. Fife Clark, a highflying information officer with prewar experience as a lobby and diplomatic correspondent, was presented to Churchill, found favour, and was attached to Swinton's Private Office well away from Number 10. The hapless Bacon, shunned by Churchill and lacking all credibility, was shunted out. Soon after, his health collapsed and he died in December 1952.[17]

Eden's premiership marked a shift of attitude. The press secretary returned to Downing Street and the job's acceptance by both major parties was now clear. Fife Clark played an important transitional role, arranging meetings and receptions at Downing Street for editors and lobby correspondents to meet Eden, and advising him on his conduct of press relations.[18] The new press secretary was William Clark, an *Observer* journalist.

For ten years after World War II the prime minister's office contained only about seven senior staff. Eden raised it to ten, Wilson to fourteen, Heath to eighteen, Thatcher to more than thirty. Part of this growth was the expansion of a *press office staff.*[19] William Clark had a deputy, who held the fort after Clark resigned, until Macmillan made his own appointment. When Macmillan retired suddenly through ill health, the deputy again (John Groves) slid into the job for Douglas-Home. Significantly, Groves's deputy, Henry James, stayed as deputy after the return of a Labour government in 1964. The office thus developed a *collective memory* of procedures and routines, both within Downing Street and in its relations with the press and the Whitehall departments.

Under Wilson the office expanded further. In addition to the deputy, who (then and subsequently) acted as office manager, there were four information officers, a filing clerk and two secretaries. By 1969 the workload justified the appointment of a night duty officer, to prevent the press secretary being woken at all hours. Heath's first press secretary, Donald Maitland, a Foreign Office mandarin, used his insider knowledge to streamline some of the details of coordination with White-

---

[17] A good summary of the arrangements under Lord Swinton and Fife Clark is in PREM 11/732, memo dated 29 October 1954.

[18] For examples, see PREM 11/1974, files for April–July 1955.

[19] Those figures are very approximate. They exclude the Political Office, not paid for out of public funds, the section dealing with honours, and various filing and support staff. For categories and variations, see Lee *et al., At the Centre of Whitehall*, pp. 30–1. Kavanagh and Seldon (*The Powers Behind the Prime Minister*, p. 300) say 'the Number Ten staff' (undefined) rose from 71 in June 1970 to 148 in December 1998. In the first Blair administration, numbers went up by about fifty per cent, compared with John Major.

hall. He had a regular note taken at lobby meetings, for circulation in Number 10. He had phone calls logged systematically.

With expansion went *diversification*. The information officers specialized by subject area. Details varied from secretary to secretary. Different prime ministers had different needs, such as help with press relations for a spouse (Macmillan's wife joined him on his long trips abroad; Heath did not have a spouse). They also had different preferences: not all wanted a daily press digest, and not all secretaries prepared it themselves. Some secretaries liked to chair the regular Monday meeting of Heads of Information in the Whitehall departments, held to coordinate the week's activities; others did not bother. Subject to such variations, a rhythm was given to the work of the office by the twice-daily lobby briefings at 11.00 a.m. and 4.00 p.m. These required the gathering and pooling of information from around Whitehall and within Downing Street (for example on Cabinet days); the briefing itself; and the follow-up. All this too was part of the coordination role.

Two factors especially stimulated these developments in the 1970s and 1980s. One was the growth of broadcasting. This introduced a new kind of press clientele and greatly increased the lobby numbers. It was also the chief cause of a dramatic change in the speed of media relations – faster communications, shorter reaction times. Press office staff whose experience at Downing Street or in Whitehall spanned the relevant period generally stressed this as the most striking development in their time.

Opportunities to broadcast added to the press secretary's advisory role, about performances both by the prime minister himself and by ministerial colleagues. Some of this included topics such as clothes and performance technique, which were not obvious press secretary skills. The secretary also became newly involved in negotiation with broadcasting executives, about programme formats, locations, preferred interviewers. As late as John Major's premiership Downing Street was not wired up for TV cameras, so arranging a broadcast from Number 10 was a performance in itself, with equipment having to be trucked in.

Already in the early 1950s, however, the potential of TV was being felt at Downing Street. Fife Clark was closely involved, in collaboration with Lord Swinton and another Churchill crony, Lord Woolton. But much of the running was made by the party organization – partly prompted by the establishment of ITV.[20] For Eden, who was keen to broadcast, William Clark tried without success to set up a New Year's

---

[20]   See PREM 11/596, esp. June–August 1952.

broadcast in January 1956. This would have been a great novelty at a time when ministers of any kind, let alone the prime minister, almost never appeared on TV.[21]

The second significant factor affecting the press office was the growth of prime ministerial travel, especially to summits. When Attlee flew to Washington in December 1950, to register his government's alarm at President Truman's possible contemplation of using atomic weapons in the Korean war, it was a big event – but a small party. Seventeen staff accompanied him, Philip Jordan among them.[22] Macmillan's travels to Africa and elsewhere, described at length by his press secretary Harold Evans, sound, in retrospect, uncomplicated and quite leisurely – if not always comfortable.[23]

Major changes came with big jets and membership of the EEC. Harold Wilson started taking lobby correspondents abroad with him (at their expense), and the press office more or less found itself in the travel agency business. Previously the lobby stayed at home and overseas coverage was left to people on the spot or feature writers. But now there were decisions to be taken about in-flight briefings and press conferences at the other end. Summits involving large numbers of heads of government required complex coordinated (or, on occasion, competitive) briefing.

Much of the expansion of press office work meant a heavier load, not a different kind. With more frequent overseas travel and the spread of terrorism, for example, the press office had to take much greater pains over 'advancing' the prime minister's trips – going over the ground (literally), to check out security, logistics, timetabling, accommodation. The proliferation of broadcast programmes meant that by the late 1980s Mrs Thatcher was getting up to thirty assorted interview requests per week.[24] Foreign media became more demanding. A very gradual relaxation of the sealed-lips Whitehall culture, too, meant there was more information to make available or respond to. In 1955, for example, it was still possible for the Secretary to the Cabinet easily to resist the suggestion that the lobby might be told the names of ministers attending the Cabinet Defence Committee. If they were not told, he reasoned,

[21]   PREM 11/819, 11 November 1955.
[22]   Francis Williams, *A Prime Minister Remembers*, London: Heinemann, 1961, ch. 15; *The Times*, 4 December 1950.
[23]   Macmillan's Commonwealth African tour in 1960, for instance, lasted six weeks and covered 18,000 miles, including a stretch at sea. He took his wife and her maid and thirteen staff, and he was accompanied by about a dozen journalists. Harold Evans, *Downing Street Diary*, London: Hodder and Stoughton, 1981, pp. 87ff.
[24]   Interview, Terry Perks (deputy press secretary), 2 March 1988.

there was a chance the lobby would not realize that meetings were taking place.[25]

In the 1980s Bernard Ingham retained the title 'Chief Press Secretary', but the accumulation of responsibilities gave his job a range, influence and status which made it a kind of 'super-secretary' and could almost have justified the name 'Communications Director'. The staff increased again: Ingham introduced training secondments, to give information officers from Whitehall departments experience of Downing Street. He developed information-networking across Whitehall in ways which computer technology was gradually opening up. Controversially (because it opened him to the charge of empire-building) he was named Head of Government Information Services in 1989. Previously the responsibility had nearly always lain with the Head of the Central Office of Information. His long tenure and closeness to Mrs Thatcher encouraged the belief that he influenced her thinking beyond what was strictly concerned with media relations.[26]

Advice on broader matters of communications strategy was available to Mrs Thatcher, through Conservative Central Office, from a variety of outsiders, especially people with marketing and advertising experience.[27] Offices within Downing Street, such as the Policy Unit (a Wilson invention) also contributed.[28] It would be wrong, therefore, to suggest that the press secretary had become an overall communications supremo, and for this reason 'Communications Director' would in fact have been a slightly misleading title. Moreover John Major took a step in the other direction, not least by limiting the tenure of his press secretaries to a couple of years and not appointing them head of the information services.

Alastair Campbell, however, was the grandest super-secretary yet. He was personally very close indeed to the prime minister. He was given a special status permitting him, as a partisan appointee, to give instructions to permanent civil servants. He went routinely to cabinet meetings (John Major's secretaries went only now and then). As a partisan, he was able to extend his work to include Tony Blair's party activities. He was head of the Government Information Services. His staff increased, and now included a press secretary for Cherie Blair and two assistants who, as political appointees, could brief on matters off limits to civil

[25]   PREM 11/1215. Minute by Sir Norman Brook, 13 December 1955.
[26]   See generally Bernard Ingham's memoirs, *Kill the Messenger*, London: HarperCollins, 1991, ch. 12 onwards.
[27]   See, e.g., Margaret Scammell, *Designer Politics*, London: Macmillan, 1995; Bob Franklin, *Packaging Politics*, London: Edward Arnold, 1994.
[28]   See, e.g., Lee *et al.*, *At the Centre of Whitehall*, ch. 7.

servants. He had responsibility for a new Strategic Communications Unit, which produced a daily grid of communication activities across the Whitehall departments and which wrote speeches and press releases. He was very actively involved in NATO's news operations in Brussels, about the military action in Kosovo in 1999. During the campaign in Afghanistan provoked by the events of 11 September 2001, he set up a round-the-clock briefing system in cooperation with the White House and the Pakistani government. It was run at different times of day from 'Coalition Information Centres' in each of the capitals.[29]

After the 2001 general election, as Director of Communications and Strategy, Campbell was one of three senior staff in the prime minister's office. The press office, the Strategic Communications Unit and a new Research and Information Unit were all under his authority. He was succeeded as day-to-day spokesman by two career civil servants, both of them styled Prime Minister's Official Spokesman. Neither had the status in Whitehall of John Major's first two secretaries, Gus O'Donnell and Chris Meyer, nor were they as close to the prime minister. Campbell still briefed in emergencies, especially when partisan questions were closely involved. He had thus created a two-tier briefing system – something that existed in embryo under Mrs Thatcher, when Ingham's deputy used to share the briefing.

Campbell's eventual responsibilities could easily have been held by a junior minister. The last stage on the circle is reached when a prime minister does delegate oversight of his media relations to a minister. This stage is most subject to variation between prime ministers. In the earlier post-1945 period, as we have seen with Lord Swinton, prime ministers might appoint a colleague simply to add political and strategic weight to the press secretary's dealings with the press, especially when editors and proprietors were concerned. They did this if they did not want to do it themselves. By John Major's time, the complexity of media relations justified not only the appointment of a minister – ultimately Michael Heseltine (deputy prime minister, no less) – but the creation of a cabinet committee, which the press secretary attended. This met four mornings a week, to coordinate policy presentation.

Downing Street was organized on this basis by 2002 more than ever before. In addition to Campbell's directorate, another political appointee, Baroness Morgan, a former Labour official, headed a 'Government and Political Relations' directorate. This included the prime minister's political office (dealing with the party), a Corporate Com-

[29]   *The Times*, 28 April 1999; *Guardian*, 10 November 2001; Lobby Briefing, 1 November 2001, Number 10 website.

munications and Direct Communications Unit and an Events and Visits Office. All, as the names show, were permeated with public communication roles. In addition the third directorate, under Blair's chief of staff, Jonathan Powell (the overall boss), contained units with communication sensitivities – a Policy Directorate, a Delivery Unit and the Honours and Appointments unit. All this was just the official picture. Informally, the advice commissioned from outsiders such as the pollster Philip Gould and his focus group research could be added in.

With the Blair administration, therefore, the wheel came full circle. Originally, the prime minister 'did everything', when 'everything' amounted to primitive press liaison. Blair too did everything – but within an expanded and increasingly specialized institutional premiership. He was his own minister for media relations. He had a 'supersecretary' heading the press secretary's office, who was assisted by a group of other offices which were better equipped than at any time in the past to cope with the diverse, complex, specialized and well-resourced world of political media reporting.

More than under any previous prime minister, too, the organization of the Blair communications machine now resembled that of the White House. This had begun to take its current shape under Reagan in the 1980s and in certain respects under Nixon ten years earlier. In addition to the press office, it included offices for media affairs (out-of-town media), speechwriting, photography, 'advance' and correspondence. The First Lady and the Vice-President had press officers among their own staffs. Out of about sixteen principal units servicing president George W. Bush in the White House in 2002, seven were concerned with public communication directly, and three others indirectly. (These latter dealt with parties, pressure groups and scheduling.) Of more than 250 staff (excluding support), the distribution was in roughly the same proportion.[30]

The Press Secretary: Who is Right for the Job?

The constitutional and political context of the press secretary's job remained essentially unchanged across the decades after 1945. So did

[30]   The first White House Communications Director, Herb Klein, was appointed by Nixon. John Anthony Maltese, *Spin Control*, Chapel Hill: University of North Carolina Press, 2nd edn, 1994, ch. 2. See also, e.g., Mark Hertsgaard, *On Bended Knee: the Press and the Reagan Presidency*, New York: Farrar, Straus, Giroux, 1988; Jeffrey K. Tulis, *The Rhetorical Presidency*, Princeton, N.J.: Princeton University Press, 1987. The Bush details are from an invaluable quarterly directory, the *Capital Source*, Spring 2002, Washington, D.C.: National Journal, 2002.

its basic tasks – spokesman, adviser, and so on. When deciding whom to appoint, each prime minister had to follow much the same decision path. Should it be a journalist or a civil servant? If a journalist, should it be a partisan or a non-partisan? If a civil servant, should it be an information officer or a policy administrator? Table 6.1 shows what prime ministers have done.

With exceptions, Conservative prime ministers have chosen civil servants; Labour, journalists. The Conservative exception was Anthony Eden, the Labour exception James Callaghan. Most of the journalists had experience in the lobby, and both Harold Wilson's secretaries were appointed from the lobby direct – Lloyd-Hughes with fourteen years experience, Haines with eleven. Alastair Campbell went from the political editorship of the *Daily Mirror* and a short stint as columnist on the now defunct *Today*, to work for Tony Blair when leader of the opposition. Almost none of the journalists had worked principally in broadcasting. By the standards of the 1950s, William Clark was experienced in interview and discussion formats, but that was not one of the reasons why Eden selected him. Tom Kelly, one of Campbell's joint successors as spokesman, had worked for the BBC in Belfast, but he was an information officer by the time of his appointment. Not until the 1980s might a press secretary have been likely to be appointed direct from a broadcasting job; and that decade and the 1990s were filled by Ingham and a succession of civil servants, until Campbell took over.

Among the civil servants (a more numerous list, partly because their tenure tended to be shorter) the majority of the information officers had joined the service after working in journalism. Sometimes this was after a considerable period – nineteen years for Ingham, fifteen for Fife Clark, fourteen for Groves. Some of these, too, had worked in the lobby (though Ingham had not). The four 'policy' civil servants were all members of the elite administrative class, whose summit was a department headship or an embassy. Ted Heath's appointment of Donald Maitland, the first of them, can be seen in retrospect as a modest elevation in the rank of the job. Maitland had already been an ambassador, and he finished his career as Permanent Secretary of a home department – Energy. What marked him out for the press secretaryship, though, was a successful period as head of the Foreign Office News Department, a post customarily occupied not by an information officer but by a diplomat. His successor as Heath's press secretary, Robin Haydon, had also done that job. So had John Major's second press secretary, Christopher Meyer. It can be taken as a sign of the secretary's status and importance in the 1990s even under a prime minister who gave, comparatively, a fairly low priority to communications management, that Meyer's career took him to

Table 6.1 Prime Ministers' press secretaries, 1945–2003

Prime Minister/Month and year of taking office	Press secretary/Month and year of taking office	Age	Preceding experience	Press officers/Total staff
Clement Attlee (7/1945)	Francis Williams (7/1945)	42	Wartime civil servant, ex-journalist	1
	Philip Jordan (12/1947)	45	Information officer, ex-journalist	1
Winston Churchill (10/1951)	Reginald Bacon (6/1951)	50	Information officer, ex-journalist	1
Anthony Eden (4/1955)	Fife Clark (early 1952)	44	Information officer, ex-journalist	1
	William Clark (10/1955)	39	Journalist (diplomatic)	2
	Alfred Richardson (11/1956)	?	Information officer, ex-journalist	1
Harold Macmillan (1/1957)	Harold Evans (2/1957)	46	Information officer, ex-journalist	2
Alec Douglas-Home (10/1963)	John Groves (10/1963)	41	Information officer, ex-journalist	2
Harold Wilson (10/1964)	Trevor Lloyd-Hughes (10/1964)	42	Journalist (political)	3
	Joe Haines (6/1969)	41	Journalist (political)	3
Edward Heath (6/1970)	Donald Maitland (6/1970)	47	Civil servant (diplomat)	5
	Robin Haydon (4/1973)	52	Civil servant (diplomat)	5
Harold Wilson (3/1974)	Joe Haines (3/1974)	46	Journalist (political)	3
James Callaghan (4/1976)	Tom McCaffrey (4/1976)	54	Information officer	3
Margaret Thatcher (5/1979)	Henry James (5/1979)	59	Information officer, ex-journalist	3 (7)
	Bernard Ingham (11/1979)	47	Civil servant (Energy), ex-journalist	5/6 (8)
John Major (11/1990)	Gus O'Donnell (11/1990)	38	Civil servant (Treasury)	6 (8)
	Chris Meyer (10/1993)	49	Civil servant (diplomat)	7 (10)
	Jonathan Haslam (2/1996)	43	Information officer	6 (10)
Tony Blair (5/1997)	Alastair Campbell (5/1997)	39	Journalist (political)	12
	{ Godric Smith (6/2001)	36	Information officer	14
	{ Tom Kelly (6/2001)	45	Information officer, ex-BBC journalist	

Note: 'Information officer' denotes a civil servant.
Sources: Imperial Calendar; various.

the topmost embassy of all – Washington.[31] The fourth in this group, Meyer's predecessor Gus O'Donnell, an economist, had done the equivalent information job in the Treasury, which followed the same practice as the Foreign Office. He too went on to the top rank of Permanent Secretary in the department. It is worth remembering as well that Ingham had been promoted to a policy job and was no longer doing information work at the time of his appointment to Downing Street.[32]

What difference might any of this make to a press secretary's crucial credibility? John Groves, reflecting on his time with Macmillan and Douglas-Home, remarked that 'it is very helpful indeed for the prime minister to have someone who has been a journalist and who preferably has worked in the lobby. But that is not quite enough, because you have to have some knowledge of the civil service system, if you are going to be trusted by all the departments as part of the machine'.[33] Like nearly all the civil service appointees, Groves had exactly that combination of experience. The 'policy' civil servants, on the other hand, lacked direct knowledge of media minds and methods, and journalists' comments about their effectiveness as press secretary reflected that fact. They were respected as efficient and dispassionate organizers, for example (Maitland being an outstanding case), but they needed to learn how to handle the lobby. The journalist secretaries, similarly, had to come to terms with Whitehall.

All the secretaries who had major difficulties and rows in the job were journalist appointments: William Clark, Lloyd-Hughes, Haines, Campbell. (Ingham's rows, which sounded fun at a distance, did not impede his effectiveness.) In each case the Whitehall context was part of the problem, if not all of it. Clark disagreed with his prime minister's Suez policy: a civil servant would have gritted his teeth and got on with it. Lloyd-Hughes appeared uncomfortable with media expectations of how freely a lobby-journalist-turned-press-secretary would brief them. Haines gave up collective lobby briefings: the relationship between departmental and Downing Street briefings was an aggravation. Campbell provoked the Government Information Services across Whitehall by his determination to reform them. He got his way, and maybe a civil servant press secretary would have failed or not have made the attempt. But to say he had a defensible case is not to say he did not have difficulties and rows. He also developed a bellicose, confrontational style with the lobby, which served the general purposes of neither side and

[31]   On retirement, Meyer became Chairman of the Press Complaints Commission.
[32]   Ingham, *Kill the Messenger*, p. 150.
[33]   Interview, John Groves, 15 January 1988.

was conducted much more publicly than it would have been twenty years ago, when lobby arrangements were less open. Campbell too often became 'the story', a fact which he later admitted was an influence in his decision to withdraw from regular briefing in 2001, and which probably also contributed to the related decision to abandon part of the lobby briefings in their traditional form.[34]

The partisan option raises the question of how and why secretaries were chosen. The decision path outlined earlier was blurred in practice by considerations such as prior acquaintance and the unexpectedness with which some prime ministers found themselves in office. Before Tony Blair, and ignoring the uninterested Churchill, only Attlee, Eden, Wilson, Heath and Thatcher were in much of a position to 'plan' for a press secretary. (Even then, Mrs Thatcher took six months to settle on Ingham, which seems short only in relation to her own very long tenure.) The other prime ministers took office generally at short notice and between elections. They tended either to keep the press secretary who was already working with them (Callaghan/McCaffrey, Major/O'Donnell); or, like Douglas-Home, to promote someone already at Downing Street (Groves). Continuity applied also to the secretaries appointed for Wilson's second term of office and for Blair: Haines and Campbell were already working for them.

Insofar as prime ministers did plan, the pattern suggests that, while some decisions were due to the different party predispositions referred to earlier, there was an element also of reacting against the practice of an immediate predecessor, rather than following it. Attlee's choice of Francis Williams was followed by a civil servant, Fife Clark. Eden then decided on a journalist. He chose William Clark because he (Eden) was used to diplomatic correspondents and that was Clark's expertise. Macmillan reverted to a civil servant. He left it to a minister, Charles Hill, to consult the lobby and appropriate civil servants and to choose one with experience of journalism. The choice was Harold Evans, who stayed throughout Macmillan's premiership and got a hereditary honour – a baronetcy – for his trouble.

Wilson, in contrast, wanted a lobby correspondent, and he knew Trevor Lloyd-Hughes as the representative of his local Liverpool paper. Joe Haines, the follow-on appointment, was a Fleet Street man. Heath planned in advance to have a civil servant. He wanted a Foreign Office man with knowledge of European issues, since this fitted his strategy of taking Britain into the European Economic Community. He was also

---

[34] Alastair Campbell, 'It's time to bury spin', *British Journalism Review*, 13.4, 2002, pp. 15–24.

influenced by the example of Konrad Ahlers, the senior and widely experienced press secretary of the West German Chancellor, Willy Brandt.[35] After another period of Joe Haines and the fairly brief Callaghan premiership, Thatcher chose a civil servant again. Major, following the contentious Bernard Ingham, avoided a prominent appointment of any kind and opted for civil servants serving roughly two-year terms. Blair, once more, did the opposite.

Whatever the reasons, that was a zigzag path, and a desire to make (rather than to avoid) a partisan appointment was rarely a strong motive. Of only two secretaries, indeed, was partisanship a strong asset. These were Haines and Campbell. Haines was appointed in 1969 straight from the *Sun* – at that time a loyal Labour daily, part-owned by the TUC until five years earlier. He was also a Labour councillor in his local borough. Campbell, similarly, had a strong background in Labour journalism. Francis Williams's Labour credentials were even stronger, as we have seen, but his wartime record as a civil servant had decaffeinated them.

None of the Conservative press secretaries was partisan, nor had been before becoming a civil servant. On the contrary, William Clark had been working for the left-of-centre *Observer*, and earlier for the left-wing *New Statesman*, before joining Anthony Eden. He was criticized by some Conservatives for *not* being partisan. Astonishingly, too, the Thatcher loyalist Bernard Ingham turned out to have been not a Conservative but a Labour candidate in Leeds local politics, before he moved to London.[36]

What prime ministers have wanted above all, clearly, is not partisanship but commitment. The former puts the party first, but the latter guarantees loyalty to *them*. It is personal, not ideological or institutional. Where there is no formal barrier, as there would be for civil servants, that may be a distinction without a difference. It is reflected, for instance, in Attlee's phrase about Williams's relation to the Labour government – 'broad sympathy'. It did not much matter what Williams felt privately, provided that he sustained credibility with the press and Whitehall and did not let the prime minister down. When party and personal loyalty clash, however, the prime minister obviously wants the press secretary to remain rock solid. This must have been one reason

[35]   Conrad Ahlers (1922–80) went from post-war journalism into the Chancellor's press office and back to senior editorial positions on *Die Welt* and on *Der Spiegel* magazine. He returned to the press office as head, with status equivalent to an ambassador, when Brandt became Chancellor in 1969. He resigned upon election to the Bundestag in 1972.
[36]   The fact was first publicized in the biography of Ingham by Robert Harris, *Good and Faithful Servant*, London: Faber, 1990.

why Macmillan and Thatcher kept the same secretary for their entire premierships. Equally, William Clark might not have survived very long with Eden, even if the Suez crisis had not precipitated his resignation, because journalists gradually realized that he did indeed have views. They were not partisan, but nor, it transpired, were they always the same as Eden's. Clark's credibility started to seep away.[37]

One advantage of a civil service press secretary is that commitment is built in to the job by definition. The appointee may not get so close to the person of the prime minister (the informal prime minister, to use chapter 1's term). But commitment to the institutional prime minister, the officeholder, will be categorical. Hence it has not mattered that the civil servants have generally had no experience of working with the prime minister before taking office. That said, however, Heath had known Maitland over a period of ten years; and both Callaghan and Major took to Downing Street the persons who had recently been working for them. Some of the press secretaries who got closest to their boss were civil servants (Ingham, O'Donnell), and some of the less close were outside appointees (Clark, Lloyd-Hughes).

Discussion of such questions shifts the focus towards the subject of the next chapter. We have seen how the press secretary's job has developed and the sort of factors affecting it. The press secretary has advanced through the Downing Street pecking order and in public recognition, reaching a peak with the incumbency of Alastair Campbell – an overarching media strategist. A Haines rule about forfeits would now produce, so to speak, bottles of wine with more body. But what are the problems that have sometimes made the office controversial?

---

[37] See, e.g., Clark's diary for 5 June 1956: '. . . very low as a result of a general persecution complex arising out of a whispering campaign designed to make me appear disloyal to the PM. The difficulty is that I no longer do see enough of the PM to feel that I enjoy his full confidence.' Bodleian Library, Oxford, MS William Clark 7, fols 10–12. Cf. Lord Hill of Luton, *Both Sides of the Hill*, London: Heinemann, 1964, p. 186: 'So intelligent a man could not fail to have his own views on current issues – and he expressed them. At times the Lobby . . . could not be sure whether he was expressing his masters' views or his own.'

7

The Downing Street Press Secretary: Getting into a Spin?

Bernard Ingham was the first press secretary to attract much criticism. It was reflected in the double irony of two books published soon after his resignation. One, Ingham's own autobiography, had a title suggesting the press secretary as butt and scapegoat: *Kill the Messenger*. The other, a biography rushed out by the journalist Robert Harris only weeks after Mrs Thatcher's fall, marshalled a case which would certainly have fitted that title – but he called it by a name which, taken literally, described exactly the role Ingham sought to play: *Good and Faithful Servant*.[1] Both books were serialized in the Sunday press, with heavy radio and TV promotion. Ingham went back to journalism and became a columnist. Such a descent from office was positively ministerial and quite unlike that of any normal civil servant. In 1947 no one made a fuss when Francis Williams retired, and no one wrote a book about him.

The criticisms of Ingham sum up the issues involving the secretaryship. Some had cropped up less contentiously under earlier prime ministers. These were deep-rooted, since they stemmed from enduring principles and practices affecting the premiership. In essence, they were charges of *constitutional impropriety*. The other criticisms were the result of Mrs Thatcher's regime and Ingham's role in it, and to that extent they were fortuitous (though not necessarily unprecedented). The charges here were of *personal impropriety* and, on Mrs Thatcher's part, a *failure of political control*.

There were three complaints of constitutional impropriety. First, Ingham behaved as a *partisan*, even though he had already been a civil servant for twelve years before going to Downing Street. Second, he behaved like a *minister* – as 'deputy prime minister', even.[2] Senior

---

[1] Bernard Ingham, *Kill the Messenger*, London: HarperCollins, 1991; Robert Harris, *Good and Faithful Servant*, London: Faber, 1990.
[2] See, e.g., *Daily Telegraph*, 29 November 1990.

ministers such as William Whitelaw admitted to thinking twice before going against things he said.[3] He behaved in this way, thirdly, behind the shield of non-attributability provided by the rules of the lobby system, which had been devised to circumvent cabinet secrecy and civil service anonymity. He was thus able to use leaks and cover-ups, to manipulate the media through *deception and 'deniability'*, and to claim to operate for the whole government in circumstances when he really just spoke for Mrs Thatcher. Ten years later, this would be called 'spinning'.

As to personal and political complaints, Ingham came across as too *combative and abrasive*: 'He presented to the world a curious mixture of aggression and good humour, touchiness and bad grace.'[4] Moreover he was an *empire-builder*, seeking to dominate the information services across Whitehall. Lastly, steeping all these features in the sediment of time, he *stayed in office much too long*. 'Well before the end', wrote Julian Haviland, former political editor of *The Times*, 'it was clear that he had been there too long, and served too controversial a mistress too well, not to have made enemies by the score.'[5] He offered to resign after the 1987 general election, but Mrs Thatcher wanted him to stay.[6] In sum, to quote Haviland again, 'here was a man grown over-mighty, whose power had dangerously increased, threatened the public good and needed to be curtailed'.[7]

Many of those complaints were made ten years later against Alastair Campbell, not as an echo but at full blast. Does the fact that at earlier periods they were also voiced, at a lower volume, mean that now they are a more or less inescapable part of the secretary's job?

Partisanship

The major issue is partisanship. This permeates most of the others, since party is the political engine of government. Because the civil service is non-partisan, the status of staff in the offices closest to the prime minister is a subject of great sensitivity. It involves matters of management, accountability, pay, security of employment, job descriptions, lines of access to the prime minister. All press secretaries without exception have been employed as temporary civil servants, if they were not civil ser-

[3]   Harris, *Good and Faithful Servant*, p. 148.
[4]   Harris, *Good and Faithful Servant*, p. 148.
[5]   Julian Haviland, 'The man with his mistress's whistle', *British Journalism Review*, 2.2, 1990, p. 58.
[6]   Harris, *Good and Faithful Servant*, p. 157.
[7]   Haviland, 'The man with his mistress's whistle', p. 58.

vants already. But by whatever route they came, the nature of the job is bound to put at least the appearance of non-partisanship at risk. This was Ingham's problem. Only in formal terms, after ten years as one of Mrs Thatcher's closest aides, did it make sense to see him as non-partisan, rather than just committed to Mrs Thatcher personally (in the sense defined in the last chapter). But his self-image and his punctiliousness about avoiding party occasions reflected precisely this very formal perception.

The pros and cons of a partisan press secretary are plain. For a Labour prime minister, the attractions have been obvious. Each time the party has come to power after 1945 (excepting 1974–9), it has done so after a long period in the wilderness: thirteen years in 1964, eighteen in 1997. Incoming Labour governments start in a hurry. As reformers, they can be forgiven for suspecting, even if wrongly, that Whitehall will be a force of inertia. A partisan press secretary, Campbell being the most prominent and forceful case, can openly share the prime minister's values and will carry confidence as his master's voice. He will have extra authority in his role as an intermediary, when strong-arming BBC and ITV executives and schmoozing with editors and publishers. Campbell's organizational initiatives, such as the creation of the Strategic Communications Unit and his blitz on the Government Information Services, must surely have been easier to push through than if he had not been a Blair intimate. Attlee's instinct to appoint a partisan in 1945 was entirely right.

A partisan press secretary in any government can enjoy the convenience of brushing aside the niceties distinguishing party from non-party activities. He can accompany the prime minister to all kinds of events organized by or for the party. Where Ingham kept clear of the annual Conservative party conference, Joe Haines was a regular attender at Labour's – and he wrote the majority of Wilson's speeches for them (and for most other non-parliamentary occasions).[8] Campbell's speech-writing and production of press articles brought such work to a new pitch of collaborative effort.

Another type of party work with which a partisan secretary can be seamlessly involved is electioneering. The relations between media and elections have been transformed over the decades of the secretary's development, and campaigns have become far less self-contained. While the idea of the 'permanent campaign' has not taken full root in British politics, the 'pre-campaign' is now a routine process of early and

[8]   J. M. Lee, G. W. Jones and June Burnham, *At the Centre of Whitehall*, London: Macmillan, 1998, p. 69.

elaborate strategic planning, in which the press secretary can help. It is bizarre to think now of what happened when Mrs Thatcher had to attend an economic summit in Venice during the 1987 election campaign. Her party staff handed her over to Downing Street officials at the airport before she left. The officials organized her media relations at the summit and then handed her back again to the party two days later, as soon as she got on the plane in Venice.[9]

What, on the other hand, are the problems? Partisanship, in various ways, may end up damaging rather than bolstering the secretary's credibility. As a partisan, he may find it harder than a civil servant to avoid entanglement in cabinet or party rows – and to avoid irritating the press if he does. If he parrots a party line, makes knee-jerk reactions to events, or persists in comments too much at odds with plausible versions of the truth, relations are likely to deteriorate. John Groves, deputy press secretary during the Profumo scandal which rocked Harold Macmillan's government in 1963, commented that 'It would have been dreadfully damaging, had we tried to pretend that all was well. We never did. We simply dealt with the facts.' As a civil servant he was able to do that.[10]

Each of John Major's three press secretaries must have derived comparable protection from their civil-service status, in an era when the lobby had become more aggressive. They had to brief about the seemingly endless waves of bad news which rolled in during much of his premiership, dumping tons of dirty water on his head. Contrast the experience of the partisan Joe Haines and Alastair Campbell. Haines told the BBC shortly after Harold Wilson's retirement, 'My job was to serve the prime minister and not to serve the press. If by coincidence these two objectives or these two servants [sic] could be taken together, that was fine. But primarily my job was to support and to protect and to represent the prime minister.'[11] Groves – or Ingham – might have said the same. But if the two objectives did clash, a partisan secretary would be more vulnerable to provocation and riposte. Haines ended up not only abandoning lobby briefings; a dispute with The Times led him also to sue that paper for calling him and his staff (who were civil servants and could not answer back) 'professional liars'.[12]

Campbell's reported jibes, teases and obscenities took him along a similar road, culminating first in his own withdrawal from briefing and

[9]   Interview, Terry Perks (Deputy Press Secretary, Downing Street), 2 March 1988. The summit was one of the regular ministerial meetings of the (then) 'Group of Seven' leading industrial countries.
[10]   Interview, John Groves, 15 January 1988.
[11]   'The Editors', Radio 4, 4 July 1976.
[12]   Ibid.

then in the partial dismantling of the twice-daily lobby conferences. He admitted these had become a 'dialogue of the deaf' – 'the press on one side saying we just spin you a line the whole time, then us on the other side saying [the press] are obsessed by trivia and process'.[13] Judging by the Blair government's continued popularity, such run-ins did not matter in Labour's first term. But an element of detachment helps when things go badly, and the run-ins must have been a factor in the decision to choose civil servants as Campbell's successors. They also meant that Campbell had few friends when his credibility was at stake in 2002, following a row about the prime minister's role in the Queen Mother's lying-in-state. In the past, journalists too seem to have valued detachment. Macmillan's secretary, Harold Evans, whose credibility remained intact for a full six years, used to turn away partisan issues successfully with a kind of 'you know what these politicians are like' approach, which the lobby evidently enjoyed.[14] The second main difficulty for a partisan press secretary is the risk of problems with the civil service. This may be no more than a straightforward lack of insider knowledge about the mind-set and machinery of Whitehall. Ingham spoke feelingly about getting information from departments as sometimes like 'dragging it from a stone'.[15] But he knew how to do it, and so did his civil-service predecessors, right back to Fife Clark. In addition, the civil-service appointees have been much the better equipped as office managers and more effective at coordinating the departmental information services. Fife Clark laid the groundwork; and Maitland and Henry James (while Ingham was being recruited) were other significant modernizers.

Much more controversial, and potentially heated, are problems about the boundaries between partisan and non-partisan matters. In the early post-1945 decades, when the parties themselves were further apart and media were less politically involved, the boundaries were simple enough to keep clear. But in an age when advice on the public presentation of policy has come to be seen as intrinsic to advice on its substance, the difference has become blurred. The best illustration of the resulting confusion was the strength of concern felt in Whitehall and Westminster about the number of 'special advisers' employed by the Blair administration. After the 2001 general election, their number rose to more than eighty. Twenty-six were in Downing Street and the rest in minis-

---

[13] *Guardian*, 9 May 2002. Campbell elaborated his argument later in the year, in 'It's time to bury spin', *British Journalism Review*, 13.4, 2002, pp. 15–24.
[14] Groves interview, 15 January 1988.
[15] Interview, Bernard Ingham, 10 February 1988.

ters' offices across Whitehall. Eleven dealt directly with the press, but another thirty were involved in public communications work of some kind too.[16]

The nub of the problem was how far a special adviser should be able to interfere with the work of the career civil servants. The extreme case was a very public dispute in 2002 between Jo Moore, special adviser to the Transport and Local Government Secretary, Stephen Byers, and the department's head of information, Martin Sixsmith. The substantive issue was trivial (the timing of news releases), and the dispute appeared to turn partly on a clash of personalities: such tensions did not necessarily arise in other departments. But the principles went to the core of party–civil service relationships, and the row reached a pitch where neither person could be kept in their job. This in itself showed how unsatisfactory it is, if these boundary lines cannot be kept clear and if they depend unduly on personal relations.

The final problem with partisanship is the risk of being accused of behaving like a minister. This is a modern charge, and it may be unavoidable, if and when a press secretary has 'super-secretary' responsibilities. The paradox in the problem is that the first press secretary accused of being ministerial (apart from the glancing remark about Francis Williams, quoted in the last chapter) was Bernard Ingham – a non-partisan. But the accusation against him was an extension of the charge that his non-partisanship was merely nominal. It would probably never have been made, if he had not been so long in the job. Campbell, the other secretary so accused, was a more predictable case and was subjected to the criticism more quickly than Ingham.

Is there some way of overcoming such difficulties and combining the advantages of both partisanship and non-partisanship? If not, on which side does the balance of advantage lie? When the press secretaryship was still at an early stage of the cycle, the issue could be fudged satisfactorily. Francis Williams's principle of 'broad sympathy' worked well. But he did not stay long enough for it to be put under strain. It is improbable that he would have had such an easy ride at any time from the first Wilson government onwards, and especially since the 1980s. Indeed 'broad sympathy' soon failed for the Conservatives during the Suez crisis, when William Clark's lack of enthusiasm for Eden's policy made his position untenable.

An alternative to the fudge of principle is the fudge of administration. To give William Clark the advantages of partisanship, a party boss sug-

[16]   Sir Richard Wilson, *Portrait of a Profession Revisited*, speech posted on the Number 10 website, 26 March 2002.

gested his salary should be paid half by the Conservatives and half by the civil service.[17] Clark reacted as though to a lobotomy, and so the idea went nowhere. Tony Blair tried a different tack. Alastair Campbell (and Blair's chief of staff, Jonathan Powell) were given the legal power, unprecedentedly, both to be partisan and to give instructions to civil servants. This had the virtue of openness. A similar arrangement might have helped Ingham avoid one criticism at least – that of behaving as a closet politician while being also a civil servant.

To some extent the fudge worked. The problem about special advisers such as Jo Moore was that they did not enjoy the same power. Among the numerous criticisms of Campbell, allegations about improper dealings with civil servants do not seem to have featured explicitly – although they may have been mixed up in the grumbles about his abrasive manner and determination to control the news agenda. Certainly the outgoing Cabinet Secretary (and head of the home civil service) responsible for cooking up the fudge, Sir Richard Wilson, was reported as believing five years later that giving Campbell and Powell their exceptional powers was a mistake.[18] In the lecture quoted earlier he also proposed different rules for special advisers dealing with media and those working solely on policy.

A different approach again was to split the secretaryship: one partisan, one non-partisan. This was tried by Harold Wilson, when the bright idea of making his local lobby correspondent the press secretary did not work. Trevor Lloyd-Hughes tended, as Wilson's aide Marcia Williams put it, 'to shrink from any part of the work of the government which could in any way be regarded as political'.[19] So Wilson appointed a *New Statesman* journalist, Gerald Kaufman (later an MP and minister) as 'parliamentary press liaison officer'. There was very strict demarcation. Anything whatever to do with government departments, Lloyd-Hughes did. Kaufman dealt with policy and party matters. These included the traditional weekly meeting of the Leader of the Commons with the lobby, and Wilson's short-lived series of ruminative sessions with selected journalists (see chapter 8). Kaufman spent most of his time at the Commons, and his Downing Street office had to be located in the private apartments, not in civil service space. Initially he had a separate telephone line there, paid for by the party. Once, a senior civil servant tore from his hand a sheet of Downing Street writing paper, lest

[17] William Clark, Diary, 10 October 1955. Bodleian Library, Oxford, MS William Clark 7, fols 10–12.
[18] *The Times*, 27 March 2002.
[19] Marcia Williams, *Inside Number 10*, London: New English Library, 1972, p. 48.

Kaufman, a party apparatchik, should appropriate something paid for by public funds.[20]

This arrangement was an expedient. Wilson did not carry it into his second term, after defeating Heath in 1974. None of these fudges, therefore, has been enormously satisfactory. A smoother arrangement has been the combination of a non-partisan press secretary with oversight by a minister – a combination discussed below. Failing that, and whatever the wisdom of past practice, it seems extremely unlikely in the modern media age that any press secretary could be an effective supersecretary or Director of Communications without being a partisan.

Spinning: the Press Secretary and the Lobby

In the same territory as partisanship are the problems of anonymity, deception, deviousness and manipulation, fused in the notion of *'spinning'*. The arguments cluster round two issues. One is the purpose and method of spinning itself. The other is part of a broader dispute about the effectiveness of the lobby system. In its contemporary political sense, 'spinning' began to enter the British political vocabulary probably in the later 1980s. It was commonplace at that time in Washington. For instance 'spin patrols' fanned out among journalists immediately after President Reagan's rare and hazardous press conferences, in order to straighten out things that Reagan was liable to say (and liability was the word).

The usage was fresh and evocative, but the purpose and practice of 'spinning' were nothing new. In the 1940s it might have been called 'propagandizing'; by the 1970s, 'news management'. For example Eisenhower's press secretary, Jim Hagerty, used to cast around Washington in the 1950s for things he could claim Eisenhower had 'done', when in fact they were done by people in the departments in the president's name. During the Suez crisis, William Clark was at one point spinning the lobby a harder line than ministers themselves, about the need to use force against Egypt.[21] 'Spinning', in this form, is just an attempt to ensure that information is understood and interpreted in a way which the person conveying it desires.

Spinning starts to become sinister when it involves an attempt to convey an unlikely or counter-intuitive meaning, as in the idea of a

---

[20]   Interview, Gerald Kaufman, 22 September 1988.

[21]   Tony Shaw, 'Government manipulation of the press during the 1956 Suez Crisis', *Contemporary Record*, 8.2, 1994, pp. 280–1.

Pyrrhic victory, or that 'the ref was blind'. The methods include partial, inaccurate and selective briefing, 'improved' interpretation, and the kind of manipulation which prevents journalists and the public recognizing that they are being conned.

This is the ground on which spin meets the lobby. The lobby might have been designed to be spun. Its bedrock (see also chapter 8 below) is the paradox, mutually convenient to government and journalists, that upon secrecy rests openness. Governments can put out more information, and media can report more, if this is done unattributably. Hence the lobby became exclusive, clannish and collaborative, enjoying high status in news organizations, and prone to present guesswork as fact, to be spoon-fed and to hunt as a pack. Such assertions were made increasingly from the 1960s onwards.[22]

Francis Williams unquestionably wanted the Attlee government to be understood as it wished: that was the point of his being press secretary. But he would have been horrified at the thought of 'spinning'. He believed, rather doggedly and – as it may seem now – naively, in giving out 'the facts' and explaining the evidence and reasoning behind them.[23] His immediate successor, Philip Jordan, may already have had a less idealist view: 'I have very few facts to impart [to the lobby]', he reported, 'and almost everything I have to say is in the nature of explanation.'[24]

The more the press secretary's job developed and made him visible, and the more the lobby itself expanded and loosened up, the more unreliable became the old methods which facilitated spinning. Yet the system's underlying logic meant both sides had reason not to abandon it. Donald Maitland was the first secretary prepared to brief attributably and on the record; it was part of his general reformist approach to the job. But the lobby would have none of it. When Joe Haines gave up collective briefings, two of the reasons he cited were that the 'non-

---

[22] For early discussions see Colin Seymour-Ure, *The Press, Politics and the Public*, London: Methuen, 1968, ch. 6, and Jeremy Tunstall, *The Westminster Lobby Correspondents*, London: Routledge, 1970. Perhaps the very earliest critique of the lobby, apart from references in the 1947–9 Royal Commission on the Press, was an article by Anthony Howard in the glossy magazine *Town* in about 1962.

[23] See, e.g., Francis Williams, 'The Motive Power of Politics', BBC Third Programme, 10 May 1948; draft in Francis Williams papers, Churchill College, Cambridge. Cf. Sir Geoffrey Cox, in a letter to *The Times* on the subject of 'spin' in 1998: 'As Lobby Correspondent of the *News Chronicle* between 1945 and 1954 I had regular contact with Williams, and I recollect no occasion on which he tried to slant the facts. He gave us the facts, but made no attempt to influence the way we presented them.' *The Times*, 7 July 1998.

[24] Royal Commission on the Press, 1947–9, Minutes of Evidence, Q.11,725, 26 May 1948.

attributable' rule was being increasingly breached and that too many suspect stories were resting 'heavily upon thin air'.[25] The lobby were annoyed, and they were pleased when the briefings resumed.

During the long incumbency of Bernard Ingham the argument became more complex. The old allegations continued, but they were made in the context of competition between the broadsheet newspapers. To readers the dispute must have seemed arcane. The *Independent*, founded late in 1986, aimed to inherit the high standards that had slipped at *The Times* during its Murdoch ownership and to find a niche between the partisan tendencies of the other broadsheets. So it challenged the circumlocutions of non-attributability. Instead of 'government sources', which was the attribution Ingham wanted, since he claimed to speak for the government as a whole, the *Independent* argued for 'Downing Street sources' or, best of all, for quoting him on the record.[26]

Ingham won, after a ballot among lobby members. The *Independent*, the *Guardian* and the *Scotsman* all stopped attending the collective briefings. They could still get copy, of course, from friendly colleagues and the wire services. The main disadvantage was exclusion from the travel-agency service and in-flight press conferences, when the prime minister took the lobby abroad. Eight months after John Major became prime minister and his press secretary declared himself happy to be quoted as 'Downing Street sources', the papers came back in.[27]

Under John Major there was a drift away from confidentiality, chiefly because of changes in the lobby. The press secretary Chris Meyer kept to the conventions, but he privately regarded his briefings as *de facto* on the record.[28] The Cabinet Office working party set up to review the Government Information Services, as a result of the Blair government's dissatisfaction, accepted that this position should be acknowledged. But Alastair Campbell insisted that he should not be identified by name; nor would he contemplate briefing on camera. Either practice might make him 'too much into a figure in his own right'.[29] He had none of Ingham's sensitivity to the government/prime minister nuances, however, and he was happy to be sourced as 'Prime Minister's Official Spokesman'.

Internet technology drove the next development – publication of a summary of lobby briefings on the Number 10 website, sourced still to the PMOS and with questioners either unidentified or sourced to their

[25]   Joe Haines to John Egan, chairman of the lobby correspondents, 19 June 1975.
[26]   Ingham, *Kill the Messenger*, pp. 203–4.
[27]   Nicholas Jones, *Soundbites and Spin Doctors*, London: Cassell, 1995, p. 93.
[28]   Interview, Christopher Meyer, 12 September 1994.
[29]   Report of the Working Group on the Government Information Services, Cabinet Office, November 1997, p. 9.

news organization. The lobby themselves might still have elements of the old exclusiveness and secretiveness, but their currency – information – had lost its original precious scarcity value. Changes in 2002 reduced it even further. As part of a package intended to show that the government was forswearing spin, the government announced that the morning lobby briefing would be open to foreign and other journalists, in larger premises off Pall Mall (those of the Foreign Press Association), and that cabinet ministers would periodically attend and be televised. The afternoon briefing would continue as before.[30]

About this long march to the openness of lobby briefings there were two ironies. One was the apparent reluctance of the media, after trumpeting the ills of anonymity, to be identified in person in the public record of question and answer. More seriously, nothing in British politics had invalidated the principle of openness resting upon secrecy. Lobby briefings therefore ceased to be opportunities for the press secretary to say things privately which would be untimely or impolitic if said publicly and identifiably. Certainly this prevented a PMOS rubbishing ministers in the manner for which, in a handful of episodes, Ingham became notorious, or gratuitously insulting journalists, as Campbell did.[31] Yet both sides needed these exchanges as much as in the past. Since ministers spent less time around the Commons itself, perhaps the media needed them even more.

Before the collective briefings were instituted in the 1930s (see chapter 8), lobby journalism was a matter of individual sleuthing and hunting in groups of two or three, with surreptitious 'swapping of blacks' (i.e., carbons). Downing Street's new openness paradoxically tipped the emphasis back towards that earlier age. The patterns of contact between the press secretary and his colleagues on the one hand, and journalists on the other, could be expected to become a little bit *more* opaque, rather than less. One or another 'inner lobby' of a few major players, meeting the press secretary privily and regularly, might presumably develop all over again. Exactly the same process happened in Washington. When the daily briefings were televised, the president's press secretary began to meet the main media privately in a back office.

One sign of the downgrading of the lobby meetings in the press secretary's priorities was Campbell's partial withdrawal as a spokesman before the 2001 election and his almost complete withdrawal after-

---

[30]   See, e.g., *The Times*, 3 May 2002. Part of the package was a decision by Tony Blair to allow himself to be cross-examined twice a year by a Commons select committee – flagged as evidence of his determination to keep parliament 'at the centre of political debate'.
[31]   Nicholas Jones, *Sultans of Spin*, London: Orion Books, 1999, e.g., ch. 6.

wards. Politically charged events in 2002, including the firefighters' strike (the first for thirty years) and Cherie Blair's flat purchases ('Cheriegate'), were handled by the two civil servant spokesmen – 'Cheriegate' with considerable discomfort, since the spokesmen proved more than once to have been inadequately briefed.[32]

What exactly was Campbell himself up to now, while in charge of the units described in the previous chapter? Dribs and drabs emerged about various managerial enterprises: the international Afghan information network; a series of meetings with Labour's regional groups of back-benchers (to make them feel involved); an improved scheme of information officer secondments to Downing Street (partly in order to improve the service at weekends).[33] But the lobby were certainly not going to be told in detail. Asked for an example of the 'business pressures' which were preventing Campbell from accompanying the prime minister on an African trip early in 2002, the PMOS told the lobby that 'it was our policy never to reveal details of Mr Campbell's diary'.[34]

One of the earliest examples of the kind of activity which would feed the suspicion that Campbell had not given up spinning came in the dispute about special advisers in 2002. It soon became clear that 'far from being uninvolved, as Downing Street had claimed, [Campbell] was at the heart of the negotiations'.[35] The same could be said about 'Cheriegate', in which Campbell advised, for instance, on the tactics of Cherie Blair's emotional public statement at the height of the media speculation about the details of the purchases.[36] Few observers can have been surprised. The question was not whether Campbell, as Director of Communications and Strategy, was still spinning, but in what way and how much. Now people knew the answers even less than when he regularly met the lobby. Clouds of suspicion and criticism rolled in.

Serving the Prime Minister or Serving the Whole Government?

Whatever he may be up to, how many masters does the press secretary serve? The conundrum here is summed up in the conventional idea – typical of the imprecision of the British constitution – that the prime minister is 'first among equals'. This is a logical contradiction: if the

---

[32] See, e.g., *Guardian*, 6 December 2002.
[33] *Guardian*, 29 October 2001, 1 November 2001, 15 November 2001, 7 January 2002; *The Times*, 22 August 2001.
[34] Lobby afternoon briefing, 6 February 2002.
[35] *Independent*, 28 March 2002.
[36] *The Times*, 11 December 2002.

prime minister is an equal, he cannot be first. Formally, the press secretary works for the government as a whole. Attlee's letter of appointment to Francis Williams said, 'The work which I should like you to
carry out would be that of the Public Relations Officer for Number 10
Downing Street, acting on behalf of the Government generally'. He also
mentioned coordinating functions, but the job was emphatically not as
PRO for the prime minister alone.[37] Forty years later Bernard Ingham,
we have just seen, was equally emphatic, despite appearing to observers
to be so loyal to Mrs Thatcher personally.

'Constitutionally it might be more exact', argue the authors of an
authoritative study of the offices supporting the prime minister, '. . . to
say that the press secretary acts for the prime minister as head of government but, as "first among equals", the prime minister is – or should
be – presenting decisions agreed collectively by Cabinet'.[38] Yet, as they
go on to point out, the press secretary's role originated in the prime minister's private office and the appointment is personal to him. Besides,
the press secretary does much more than deal with business already
agreed. The media like nothing more than stories about splits and rows.
Moreover all press secretaries agree on the importance of encouraging
departments and ministers to speak for themselves. So even if one makes
a distinction between the press secretary working *to* the prime minister
and *for* (meaning 'in the interests of') the whole government, the relationship is inherently subject to tensions.

How far serving the prime minister and the government do amount
to the same thing has depended firstly on trends in the scale and complexity of government activity. Haines gave as another of his reasons
for abolishing the lobby briefings in 1975 the impracticability of the
Downing Street office trying to speak on behalf of the departments, even
though 'the traditional role of the press secretary has always included
answering questions over the broad field of Government policy'.[39] Tony
Blair added a new layer of complexity by permitting ministers to have
their own press secretaries, often in the guise of 'special advisers' such
as Jo Moore. Whatever their usefulness as spinners for individual ministers, they were a bane for Campbell. Their primary loyalty was to their
minister, to whom in many cases they had been close before entering
government. They were not so easy to coordinate and control as the
civil service information officers. The extreme case was the Chancellor
Gordon Brown's secretary Charlie Whelan. He was a divisive force,

[37] Attlee to Williams, 27 September 1945. Churchill Archives Centre, Francis Williams
papers, FRWS 8/1, Churchill College, Cambridge.
[38] J. M. Lee et al., *At the Centre of Whitehall*, p. 75.
[39] Joe Haines to John Egan, 19 June 1975.

briefing the press from the perspective of his boss rather than Downing Street, when Brown and Blair did not always see eye to eye. After five years working together (mostly in opposition) Brown agreed he should resign, early in 1999.[40]

The second critical factor, important in the short run, is how far the government itself sings one tune. For example, it is inescapable that the press secretary becomes involved in competing leaks and rivalries among departments and ministers, because these are the prime minister's responsibility to sort out. Attlee's stalwart minister, Ernest Bevin, saw Francis Williams clearly as one of Attlee's protectors against Bevin's enemy Herbert Morrison, Leader of the Commons.[41] George Brown, Deputy Leader to Harold Wilson, and often at loggerheads with him, tried to make the industrial correspondents' organization into a kind of personal press corps.[42] Even civil servant secretaries cannot always distance themselves successfully from such rows and schisms.

Disputes will not necessarily have been caused by personal rivalry and party considerations. A cabinet may simply take time to reach a collective view or may be seriously split on a matter of policy, like Wilson's cabinet over Common Market membership in the 1970s and Major's over the same general issue twenty years later. Or the prime minister may move in and take over the running from a ministerial colleague at critical moments. Prime ministers not infrequently start becoming their own Foreign Secretary, for instance, like Tony Blair after 11 September 2001; and Blair was closely involved at key stages of negotiations about Northern Ireland. At the very least, these moves need tactful coordination by the press office.

The press secretary must expect to cope with the occasional messy resignation. One of the greatest threats to Mrs Thatcher's position as prime minister, for instance, was the 'Westland crisis' in 1986 (discussed in chapter 3), which involved the Trade and Industry Secretary, Michael Heseltine, resigning in the middle of a cabinet meeting on 9 January and striding away along Downing Street. How could a press secretary avoid at the very least the appearance of taking sides in a crisis such as that?[43]

---

[40]   Andrew Rawnsley, *Servants of the People*, London: Hamish Hamilton, 2000, ch. 12; Peter Oborne, *Alastair Campbell*, London: Aurum Press, 1999, ch. 12; Nicholas Jones, *Sultans of Spin*, ch. 8.

[41]   Francis Williams, *Nothing So Strange*, London: Cassell, 1970, p. 218.

[42]   Groves interview, 15 January 1988.

[43]   Ostensibly this row was about the failure of the small Westland helicopter company. The twist was that, in circumstances never clarified, Heseltine's position was undermined by the deliberate leak of a letter to him by the Solicitor-General, suggesting that some of Heseltine's claims about the implications of the Government's plans for Westland were inaccurate. In addition to the row about whether Bernard Ingham authorized the leak,

The press secretary cannot escape, either, the controversial reshuffles – rumoured, foreshadowed, or actual – which are a fact of cabinet government. Ingham, in theory unattributably, foreshadowed the dismissal of senior ministers. The most celebrated example was his description of the Commons Leader, John Biffen, as a 'semi-detached' member of the cabinet. This drew the riposte from Biffen that Ingham was merely 'the sewer not the sewage'.[44] Comparable signals, equally accurate, were sent by Alastair Campbell about two of the first ministers to be reshuffled in the Blair government, Harriet Harman and Frank Field.[45] In any such resignations and dismissals, the secretary can never aspire to be an exclusive news source, and if he turns aside too many leading questions, he eventually jeopardizes his credibility. Alternatively, if he enters the fray with a will, he may be seen too uncompromisingly as the prime minister's man – again, at risk to his credibility.

The press secretary is more likely to be perceived as the prime minister's man, whether or not that is how he perceives himself, when he is a partisan. The nature of the appointment, most clearly in the case of Haines (in his second term) and Campbell, with their prior experience of working with the prime minister, makes this an understandable basis on which to start. Equally, the longer a secretary is in office, the more one may assume he is committed to the prime minister personally. Bernard Ingham is the prime example. 'He did not merely speak for Thatcher, he out-Thatchered Thatcher', wrote Robert Harris, 'to an extent she may not have fully realised.'[46] Ingham flatly denied that he ever had instructions to rubbish ministers: 'Mrs Thatcher never once asked – let alone instructed – me to criticize a Ministerial colleague in my dealings with journalists. Nor did she ever imply that I should do so.'[47]

But how could people tell, since prime minister and press secretary were so close? Maybe Ingham did not need instruction. If he said Mrs Thatcher was incandescent about something, journalists could be entirely confident it was true. Yet where lay cause and effect? Was she incandescent because Ingham put it that way, or did he describe an

---

there was a row about the extent of the prime minister's personal knowledge of it – in other words, about a possible cover-up. Ingham's account, which is conveniently succinct and gives a taste of the issues, is in *Kill the Messenger*, pp. 333–8.

[44]   Quoted by Ingham in *Kill the Messenger*, p. 361.

[45]   Harman was Secretary of State for Social Security, Field Minister of State (not in the Cabinet) for Welfare Reform. Leaked faxes showed Campbell rebuking them, in a manner unexpected of a civil servant, for not sticking to the rules about media briefings. Nicholas Jones, *Sultans of Spin*, pp. 208–12.

[46]   Harris, *Good and Faithful Servant*, p. 87.

[47]   Ingham, *Kill the Messenger*, p. 319.

observed combustion? A similar degree of instinctive sympathy appeared to exist between Tony Blair and Alastair Campbell: 'The two men are on terms of complete equality. Often, indeed, Campbell has the upper hand.'[48] In such cases, the identification of secretary with prime minister is total, and the secretary can be seen as serving the whole government only by being the prime minister's instrument in keeping the rest of the cabinet to heel. 'The press secretary serves the prime minister; the government is the prime minister's; therefore the press secretary serves the government.' This is a formulation Campbell or Ingham could not easily refute. For them, so it appeared, the prime minister was first among *un*equals.

Ministerial Back-up for the Press Secretary?

Francis Williams, Bernard Ingham and Alastair Campbell are the three press secretaries described (the two latter, critically) as behaving ministerially. In the terms of the cycle outlined in the previous chapter, their closeness to the prime minister gave them an informal authority enabling them to carry out their roles as spokesman, adviser, intermediary, manager and confidant, with the status and in the manner of a senior political colleague.

The more usual arrangement has been a press secretary operating at an executive level, with a minister responsible for political and strategic aspects of the secretary's work. The priority for the job has varied, especially in the coordination of government information services and dealings with proprietors and broadcasting executives. There has always had to be a minister to answer questions in the Commons about the information services. Conventionally, too, the Leader of the Commons has met the lobby correspondents every week, to discuss forthcoming parliamentary business. Ministers have also played an important part in backing up the press secretary during crises such as Suez (1956), the Falklands (1982) and the Gulf War (1991).

Attlee saw no need for a coordinating minister. Herbert Morrison had the important task of reorganizing the large wartime information services onto a smaller and less propagandist peacetime basis, but this was a different kind of work. Churchill's complete delegation of media rela-

---

[48]   Peter Oborne, *Alastair Campbell*. For that remark, and more of the same, see pp. 151ff. Cf. Nicholas Jones, *Sultans of Spin*, p. 38: 'The coordination which the two men display is almost subliminal. . . . So seamless is their joint operation that political journalists frequently cannot remember precisely from whose lips it was that they first heard mention of a particular phrase or idea.'

tions to Lord Swinton in 1951 was simply a result of predisposition. His press secretary Fife Clark reported to Swinton in the same way that Williams had reported to Attlee; and Swinton and R. A. Butler (Chancellor of the Exchequer) alternated as sources and spokesmen.[49] So the first prime ministers to see the advantages of combining partial delegation to a colleague with a measure of personal involvement were Eden, Macmillan and Douglas-Home.

Eden took the initiative, because he wanted information policy reviewed in the aftermath of Churchill's inertia, and because of his awareness of the potential of television. Conservative backbenchers and party officials were pressing the importance both of its long-run significance and of the immediate need to train MPs and candidates in broadcasting technique. To take the lead ministerially, Eden chose Dr Charles Hill, a populist Conservative who had become extremely well known in the 1940s, the heyday of radio, as 'the Radio Doctor'. Eden made him Postmaster-General, a non-cabinet minister whose responsibilities included broadcasting. Hill was to advise both on political broadcasting and on the working of the government information services.[50] Routine dealings with the press and back-up for the press secretary were provided principally by R. A. Butler, Leader of the Commons.

Hill did not make much progress before Eden's premiership became mired in the Suez crisis. During this, Walter Monckton (successively minister of Defence and Paymaster-General) briefed editors and defence correspondents. In the invasion period itself (November 1956) he, rather than the press secretary William Clark, held a daily coordinating meeting of the information heads of the relevant government departments. Clark reported both to Monckton and – less often – to the prime minister.[51]

When Harold Macmillan succeeded Eden in January 1957, he increased the priority attached to media relations by promoting Hill to the cabinet and removing his departmental responsibilities as Postmaster-General. His work ranged from briefing the lobby – daily at 2.30, if they wished – to the coordination of the information services and the continued strategic review of broadcasting and politics.[52] After four

[49] A good summary of the arrangements under Fife Clark is in PREM 11/732, 29 October 1954.
[50] Lord Hill of Luton, *Both Sides of the Hill*, London: Heinemann, 1964, pp. 176–8.
[51] Relevant cabinet papers include minutes of the cabinet's Egypt Committee, EC(56)10, 3 August 1956; EC(56)12, 9 August 1956; EC(56)37, 1 November 1956; PREM 11/1162: GEN 558/1, 1 November 1956; Monckton to Eden, 10 August 1956, PREM 11/1162. See also the William Clark and Monckton papers (Box 7) in the Bodleian Library, Oxford.
[52] Hill, *Both Sides of the Hill*, chs 10 and 11.

years, he was replaced by Bill Deedes, a backbencher since 1950 and a journalist since leaving school in the 1920s. (Later he became editor of the *Daily Telegraph* and a member of the House of Lords.)

Deedes, styled minister without portfolio, covered much the same ground. He sat on cabinet committees, to advise about presentation; and he gave off-the-cuff advice in cabinet, when requested. He took the weekly meeting of departmental information officers, met the foreign press every week, kept in regular touch with proprietors and editors, encouraged ministers to go on TV ('possibly my most useful function'), and sat on the liaison committee linking Downing Street with the Conservative party. He briefed Macmillan's press secretary, Harold Evans, about cabinet proceedings, and he briefed the lobby on political matters himself. He was also in charge of a campaign to explain the implication of EEC membership to the public.[53] Altogether, the portfolio which he did not have amounted to a comprehensive brief for a minister of media relations. Had he and Hill not carried it out, it is unlikely that Evans, as a civil servant, could have survived so uncontroversially throughout Macmillan's administration. Moreover Deedes stayed in the job during Douglas-Home's year-long premiership, providing similar back-up to Evans's successor John Groves. Now there was an added political urgency, due to preparation for the general election which would be coming in the autumn of 1964.

There is little doubt that the Hill–Deedes arrangement worked well for each of the three persons involved – prime minister, press secretary and media relations minister. The chief reasons, probably, were Macmillan's temperament, the comparative popularity of his government until the summer of 1962, and his shrewd choice of appointments – at both ministerial and official level. Deedes was acutely conscious, for example, of his own potential for getting across departmental ministers, who were formally responsible for managing their own media relations; and also for his capacity to cause difficulties for colleagues by remarks he might make to the lobby. His tact and good humour prevented this.

If the Hill–Deedes arrangement was, so to speak, 'Type A', Harold Wilson and his two successors, Heath and Callaghan, represent 'Type B'. None saw the need for a minister to share overall responsibility with themselves. Wilson fancied himself as a media operator. Heath felt he was giving his press secretary all the authority the work needed. Callaghan simply does not seem to have given public communication a high priority. Each administration therefore saw a succession of minis-

---

[53] Deedes interview, 19 December 1987; W. F. Deedes, *Dear Bill*, London: Pan Books, 1997, ch. 11.

ters with minor roles – essentially as chairmen of coordinating meetings, occasional briefers (like the Leader of the Commons), and intermediaries with news organizations and the party bureaucracy. Taking Heath as an example, William Whitelaw, Leader of the Commons, was available to back up Donald Maitland in dealings with broadcasters (and sometimes to persuade ministers to broadcast). But Maitland did his own strategic thinking – the initiatives in information services coordination and the experiment with prime ministerial press conferences, for instance (see chapter 8). If there had been a supervisory minister, he reflected later, 'one of us would have begun to feel redundant'.[54]

The appointment of Henry James to set up Mrs Thatcher's press office in 1979 suggests that she too might have evolved a 'Type B' system, for James had worked in that way in the Press Office under both Wilson and Heath. If so, then Ingham's evolution from functionary to quasiminister was unintended. It can be explained by the remarkable compatibility of temperament in what one Thatcher minister called 'two over-doers',[55] by the efficiency of Ingham's press office, during a period when media developments were not putting the procedures under strain, and thirdly by the passage of time. Mrs Thatcher's first 'coordinating minister' (till 1981), Angus Maude, chaired the weekly meeting of heads of departmental information services – but then Ingham took over that job himself. Ingham writes in his memoirs, in a throwaway remark, that by 1982 John Biffen, as Leader of the Commons, had 'responsibility for coordinating presentation policy, *which he left to me*'. *The Economist* commented that 'the "information coordination" function once performed by [the minister] is all but defunct': responsibility had passed to Ingham.[56] When Mrs Thatcher later gave responsibility to John Wakeham, by then her cabinet 'fixer', it was allegedly just a pretext for putting him on any cabinet committee which she wanted to keep an eye on.[57]

Ingham, in the view of his sternest critics, was not a minister without portfolio but holder of a portfolio without a minister – with himself unofficially plugging the ministerial gap. This, not the press office 'portfolio' itself, was the basis of the complaints of constitutional impropriety. Nor were his methods (the rubbishings and spinning) open to criticism as political infighting: the problem was, Ingham was not employed as a politician. Mrs Thatcher, on this analysis, followed 'Type

[54]   Maitland interview, 5 April 1988.
[55]   David Howell, *Daily Mail*, 27 July 1989.
[56]   Ingham, *Kill the Messenger*, p. 325 (my italics); *The Economist*, 5 February 1983, quoted in Lee et al., *At the Centre of Whitehall*, p. 80.
[57]   Lee et al., *At the Centre of Whitehall*, p. 80.

A' practice – only she never made her media relations minister a real minister.

Twice Mrs Thatcher may have paid a price for not having a 'real minister'. The first time was in the Falklands War, when there was no one in the inner 'war cabinet' with a clear and specific responsibility for media relations. Military success meant the consequences were only trivial – media grumbles about briefings.[58] (Next time, in the Gulf War, the omission was rectified. The Defence Secretary gave briefings, and the Downing Street press secretary sat in on the war cabinet.) The second occasion was the leadership contest in November 1990, when Mrs Thatcher badly needed effective campaign management, in order to stave off Michael Heseltine's challenge (strictly, to her leadership of the Conservative party but indirectly to her premiership). This time, the consequences were fatal. Her defeat was partly due to a feeble campaign among Conservative MPs (with whom the choice lay), but this made the contest narrow enough to mean that better press support might have made a difference.

Lacking an Ingham, and unenthusiastic about communications management, John Major started with 'Type B' news operations. But the depths of his and his government's unpopularity forced him – much too late – to shift to 'Type A' in 1995, when he put the deputy prime minister, Michael Heseltine, in charge.

The distinctive feature of Blair's first government was that he combined Types A and B. Campbell started with the power and status of a strong press secretary. With him worked Peter Mandelson – like him, a party apparatchik in opposition. But Mandelson had also been an MP since 1992, while Campbell was now a temporary civil servant. Formally, the two could not remain colleagues in quite the same way as before. Soon, Blair made Mandelson a junior minister in charge of media relations, on a 'Type A' basis (including, for instance, chairmanship of the cabinet presentation committee instituted under Major[59]). His closeness to the prime minister made him more like a cabinet minister in practice. Similarly, his relationship with Campbell must have been quite unlike that of any press secretary with Hill or Deedes during the original 'Type A' era.

[58] Cecil Parkinson, Conservative party chairman and a newly elevated cabinet minister, joined the war cabinet with a general responsibility for presentation. But the Commons Defence Committee post mortem found it difficult to discover what his role had actually been. Defence Committee, The Handling of Press and Public Information during the Falklands Conflict, Session 1982–3, First Report, London: HMSO, para 105.
[59] Report of the Working Group on the Government Information Services, pp. 7–8.

While Blair gradually stamped his authority on Downing Street, Mandelson proved personally accident-prone.[60] By 2002, Blair was operating a system which, more than any other, resembled Mrs Thatcher's, updated for the twenty-first century. This was because he dispensed formally with a designated media relations minister and made Campbell even more of a super-secretary than before. Campbell's partisanship, personal closeness to Blair and responsibility for a centralized media relations machine all made him quasi-ministerial (and fairly impervious to attack when reporters felt they were being hoodwinked, as they did during 'Cheriegate'). The corollary of the conclusion to the previous section – that an Ingham or Campbell is *de facto* the prime minister's man, not the cabinet's – is that such a secretary may need ministerial back-up only for emergencies such as war, or for certain routine minor tasks.

Conclusion: the Super-Secretary and Accountability

Prime ministers and media do not have identical interests, and so the relations between them tend not to be in equilibrium for long. These relations are a product of the periodic reactions of each side to changes in the other: new parliaments and prime ministers; new media organizations and technologies. The balance of advantage tips from side to side. Caught between the two, the press secretary either absorbs or radiates heat. The history of the office could be traced through alternating phases. Prime ministers come to see themselves as the victims of irresponsible, ill-intentioned or incompetent media; while media see themselves bludgeoned and manipulated by cynical news managers. Memoirs on either side thud with the banging of heads on walls.

This unsteady alternation makes the press secretaryship difficult to evaluate. For example, was John Major's low-key operation no more ineffective than a larger-scale alternative would have been, given the divided state of his party and the tenor of the times? In contrast, was the Blair–Campbell system less effective than it seemed? Already in 2001 there were voices claiming that the unprecedented repetition of the 1997 electoral victory was achieved regardless of Campbell's activity, rather

---

[60]   Mandelson was sacked from the cabinet in December 1998, for failing to declare a large house-purchase loan from a fellow minister. Brought back a year later as Northern Ireland minister, he became embroiled in allegations about lobbying by wealthy Indian businessmen for British passports. He resigned early in 2001.

than because of it.[61] A year later, 'spin' had become a dirtier word than ever – as Campbell publicly admitted – and a potential electoral liability.[62] The government's credibility was low, and it remained ahead in the polls, arguably, more than ever for want of an alternative.

Beyond the difficulty of showing cause and effect, it is difficult, secondly, to separate the effectiveness of the secretary's system and procedures from the persons operating it and with whom it deals. Downing Street is a 'family', to quote Ted Heath again, and families dwell in varying amity. In the extreme case, if a press secretary (Bacon) is trying to work for a prime minister (Churchill) who does not want to acknowledge his existence, the system cannot work.

The history of the secretaryship suggests the following conclusions. Most important, the natural job description now is surely that of a super-secretary. The scope of the job has increased and, within it, the traditional role as spokesman (principally to the lobby) has declined, compared with other tasks. An appointee who does not have a full range of super-secretary responsibilities is more accurately described – in the Campbell terminology – simply as Prime Minister's Official Spokesman. On the media side, too, electronic glut in its various forms demands a super-secretary – unless the prime minister enjoys tossing on high seas in an open boat without a tiller. But this brings us back to the argument discussed in earlier chapters – that a prime minister who does not try to manage his public communication puts his reputation and his programme at risk.

The more one accepts the claim about electronic glut, the more important is the secretary as an instrument to help the prime minister manage his colleagues. The press secretary's routine tactics in encouraging some ministers to go on television and others to keep quiet, some stories to be played up and others down – all the realities of 'coordination', not to mention the types of spinning *against* people – give him an unrivalled role in ensuring that the overall pattern of communication about policies and people bears so far as possible the stamp that the prime minister wishes.

There is nothing new in principle about this role. Some of the resentment about Ingham was actually about Mrs Thatcher using him as a surrogate for briefings which could promote her purposes without

---

[61]   See, e.g., Anthony King, 'Tony Blair's first term', ch. 1 in Anthony King (ed.), *Britain at the Polls*, 2001, New York: Chatham House Publishers, 2002; Nicholas Watt, *Guardian*, 16 February 2002; Steve Richards, *Independent on Sunday*, 17 February 2002.

[62]   Alastair Campbell, 'It's time to bury spin', *British Journalism Review*, 13.4, 2002, pp. 15–24.

requiring her to muddy her own hands. Further back, there are nice examples of Wilson seeking to keep control of his government's message. Six months into office, he sent to departmental ministers a note headed 'Lobby Conferences', warning that conflicting and confusingly timetabled briefings risked giving 'an impression . . . of inadequate co-ordination at government level'. A personal minute to all ministers, some time later, stressed that 'what is essential is that Ministers speaking outside their own departmental jurisdiction should not embarrass their colleagues by private enterprise forays which have not been cleared with the Minister concerned, and where necessary with me'.[63]

Wilson's memos imply an itch to centralize. This is different from coordination but may be facilitated by it. Ingham wanted merely to be informed when ministers intended to go on television, in general. Wilson (through Haines) wanted the opportunity to make the decision himself; and so, in the glut era, did Campbell.[64] From the mid-1990s internet and e-mail technology made central control easier to organize, with innovations such as the daily grid of departmental communication activities and the cabinet presentation committee. Ingham's desire to be head of the Government Information Services was entirely logical. So, at a later stage of technology, was Campbell's. These were steps in the process of institutionalization and professionalization of Downing Street news operations started in 1945. A government would have been rash not to take them.

Centralization of control (up to the point where it becomes counter-productive) must be attractive to the press secretary also because new technology tends to create or strengthen his competitors too. In the Blair administration the obvious example were the special advisers, spinning for their own ministers. Even where they worked for the government's common good, they were inevitably a source of contradictory and discordant stories for eager journalists.

If the trend is towards super-secretaries, this highlights the political questions. Must a super-secretary be political? Does this mean 'partisan'? Does it also mean quasi-ministerial? One may plausibly argue that the relationship between 'political' and 'partisan' became less clear-cut from the 1990s. This was due to the decline in explicit party identification (membership), in enduring loyalty (more volatility among voters), in ideology, and in programmatic policy differences. The difficulty of a

---

[63] Derek Mitchell (Wilson's Principal Private Secretary) to ministers' private secretaries, PREM 13/504, 8 March 1965; prime minister's personal minute No. M67/68, 21 October 1968.

[64] Ingham interview, 10 February 1988; Report of the Working Group on the Government Information Services, p. 7.

super-secretary performing the full extent of advisory and intermediary roles for his boss, while maintaining the formal boundaries inherent in bureaucratic rules, is surely overwhelming. A PMOS finds it difficult enough, simply at the briefing level.

The cases of Ingham and Campbell showed that the loyalties of a super-secretary are almost bound to cut across the partisan–non-partisan boundary, whatever the niceties of formal rules and job descriptions. In the same way, they make almost inescapable the appearance, and maybe the fact (Downing Street secretiveness means we can never be sure), of the secretary behaving like a minister. The significance of this is partly just that it makes real ministers and parliamentarians annoyed – but this need not matter, unless it costs the prime minister goodwill. More important in theory is the issue of the super-secretary's accountability. If he were appointed as a minister, he would be answerable to parliament and vulnerable to dismissal, in circumstances where the loss of his parliamentary reputation made it dangerous to the prime minister to keep him. But press secretaries are not accountable in that way: hence the claims by Edward Heath that the use of the Press Office to criticize Thatcher's ministers was 'corrupt', and by the Conservative elder statesman Lord Hailsham that it was unscrupulous and dishonourable.[65]

If the press secretary were a career civil servant, on the other hand, he would be accountable to his line manager (probably the Cabinet Secretary) for sticking to the terms of his employment. A partisan and temporary civil service appointee such as Campbell, however, works within a large enough grey area to mean that these official rules may not be a comprehensive restraint. Campbell did put in several appearances before Commons Select Committees, to talk about aspects of his job; but that was trivial – and there were other, more serious inquiries which he refused to assist.[66] Similarly, Ingham had discussed Falklands news operations with the Commons Defence Committee, but Mrs Thatcher protected him from having to discuss his much more controversial part in the sensational Westland affair.

An extreme example of these various issues developed in June 2002, when Campbell came under intense pressure from the media and from politicians (including some Labour). What were now familiar allega-

[65] House of Commons Debates, 2 February 1989; Harris, *Good and Faithful Servant*, p. 175, quoting Lord Hailsham.
[66] Notable was the Wicks Committee on Standards in Public Life, chaired by Sir Nigel Wicks, the Parliamentary Commissioner for Standards. Like Alastair Campbell, Mr Blair's chief of staff, Jonathan Powell, also refused to give evidence. *The Times*, 5 July 2002.

tions, ranging upwards from loss of touch and judgement to lying, bullying and the complete collapse of credibility, fused in a row about the lying-in-state of the Queen Mother in Westminster Hall. Claims and counter-claims about whether Downing Street had sought a high profile for Tony Blair on this symbolically charged occasion led to Campbell first complaining to the Press Complaints Commission – and then backing off. The Downing Street PMOS, Campbell's subordinate, had the paradoxical task of assuring the lobby that the prime minister retained full confidence in Campbell.[67] As a minister, Campbell – rightly – would have had to justify himself on the floor of the Commons. In his original role as PMOS, he would have been explaining himself to the lobby. As a career civil servant, he would not have got into this position anyway. If he had been a minister, moreover, there would have been more room for manoeuvre by the prime minister. Campbell could have been moved in the next reshuffle – or returned to the backbenches, like Mandelson. As an appointee, it was difficult to see that he could be anything other than right in or right out.

Campbell's example shows that for purposes of accountability, the quasi-ministerial super-secretary would be more at home in Washington, as part of the president's White House staff. Not surprisingly, therefore, in view of the centrality of public communication to prime ministerial leadership, the secretaryship proves (on these arguments) to be one more brick in the building of a British 'presidency'. To the longer-term claims about this, going back to Richard Crossman's arguments in the 1960s about the growth of prime ministerial power at the expense of the cabinet, can be added evidence from the Blair administration. This includes both the creation of a 'Prime Minister's Department' at Downing Street (the next stage in which, ironically, was taking place at the same time as the Campbell row), and also the signs of a creeping spoils system, at the expense of the senior civil service, through the recruitment of political special advisers to ministerial entourages across Whitehall.

To argue in this way is to say how prime ministers might be expected to treat the press secretaryship, if they take the management of their public communication as seriously as they ought. But the flexibility of the job means that a prime minister can still choose otherwise. The 'Type B' system – prime minister plus career civil servant – does seem less likely than in the past; and if it were to be adopted, the civil servant might find himself restricted to the 'PMOS' routines, with a super-secretary wearing a Communications Director label as his line manager.

[67] Lobby morning briefing, 13 June 2002.

More likely would be reversion to 'Type A', with the appointment of a cabinet minister to have responsibility for the full range of the government's public communications. So central is communication to the prime minister's personal fortunes, however, that prime ministers may prefer the Thatcher–Blair expedients of unofficial quasi-ministers and remain content just to shrug off the criticisms.

Whatever a prime minister's preference, the secretary is likely to go on attracting criticism. Much of it will be the scuffle of politics, ephemeral and partisan. Some may take the high constitutional ground – though none the less politically motivated, perhaps. Criticism feeds curiosity, and curiosity may help to ensure that the secretary's job gets the public scrutiny it deserves.

8

Prime Ministers and Press Conferences

Why did British prime ministers not give regular press conferences, until Tony Blair started doing so in June 2002? (See figure 8.1.) One answer is that they did. For example Wilson often schmoozed with lobby correspondents, until he fell out with them. Heath held three big conferences in the grand surroundings of Lancaster House (see chapter 4). Press conferences are a feature of general election campaigns. Summit press conferences have become common.

But either such conferences have been given less as prime minister than as party leader, or they are shared with other people (ministers, overseas visitors, industrialists), or they are about some particular topic and place (Irish developments in Belfast; urban regeneration on Tyneside). What British prime ministers before Blair did not do was give regular, wide-ranging press conferences, generally 'open' both in the sense of on the record and accessible to a variety of journalists, on the classic model of American presidential press conferences. It is these which are the focus of this chapter.

A few prime ministers have been exceptions to that rule – but their conferences were occasional, not regular. John Major held a conference in the Downing Street garden on 13 June 1994. As it was planned the same morning, it caught journalists on the hop; some were unsure what its point was.[1] Tony Blair himself gave a conference in the Downing Street state dining room on 12 July 2000, three years into his premiership. It was billed as the first of a series leading up to the next election. What Blair's press secretary could not know was that the next in the series would be three emergency conferences on successive September evenings during an unexpected petrol blockade crisis.[2] Exactly a year

---

[1] Anthony Seldon, *Major*, London: Phoenix, 1998, p. 470.
[2] *The Times*, 13 July 2000. The petrol blockade conferences were on 12, 13 and 14 September 2000.

Figure 8.1: *Tony Blair's first monthly press conference, 20 June 2002.*

Tony Blair speaks to reporters in the state dining room of 10 Downing Street, in the first of his monthly press conferences. They were 'open' in several senses: on the record, televised, accessible to a much wider range of journalists than the lobby (including overseas journalists) and unrestricted in subject matter.

Photograph: Glen Corpus/Reuters.

later Blair was again having to address the press about an emergency infinitely worse – the terrorist attacks on New York and Washington. Grave events gave all those occasions special weight. So perhaps it did not seem surprising, some months later, to hear that 'presidential' press conferences had come to stay. But why had they not come earlier, and what are the issues involved?

What Makes a Press Conference?

The essence of a press conference is the questioning of the prime minister by journalists meeting for that purpose. If very brief or unorganized, the meeting cannot be considered a 'conference'. If conducted with a single journalist or very few, it is an 'interview'. If the group includes non-journalists, it is not truly a 'press' conference. All those occasions are likely to have different rules of exchange from press conferences.

There are obviously many variations on that basic model. Because it is an exchange, the format is the result of negotiation. This need not be formal or explicit. When the prime minister gives an in-flight conference while travelling abroad, for example, the rules are well understood, since most of the journalists will be lobby regulars. In other circumstances the arrangements may have been discussed and agreed far in advance. On all occasions, the outcome will probably be a compromise, because of the normal underlying tensions between the respective purposes of prime ministers and of news media.

The elements in such compromises can be analysed under four interrelated headings (similar to those concerning a prime minister's use of different locations, discussed in chapter 4):

- Who takes part?
- What is the procedure?
- How may the information be used?
- Where and when does the conference take place?

In each of the four, the prime minister and the press will seek to maximize their own control, with the aim of influencing the overall outcome.

Who takes part?

The classic presidential press conference pits the president as lone hero against an assembled horde. As head of a collective executive, the prime minister need not so obviously stand alone in the firing line. At summits or overseas, prime ministers may have no choice but to share a platform, with some loss of control over the proceedings. The same is true during election campaigns, when strategy usually suggests that the limelight is shared. Again, when launching a government initiative departmental ministers will be in support. On occasion, too, the prime minister may be chaired by his press secretary, who will in any case never be far away. From the 1980s, one of the commonest types of conference, generally little more than a photo opportunity, was the ritualistic performance with an overseas visitor. Sometimes these occasions had real substance, as with the joint announcement by John Major and Albert Reynolds, outside Number 10, of the Anglo-Irish Downing Street Declaration in 1993.[3]

On the media side, the key issue is access. How many journalists can attend? Should they be specialists? Who decides? For Blair's first

---

[3]   15 December 1983. The doorstep event was followed later by a press conference in the Downing Street state dining room. Seldon, *Major*, p. 428.

'regular' press conference at Downing Street in 2002 the lobby were asked to select forty-five names and the overseas correspondents group thirty, and Downing Street invited fifteen political commentators. (That was the maximum the state dining room would hold.) Size is likely to be inversely related to efficiency, if the object is some kind of dialogue. But if the prime minister wants to put on a show, which can be said of that conference or the three big conferences Heath gave experimentally in Lancaster House, it matters little who comes and how much they participate, provided there is a full house. The object is to demonstrate competence and control. On less self-conscious occasions, such as Wilson's attempts to ruminate and try out ideas with lobby correspondents, numbers should be small and carefully selected.

In practice there have been natural groupings. Some prime ministers (Eden, Major, Blair) have had meetings with a handful of editors or proprietors. The foreign press have historically been treated separately, and the Americans separately from the others during most of the twentieth century. The lobby correspondents, like the White House press, effectively make the rules about their own membership, and the history of the lobby confirms the inverse relation between size and utility. In its post-1945 heyday the lobby were extremely exclusive and would refuse to take part in a press conference with non-members. Heath's first broadcast press conference in Lancaster House provoked a general sulk: the lobby did not want to be stooges in his theatre, nor see television get first bite at the answers to their questions. For the second the format was changed. Heath made a televised statement, followed by questioning without the cameras on, and finishing with separate televised interviews after the main event was over.

What is the procedure?

Who comes can make a big difference to what happens at a press conference. For example at routine lobby conferences the lobby chairman is in charge of starting and ending the proceedings.[4] Normally the problem is to shape the agenda to a limited time. In their very rare meetings with the taciturn Attlee, the chairman's job, perversely, was to try and keep discussion going. Sometimes journalists do not ask questions the prime minister wishes to answer. More problematically they press questions he wishes to avoid. Prime ministers have to duck questions or

---

[4]   This convention extends to in-flight conferences. On a Blair flight from Tokyo the chairman reportedly got into trouble with colleagues for wanting to watch a movie instead of agreeing to a prime ministerial briefing. *Guardian*, 25 July 2000.

rule subjects off limits in advance, if they can. Usually they make an opening statement, if only to get the ball rolling. In a broadcast conference, their staff may have tried to plant questions in advance, in order to ensure a subject is raised. They may avoid catching the eye of unsympathetic questioners, although the main national media cannot easily be ignored – especially the BBC and ITV. Even from these, however, supplementaries can often be squashed, particularly if the conference is a big one. A large conference, too, makes the development of a line of probing questions difficult.

In the United States, presidents quickly refined such expedients for controlling conference agendas. To cope with hostile questioning about the Vietnam War, for example, Lyndon Johnson made very long opening statements. These ate up nearly two-fifths of the available time on average, compared with ten to fifteen per cent for Kennedy, Nixon and Ford. Johnson also held impromptu conferences, sometimes on the trot in the White House garden, to prevent journalists having time to prepare questions in advance.[5]

How may the information be used?

The key questions about use are whether what the prime minister says is on or off the record and whether it can be broadcast. There are advantages to both sides in staying off the record. The prime minister will probably speak more freely and provide better copy. He should find it easier to spin the news, and speaking off the record allows him 'deniability'. For his part, the journalist's privileged position in his news organization is strengthened: his possession of the news is exclusive, and lack of personal resourcefulness is easier to conceal.

If the prime minister agrees to speak on the record, there is little reason why a conference should not be broadcast, in full or part. This became a realistic possibility in the early 1960s, when the rules about political broadcasting began to be relaxed. Broadcasting had the potential to transform press conferences. When TV or radio eavesdrops, a third party is introduced. The existence of a broadcast audience destroys intimacy and confidentiality. The prime minister will talk past the journalists, as Blair did in his petrol crisis conferences in September 2000. The journalists themselves may posture; and their performance, like the prime minister's own, will be an object of scrutiny. When Kennedy gave the first live televised conference, after less than a month in office, the essence of the traditional Roosevelt press conference was at a stroke

[5]   George C. Edwards III, *The Public Presidency*, New York: St Martin's Press, 1983, pp. 116, 113.

changed and, in the eyes of many print journalists, diminished. The change was captured in the reaction of Ben Bradlee, later editor of the *Washington Post*, to a group TV interview with Kennedy: 'I watched it at home, and felt professionally threatened as a man who was trying to make a living by the written word.'[6]

If he agrees to a broadcast conference the prime minister's purpose will therefore be substantially different from what it would be at an off-the-record event. The natural alternatives would be the broadcast interview or the face-to-camera address to the nation – a format signalling high seriousness. The choice of a press conference, whether broadcast or not, cedes to journalists the task of reporting and interpreting. Their personalities and their reputations are enlisted. This may bring benefits to the prime minister; but it is a risk, compared with talking directly through the screen, for it is a loss of control.

Where and when does the conference take place?

This question puts a press conference into its wider context. It raises issues of routine and regularity. The location of a conference has practical implications for control of conduct and content, in addition to such symbolic connotations as were discussed in chapter 4. Prime minister and media enjoy advantages in spaces they respectively 'own'. Historically, the lobby 'invited' the prime minister to meet them, and their territory was (and is) the turret room at the Commons.[7] Part of the dismantling of the old lobby system in 2002 was a plan to move the morning lobby conferences elsewhere in Whitehall, away from Downing Street. Other locations, such as airports and aeroplanes, as we have seen, are neutral. Canadian journalists, in the early days of in-flight interviews, 'petitioned' the prime minister Trudeau in Latin for a conference – defusing uncertainty about the location through a joke.[8]

---

[6] Kennedy's comment, when Bradlee told him, was: 'I always said that when we don't have to go through you bastards, we can really get our story over to the American people.' Benjamin C. Bradlee, *Conversations with Kennedy*, New York: Pocket Book, 1976, p. 123.

[7] 'The Lobby meetings are very informal, and held in conditions of physical discomfort in a small room reached by an iron staircase at the very top of the House of Commons building. The traditional style for these weekly meetings is chatty, personal and not too heavy. On the other hand, every word said, particularly by a Prime Minister, is most carefully examined for all possible implications, and may be "written up" well above the level of Ministerial intention.' Brief for Anthony Eden before his first meeting with the lobby. F. Clark to D. Pitblado, 28 June 1955, PREM 11/975.

[8] Patrick Gossage, *Close to the Charisma*, Toronto: McClelland and Stewart, 1986, p. 192.

A regular location goes with regular rules of conduct. These favour the prime minister, in the sense that he is more likely to make a gaffe if unprepared, on unfamiliar ground or out of his routine. Major, for example, admitted that 'trying to think up snappy replies' in doorstep encounters was 'much more difficult than coping with a structured interview'.[9] But regularity is not the same as frequency. How often to hold conferences is a difficult judgement. The general problem is that a habit of press conferences when the prime minister has something to say is not easily broken when he badly wants to say nothing. Blair might find his monthly press conferences started in 2002 an awkward commitment at some future date. Too frequent a cycle, furthermore, risks devaluing the currency – a factor to which John Major's press secretary was naturally alert after the Downing Street garden conference. Wilson arguably made a mistake by meeting the lobby too often in the early months of his premiership; relations became the more sour for being at first so sweet. Prime ministers should ideally have press conferences preferably when both they and the media think they have something special to say.

The press conference format: tendencies

This brief analysis suggests three comments. First and not surprisingly, *the press conference idea works best when the format fits fairly closely the purposes of both sides.* Wilson's sessions with the select lobby group failed, as did Heath's grand public conferences, because they met the prime minister's needs but not the journalists'. In the United States the golden age of the presidential press conference was Franklin Roosevelt's era, from 1933–45, when president and reporters each knew exactly where they stood and were happy about it. Once the system got going, relations were characterized by 'intimacy, informality and a set of institutionalised procedures'.[10] The same principles surely apply in Britain. If the press is bored, cowed, or alternatively rampant, their exchanges with a prime minister are likely to become mired in frustration, bad temper and fruitless point scoring.

Once instituted, secondly, *press conferences tend to become formalized.* This is because of both sides' desire for control. A regulated format, even if the rules are implicit, is likely to be more productive. When a conference is scheduled well in advance, to take an obvious

[9] Nicholas Jones, *Soundbites and Spin Doctors*, London: Cassell, 1995, p. 36.
[10] Daniel J. Boorstin, 'Selling the President to the people', *Commentary*, July 1955, p. 427; quoted by S. Kernell, *Going Public*, Washington, D.C.: CQ Press, 1986, p. 66.

example, there is time for preparation and to ensure the results fit conveniently into political and media timetables. After Blair started regular press conferences, the lobby persistently badgered his press secretary about when the next one would take place. They were given roughly a month's notice.

Within the general press conference format, thirdly, prime ministers have held four types. One is the *press conference as routine*. This is characterized by predictability of timing, conduct and value. It includes the monthly Blair conferences. General election conferences and many of the now familiar Downing Street doorstep events provide other examples. A second type is the *press conference as culmination*, signalling the end to a summit or some other possibly fraught process of negotiation. Such conferences can be either ritualistic or full of urgency. If the latter, they overlap with *the press conference as hot news*. Wilson announced his wholly unexpected resignation as prime minister in 1976 at a press conference. Mrs Thatcher broke the news of the recapture of South Georgia in the Falklands War in 1982 in a doorstep conference outside Downing Street. Major briefed the lobby in his room at the Commons when Michael Heseltine provoked a sudden row about pit closures in October 1992.[11] Blair's petrol crisis conferences in 2000 were extremely hot news, otherwise he would not have held three in succession.

In contrast to hot news, the last type is the *conference as stocktaking*. Wilson's ruminative sessions would have come in this category, if they had worked. Although Major's 1994 Downing Street garden conference was organized at a few hours' notice (it seems to have been inspired by better-than-expected Conservative results in the European parliamentary elections), he had nothing remarkable to announce. Blair's Downing Street conference in July 2000 had stocktaking elements too. In such cases the precise timing of the conference does not greatly matter.

The Presidential Press Conference

Kennedy's innovative televised conferences prompted Harold Macmillan, prime minister at the time, to think hard about copying them. He had already proved an adept television performer. A few years later Wilson, a keen observer of the Kennedy style, was tempted too. What exactly has been the American experience?

---

[11] Nicholas Jones, *Soundbites and Spin Doctors*, p. 106. Jones comments: 'Most of us had never set foot in the room before.'

Presidents as early as Andrew Johnson (1865–9) gave private interviews to journalists, but the modern press conference had its first boost from Theodore Roosevelt (1901–9). He saw the value of cultivating reporters, as distinct from editors and publishers. On his first day in office he laid down rules permitting reporters unprecedented access to the White House but giving him considerable control over how they gathered and used their information. For example they were allowed to hang around in the White House anteroom and portico – but not to address the president unless he stopped spontaneously. (A virtually identical rule applied to reporters in the House of Commons lobby.) Above all, information given in confidence had to remain confidential.[12]

Theodore Roosevelt was able to get his way by dividing reporters into insiders and outsiders and playing on their resulting fears and aspirations. Woodrow Wilson (1913–21) started with a more free and easy approach. He opened his weekly Oval Office meetings to reporters at large. At first more than two hundred turned up, so increasingly he dealt with a small group of insiders. He refused to be quoted on the record without permission. After a row when that rule was broken, he agreed that the conference should be policed by the journalists themselves – a move which greatly increased their leverage. This led to the foundation of the White House Correspondents Association (again, very much like the lobby correspondents' group).

Wilson's less celebrated successors, Warren Harding (1921–3), Calvin Coolidge (1923–9) and Herbert Hoover (1929–33), each began with regular open press conferences but backtracked. Harding's conferences became dull because he required questions to be submitted in advance and refused supplementaries. Coolidge kept the former requirement, refused to be quoted and was the first president to make reporters source their information to 'a White House spokesman'.[13] Hoover made himself unpopular by having favourites and ignoring questions from others.

The press conference took a great leap forward under Franklin Roosevelt (1933–45). From the start he promised 'hard news openly conveyed' – and he provided it every Tuesday and Friday in the Oval Office.[14] By the time of his death he had held 998 conferences. He kept strict rules and maintained them by charm and even-handedness – the 'intimacy and informality' referred to earlier. The rules produced four

[12] An excellent account of the development of the presidential press conference is in Samuel Kernell, *Going Public*, ch. 3.
[13] Howard H. Quint and Robert H. Ferrell, *The Talkative President*, Boston, Mass.: University of Massachusetts Press, 1964, pp. v–vi.
[14] Kernell, *Going Public*, p. 3.

types of information: occasional direct quotations; remarks attributable but not in direct quotation; background information not attributable to the White House; and remarks off the record not to be repeated outside. The rules and procedures were backed up by the appointment of the first influential presidential press secretary, Steve Early. The system gave reporters lots of news and very high status within their news organizations (most of which, of course, were far away from Washington). Roosevelt, in return, got a friendly press corps – which helped to counter a hostile (because Republican) news industry.

Roosevelt's system had much in common with the Westminster lobby in the lobby's heyday – say, the mid-1930s until the mid-1960s. But there were two big differences. Most of the time at Westminster a surrogate, the Downing Street press secretary, spoke for the prime minister, as we have seen in the preceding chapters. Secondly, while much of what he said remained opaque or confidential, the president could at least sometimes be quoted. The same factors which upset the equilibrium under Roosevelt's successors accounted, too, for the degeneration of the lobby: the loss by newspapers of their media monopoly (including, in the United States, the far greater presidential reach permitted by air travel), and a corresponding loss by the press corps of its corporate identity.

Truman (1945–53) lacked Roosevelt's skill but initially kept the same format. A foretaste of the future came when he gave permission in his second term for the conference to be recorded and extracts broadcast on radio. This meant the whole conference, in effect, was designed for the record. A corollary was that Truman began to prepare and practise. In 1950 he cut the conferences to weekly and moved them out of the Oval Office. All these changes reduced their spontaneity and news value. Eisenhower (1953–61) went further. He held only two conferences a month, worried about letting secrets slip, perplexed reporters with his 'circular sentence construction',[15] and compounded those difficulties by publishing verbatim transcripts and, from 1955, letting TV cameras record the proceedings.

The significance of the decision by Kennedy (1961–3) to televise his conferences was that he had the panache to broadcast them live, and in a period by which TV news had taken off. The inaugural conference in January 1961 attracted 418 reporters to the State Department auditorium and sixty-five million viewers. The predictable consequences fol-

---

[15]   James E. Pollard, *The Presidents and the Press*, New York: Macmillan, 1958, p. 79, quoting a news agency correspondent, Merriman Smith, who found Eisenhower 'the most difficult President in recent years to follow on pencil and paper'.

lowed. Reporters became props and prima donnas. The vast majority of participants were just set decoration. Questions became soggier, supplementaries fewer and the conference as a whole less coherent. 'As background briefings and sustained questioning on issues gave way to presidential position-taking and evasion, the print journalists lost their hard news.'[16]

Kennedy had created *the press conference as public spectacle*. As such, it could not be staged too often, if it was to remain effective, and it was likely to have a large element of stocktaking. Kennedy therefore – a stylish communicator – paradoxically averaged fewer conferences than the bumbling Eisenhower. His successors gave fewer still. Nixon (1969–74) and Reagan (1981–9) averaged one every two months and Carter (1977–81) fewer than one a month. Moreover live conferences were fine for a youthful president in a Camelot climate, but they were potentially hazardous in the dark Vietnam and Watergate years. Nixon gave none at all between late July and early November, 1970 – the longest gap since Hoover – and by his fourth year he almost never had them televised.

Presidents turned to other methods of conveying the kind of information for which Roosevelt used the press conference. Roosevelt had never given exclusive interviews: Kennedy did not hesitate. Reagan, whose lack of grip on detail made his rare conferences nerve-wracking (they were scheduled late in the day, to allow less time for unsympathetic editing in news clips), gave 194 press interviews in his first three years and 150 special White House briefings for media from outside Washington. The many forms of public communication and media management which developed were represented in the increasing number of offices devoted to them – at least eight, in addition to the press office, by Clinton's time.[17]

Along with that diversification, electronic developments enabled the president to retain some of the traditional press conference characteristics within more complex formats. By the end of the century, Clinton could be interviewed by journalists in a very wide range of settings. These commonly featured distant or dispersed participants, linked elec-

[16] Kernell, *Going Public*, p. 71.
[17] In 1999 Clinton's White House had offices for Communications, Speech Writing and Research, Political Affairs, Public Affairs, Public Liaison, Scheduling, Advance, and Correspondence, plus the Press Office. *The Capital Source*, Washington, D.C.: National Journal Group, Fall 1999, pp. 6–12, lists 111 staff in these offices, with another five working on media and communications in the First Lady's Office. Arrangements in the George W. Bush White House at the beginning of his presidency were on a comparable scale.

tronically, and a mixture of journalist and non-journalist questioners. The former included electronic conferences with out-of-town journalists and simultaneous interview sessions with people in several different places. The latter included 'electronic town meetings', of which Clinton gave at least half a dozen in his first year. In addition, Clinton continued to give occasional traditional open press conferences on televised post-Roosevelt lines. There was no reason to suppose this format would disappear altogether, but a measure of its declining significance was that the TV networks did not consider all of Clinton's important enough to carry live. Another measure is that George W. Bush's first traditional press conference did not take place until 12 October 2001 – nearly nine months after he took office and one month after the terrorist attacks.

Prime Ministers' Press Conferences with Lobby Correspondents: from the Roosevelt to the Kennedy Model

Right up to the new millennium the prime minister's natural clientele for a press conference was the lobby. But the majority of prime ministers did not want press conferences, so they delegated the task to their press secretaries. Relations between the Downing Street press secretary and the lobby became very similar in form to those of Franklin Roosevelt with the White House press (though the secretary/surrogate could obviously never have the authority or gravitas of the chief executive himself). The closest a prime minister personally came to the Roosevelt model – and during precisely the same period – was Neville Chamberlain in the later 1930s. When change eventually came in the 1990s, it did so in stages. First, John Major's experiment with a press conference in June 1994 was held on the record and included a few non-lobby journalists. Next, Blair's *ad hoc* conferences, notably on the petrol blockade in 2000 and the New York attacks in 2001, were broadcast on television and open to a wider clientele. Thirdly, Blair started to hold conferences at regular monthly intervals from the summer of 2002. With this last stage, adjustment to the essential features of the Kennedy model was complete.

Until the end of World War I prime ministers never saw lobby men singly, let alone collectively. At most they confided in favoured editors or used intermediaries. After the war Lloyd George had one big public press conference during the Chanak crisis near the end of his premiership.[18] Stanley Baldwin used to talk to individual journalists in the

18 The cabinet approved both a proposal that the prime minister should brief the press and the main points to be emphasized. The two-column report in *The Times* was pre-

Commons lobby – the original place of contact from which the lobby system takes its name.

Collective meetings started after the appointment by Ramsay MacDonald of the first Downing Street press secretary, George Steward, who gave regular briefings from 1930. The prime minister himself started seeing the lobby in a Roosevelt-style conference (in fact a few years before Roosevelt started) every Thursday in his room at the House of Commons. (See summary in table 8.1.) He talked informally and not just about politics. Other ministers – Chamberlain among them – were quick to see the advantages and joined in. When Baldwin became prime minister in 1935 he was content to let Chamberlain take lobby meetings on his behalf. So by the time Chamberlain in turn became prime minister in 1937 he had come to see the lobby as his 'personal service'.[19] The lobby's written rules imposed strict non-attributability and extreme confidentiality: members were not even to mention that the meetings took place. The prime minister's forthcoming attendance was signalled in a bizarre code about the day when 'the mantle will fall'.[20] The system made it simple for Chamberlain to manage the news, especially with Steward's backing. He even started requiring the submission of questions four hours or more in advance, if reporters wanted to be sure of getting a reply. He continued these weekly meetings until after the outbreak of World War II. Unlike Roosevelt, who provoked very strong resentment when he once gave an exclusive interview in 1937 (he promised not to do it again), Chamberlain had no problems about seeing individual lobby journalists from time to time too.[21]

Here was a prime minister, then, managing a very effective weekly press conference for several years. But no one knew it was happening, unless they were privy to the meaning of such phrases in their paper as 'an authoritative source' or 'unofficial and semi-official contacts'.[22] The system did not survive the war, however. There were practically no

---

ceded by an explanation that 'Mr Lloyd George made a long and important statement on the Government policy in the Near East to a party of newspaper representatives who were invited to attend at 10 Downing Street on Saturday'. Cabinet minutes, 23 September 1922, CM 50 (22), min.3; *The Times*, 25 September 1922. The crisis was part of the complex pattern of British and French involvement with Graeco-Turkish relations.

[19] 'Whitehall and the press', letter to *The Times*, 8 July 1976, from Norman Barrymaine, a retired lobby correspondent; Richard Cockett, *Twilight of Truth*, London: Weidenfeld and Nicolson, 1989, pp. 5–6. Cockett's account of the development of collective lobby briefings is highly perceptive.

[20] Interview, William Deedes, 19 December 1987.

[21] Cockett, *Twilight of Truth*, p. 7.

[22] These examples are from the *Guardian* and the *Daily Telegraph*, quoted in Cockett, *Twilight of Truth*, p. 104.

Table 8.1 *Prime Ministers' press conferences, MacDonald to Blair: summary*

Prime Minister and dates	Approx. number of lobby journalists: Maximum / Active	Private meetings with lobby?	Open or televised press conferences?
MacDonald (1929–35)	45 / 25	Weekly	No
Baldwin (1935–7)	Same	Not interested	No
Chamberlain (1937–40)	50 / 25	Weekly	No
Churchill (1940–5; 1951–5)	Same	No	No
Attlee (1945–51)	100 / 35 Evening papers join	Almost none	No
Eden (1955–7)	Same	Two or three with lobby; three or four with editors	No
Macmillan (1957–63)	120 / 45 Broadcasters join; 'alternate' members permitted	Several in early years	Considered copying Kennedy in 1961
Douglas-Home (1963–4)	As for Macmillan	Few if any	No
Wilson (1964–70; 1974–6)	130 / 50? by 1970	Often in first two years; short experiment with select group; in-flight conferences start	Considered copying Kennedy; at least one experiment
Heath (1970–4)	As for Wilson	Two or three times a year; in-flight conferences	Experiment with three at Lancaster House
Callaghan (1976–9)	200 / 60? Multiple membership permitted	Not interested? In-flight/airport conferences	No
Thatcher (1979–90)	230 / 60? by 1990	Not interested; in-flight/ airport conferences	Began Downing Street 'doorsteps' in 1982
Major (1990–7)	240 / 65?	Few if any after 1992; in-flight/airport conferences routine	'Doorsteps' regularized; open conference in garden (not televised)
Blair (1997–)	Same	Lobby system reformed; in-flight/airport conferences routine	Regular 'doorsteps'; crisis conferences in State Dining Room; monthly general conferences from June 2002

Notes

Lobby correspondent numbers are very tentative. Many members attended irregularly. Until the 1960s some (e.g., Sunday journalists) were excluded from the collective briefings. 'Alternate' membership meant only one of a news organization's members could attend at a time.

Overseas conferences, shared or specialized conferences and election campaigns are omitted.

prime ministerial lobby conferences until Anthony Eden's premiership nearly twenty years later, and not many thereafter. The reasons were a mixture of prime ministers' reluctance, through temperament or social background, and changes in the character of the lobby. Churchill (1940–5, 1951–5), Eden (1955–7), Macmillan (1957–63) and Douglas-Home (1963–4) did not move in lobby circles: they were more used to editors and proprietors. (Chamberlain, in contrast, had not mixed much with proprietors.) Attlee (1945–51) told his press secretary flatly, when appointing him: 'I am allergic to publicity'.[23] Heath met the lobby two or three times a year. Callaghan was uninterested. Thatcher seems not to have given a lobby conference in her entire premiership. When a leading correspondent asked Bernard Ingham if she would consider giving even an annual press conference, the request was turned down.[24]

Attlee's reluctance was not resented, because his press secretary, Francis Williams, was an excellent substitute. Besides, Attlee's very occasional meetings, as has been said, were frustratingly terse. One of these took place on 3 June 1947, immediately after his announcement in the Commons of the date for Indian independence.[25] Churchill was classically an editor/proprietor man, and he was hardly going to change the habit of a lifetime in his post-war premiership, which started when he was 76. James Margach, a lobby veteran, claimed Churchill never once met the lobby correspondents. One botched attempt involved an abortive expedition to Southampton, to meet the prime minister on his return from a meeting with President Truman.[26]

A memo by Churchill's arm's-length press secretary, Fife Clark, gives a whiff of the social distance typically separating prime ministers from reporters until the 1960s. Clark, confirming arrangements in 1955 for the new prime minister, Anthony Eden, agreed that Eden 'could not fairly be asked to see individually anyone except top-rank proprietors

---

[23] Francis Williams (Attlee's first press secretary), quoted in *The Times*, 3 December 1947.

[24] Anthony Bevins, memo to the editor of the *Independent*, 20 April 1986.

[25] The Secretary of State for India was deputed the task of briefing the Indian, Empire and overseas press. 29 May 1947, PREM 8/551.

[26] The lobby correspondents went down to Southampton the night before Churchill was due to land, after his first meeting with President Truman in the United States since becoming prime minister. They were ferried out to the *Queen Elisabeth* in the early morning. Churchill, who had a heavy cold, kept them waiting and then said that, as had no doubt been explained at Downing Street, he had nothing to say on policy. Much of the brief report next day in *The Times*, for instance, was about Churchill's attempt to engage with a man in the quayside crowd, who booed him. *The Times*, 29 January 1952; interview, Francis Boyd (former *Guardian* lobby correspondent), 10 February 1988; James Margach, *The Abuse of Power*, London: W. H. Allen, 1978, pp. 66–7.

and editors'; but 'he would meet political correspondents collectively from time to time'.[27] Eden thus started with good intentions and did indeed carry them out, if only on a couple of occasions, in the brief period before his premiership foundered in the 1956 Suez canal crisis. During this crisis he saw groups of editors, sometimes as many as twenty, in preference to the lobby. Eden 'talked freely and with great friendliness to a group of people who spend half their time trying to strangle him', noted his press secretary William Clark in January 1956. He saw editors at least twice more during the summer and Clark had to dissuade him from doing so repeatedly; Eden seemed to think he could manage his complete Suez publicity by that means. In contrast he actually refused to have a conference with the lobby in April, which would have marked the anniversary of his entertaining them in Downing Street.[28]

Harold Macmillan, with a comparable background to Eden, began with a similarly dutiful attitude. He saw the lobby several times before falling out for reasons which remain obscure.[29] He disliked press conferences, which generally happened overseas, at the best of times: ' "Why do you make me do these things?" was an almost standard flash of annoyance before a conference.'[30] But Macmillan (and Douglas-Home, for his short premiership) were the last of the patricians. The arrival of Harold Wilson in Downing Street in 1964 brought a prime minister who was both interested in lobby conferences and not inhibited by social distance.

Wilson's lobby conferences got off to a rousing start, part of the general freshness following thirteen years of Conservative rule. The honeymoon lasted only months. The lobby quickly saw that Wilson expected to have them in his pocket. 'They began to resent being summoned at all hours to Number 10 to be told by the great man what wonderful new thing he had done' – not least because of the convention that the lobby, not the prime minister, does the inviting.[31] The selec-

[27] F. Clark to D. Pitblado, 25 April 1955, PREM 11/974. Eden agreed to see individually the *Observer* journalist Hugh Massingham. Massingham, an influential columnist (and a gent) was excluded from lobby membership at that time, because he did not work for a daily paper. F. Clark to D. Pitblado, 6 July 1955, PREM 11/974.
[28] William Clark, diary entries for 24 February 1956, 4 September 1956, 27 March 1956. William D. Clark papers, Bodleian Library, Oxford University.
[29] There may have been a row at a lobby meeting. Interview, John Groves, former Downing Street press secretary, 15 January 1988.
[30] Harold Evans, *Downing Street Diary*, London: Hodder and Stoughton, 1981, p. 63. Evans was Macmillan's chief press secretary for most of his premiership.
[31] Groves interview, 15 January 1988.

tive 'white Commonwealth' meetings began well but palled. They took place fortnightly, often lasting three or four hours into the evening, 'assessing the whole political scene, including the Tories', and 'run like a seminar'.[32] The selection was based partly on Wilson's likes and dislikes, which meant key correspondents from *The Times* and the *Daily Express*, for instance, were excluded.[33] Wilson also attended hard news lobby conferences regularly during his first two years or so, 'feeding out the daily tightrope sagas himself'.[34] But by the end of his government in 1970 such personal contacts had ceased. During his second government in 1974–6, relations with the lobby became so bad that his press secretary too stopped giving daily lobby briefings.

It was ironic that the most well-disposed prime minister since 1945 should have failed so badly with the lobby. What he ideally wanted, wrote his assistant Marcia Williams, was a dual system of off-the-record lobby meetings and regular open press conferences.[35] His failure was no doubt partly due to personality and the turn of events – especially economic and industrial troubles. But the very lack of social distance between prime minister and journalists, which reduced deference and formality, probably made confrontation more likely. In Chamberlain's time the lobby really had very little leverage. If they irritated Chamberlain, he could have brushed them away. Still in Eden's time, they struck the press secretary William Clark (himself a former diplomatic journalist) as 'a tight, loyal, professional body of people with a devouring interest in rather dull "scoops"; e.g. all fear that one day the announcement of cabinet changes will find them napping'. Fife Clark, too, reassured Eden that he had nothing to fear from them: 'they will not press their questions in the American style; and they will be satisfied with less information'.[36] It would be absurd to imply that lobby correspondents were in thrall to Old Etonian prime ministers. But with Wilson they were more likely to argue – and maybe even to do so publicly, since the existence of the system began to attract occasional media comment in the early 1960s.

[32]   Marcia Williams, *Inside Number 10*, London: New English Library, 1975, pp. 184–5. The term 'white Commonwealth', used ironically, was borrowed from the distinction, common at the time, between the old dominions such as Canada and Australia, and the more recently independent African and Asian members of the Commonwealth.
[33]   Interview, Ian Waller, former *Sunday Telegraph* lobby correspondent, 23 April 1976.
[34]   Marcia Williams, *Inside Number 10*, p. 180.
[35]   Marcia Williams, *Inside Number 10*, pp. 179ff.
[36]   William Clark, Diary, 3 October 1955. MS William Clark 7, Bodleian Library, Oxford. F. Clark to D. Pitblado, 22 June 1955, PREM 11/976. At Eden's lobby conference in June 1956, William Clark was 'amazed' at 'how bad the press was at asking questions; they seemed so terribly shy'. Diary, 25 June 1956.

Wilson's willing familiarity coincided with a crumbling of that tight loyalty. Increasing numbers in the lobby went with higher turnover, looser adherence to the rules and thus, from a prime minister's perspective, declining trustworthiness. In the 1930s the lobby regulars numbered fifty to sixty, of whom up to twenty were prominent. Fife Clark briefed Eden to expect sixty when he met them in 1955. Twenty years later 'up to one hundred' came to Haines's major Thursday briefings, before he abolished them.[37] James Callaghan reflected, some years after his premiership, that 'there are too many people, we have lost the basis of confidentiality and trust. If you go to a lobby convention [sic] you do not know half of the people there, anybody seems to be able to get a ticket.'[38]

Increased numbers also went with the decline of anonymous journalism, the huge growth of electronic outlets and a heightened 'decibel count' (such as stronger headline language), as Bernard Ingham called it. Ingham 'conceived the idea of Mrs Thatcher briefing small pre-arranged groups of political editors, so that they could have a fuller discussion with her than was possible with the lobby as a whole'. Perhaps predictably, 'this was immediately seen as a revival of the "white Commonwealth"', and he abandoned it.[39]

Ten years earlier, all those changes had influenced Ted Heath's press conference experiments. The lobby correspondents, in his press secretary's view, too often editorialized the facts. The Lancaster House conferences were supposed to enable Heath to 'speak simultaneously through the media to the people'. Thus the first one (12 July 1971) launched the government's campaign to win popular support for entry to the European Economic Community and was held in advance of the party conference and the key Commons debate.[40]

These conferences were only the most ostentatious of Heath's initiatives. He saw the lobby two or three times a year, but he preferred on-the-record briefing. He gave conferences about prices and incomes policy and about the miners' strike which brought him down.[41] His first press secretary, Donald Maitland, pushed unsuccessfully for lobby meet-

[37]   F. Clark to D. Pitblado, 18 April 1955, PREM 11/974; interview, Joe Haines, 11 April 1988.
[38]   Oral evidence to House of Commons Treasury and Civil Service subcommittee, HC (1985–6) 92.II, p. 226.
[39]   Interview, Bernard Ingham, 10 February 1988; Bernard Ingham, *Kill the Messenger*, London: HarperCollins, 1991, p. 347.
[40]   Interview, Sir Donald Maitland, 5 April 1988; Douglas Hurd, *An End to Promises*, London: Collins, 1979, pp. 66–7, 82.
[41]   Interview, Sir Robin Haydon, 22 March 1988.

ings to be held on the record; and he also explored the idea of a weekly on-the-record government press conference, which would have featured a variety of ministers – the prime minister occasionally among them.[42]

The lobby had grown to 226 members when Ingham left office in 1990. Voracious competition between individuals and between print and broadcast media meant that during John Major's premiership the conferences with his press secretary were in practice more or less on the record anyway.[43] A lobby conference with the prime minister would have had even less chance of being successfully conducted in confidence. This was one reason why Major saw the lobby privately very rarely during the second half of his premiership.

By the time Tony Blair took office, therefore, the only realistic option, if the prime minister wanted an occasional press conference with the lobby, was to hold it openly. The Roosevelt model was no longer practical. If it was open, however, why limit it to the lobby? Both Major's and Blair's Downing Street conferences had a wider clientele.[44] In this respect their experiments resembled a solitary effort by Wilson some months before his retirement. This was announced as the first of several, after Haines stopped briefing the lobby. It was held in a marbled room in the Treasury and was open to all comers, British or foreign. The subject was the government's industrial strategy. Wilson explained that he wanted industrial specialists to participate in addition to the lobby, but *The Times* reported that 'most of the audience were familiar lobby faces'.[45] If a press conference was open, furthermore, why not broadcast it? Wilson was asked this question, but there is no record of the reply.

Although Major's decision to have an open press conference owed something to the scepticism of his press secretary about private lobby contacts, the timing was spontaneous, the subject was unrestricted, and the meeting was wrapped up by the prime minister when he had had enough. He gave one other conference on the same lines, on the afternoon of 16 January 1995 in the Downing Street state dining room. The lobby were forewarned at 11.30. The purpose was a look ahead to 1995 and to show Major had the political initiative.[46]

---

[42]   Maitland interview, 5 April 1988.

[43]   Interview, Christopher Meyer, 12 September 1994.

[44]   Most of the questions at Wilson's conference were asked by the lobby. Major's conference was described by his press office as essentially for the lobby, with the possibility of expanding the attendance in later cases. Interviews, 12 September 1994, 5 October 1994.

[45]   *The Times*, 26 June 1975.

[46]   Nicholas Jones, *Soundbites and Spin Doctors*, p. 117; Seldon, *Major*, p. 521.

Tony Blair's first conference along those lines, mentioned in the introduction to this chapter, did not come until 12 July 2000, three years into his premiership. Its aim was to 'set out the "economic narrative" on which he plans to fight the next election' (expected within a year).[47] His next three – unplanned – conferences on 12–14 September 2000 were designed to show that the government was on top of a rapidly escalating transport crisis caused by fuel delivery companies picketing depots to protest about the level of fuel tax. The conference format was particularly suitable because parliament was not in session. Blair talked across the heads of the press direct to the people ('Let me assure the public . . .'). He hammered two main points about being a 'listening' government and not giving in to intimidation, and he was asked about a dozen not very challenging questions each time.

The conferences on 12 and 25 September 2001 were on a different scale of significance. The first, like the previous ones, was held in the state dining room, which by now had become the routine press conference venue. Blair took eight questions after an opening statement. Parliament was again in recess but met for a single day on 14 September. On 25 September Blair gave a rather longer 'update' conference in the Downing Street garden and answered ten questions. The timing of this conference caused speculation about the imminence of military action, which started in early October.

All those conferences (except 12 July 2000) took place during crises in which – certainly at those particular moments – the media were likely to be quite supportive. The fact that they were called at all was in itself a portent. The monthly conferences beginning on 20 June 2002 were announced as a routine, so their atmosphere and rhythm were somewhat different, with more sceptical and needling questions. The first conference was a self-conscious affair, lasting 75 minutes, with 45 questions on 16 topics – many of them about the government 'spin'. The second (on 25 July) included 54 questions covering 24 topics, many of them about international affairs, especially Iraq. Iraq was the subject of 35 out of 49 questions (covering 11 topics) at the third conference on 3 September. This one took place in Blair's constituency of Sedgefield, County Durham. Of the three, the last attracted most media coverage, because it dealt with an issue of great topical concern, during the parliamentary recess.

By adopting the Kennedy model of press conference, Blair made a clear break, therefore, with all his predecessors. But he was adding to

---

[47] *The Times*, 12 July 2000.

the range of methods of meeting the press, not substituting for any of them, and some of these alternatives should now be looked at.

Prime Ministers and Press Conferences: the Broader Pattern

Prime ministers have met the press in a number of formats sharing features of the presidential type of conference. To explore them in detail would overload the chapter and distract from the focus on the presidential type, but they can be illustrated briefly. One type is the *policy launch or update*. This can closely resemble a lobby or presidential conference. Perhaps the clientele will be different, and the subject will be narrower. Attlee's India conference, mentioned above, could strictly have been classed here. So might Eden's meetings with editors about Suez and Wilson's industrial strategy launch. Heath's third Lancaster House conference was on the specialized topic of Stage 3 of his incomes policy, about which the prime minister 'allowed himself to become too technical'.[48]

John Major held open press conferences in 1991 to launch education policies and his favourite Citizen's Charter, the latter in the Queen Elizabeth II conference centre in Parliament Square. At Lancaster House on 24 May 1994 he launched a competitiveness white paper. In Belfast, with Irish prime minister John Bruton on 22 February 1995, he launched the Irish framework agreement. This last was preceded, the day before, by an extremely confidential briefing round the cabinet table with a tightly restricted group of key political journalists.[49] Blair's premiership provided many comparable examples. To cite just three, he gave a conference in Belfast with Irish prime minister Bertie Ahern, to condemn a bombing in Omagh which killed twenty-eight people (August 1998), a conference in London about American bombing of Iraq (December 1998), and a conference highlighting increased government investment plans (November 2000).

A second type of conference, which was referred to in the chapter about capital cities, is the *Downing Street 'doorstep'*. This had its origin in catching the prime minister on the move. In Harold Macmillan's time it would have been unthinkable, reminisced a lobbyman turned press

[48] 'Much of his matter was incomprehensible to the journalists at the press conference, let alone the television audience that evening.' Douglas Hurd, *An End to Promises*, pp. 82–3.
[49] Nicholas Jones, *Soundbites and Spin Doctors*, p. 118. The journalists entered from Whitehall, not Downing Street. Jones says he was not among them.

officer, that the prime minister would actually have addressed remarks to a TV camera outside Number 10, or that journalists would anyway have shouted questions at him.[50] These press conferences-in-miniature began with Mrs Thatcher's announcement of the recapture of the island of South Georgia during the Falklands War of 1982. Thatcher's own account simply says that after John Nott, the Defence Secretary, read out his statement, 'journalists tried to ask questions'.[51] Certainly the encounter contained only the germ of a conference, but the questions provoked her loud rejoinder, for which it was long remembered, to 'just rejoice at that news'.

Mrs Thatcher claimed her 'rejoice!' remark was misinterpreted as heartless triumphalism about the war itself. This illustrates well the anxiety repeatedly expressed by press secretaries about the hazards of encounters without pre-arranged rules of exchange. But the doorstep format proved so convenient for fairly brief exchanges that it quite quickly became formalized, with a podium, microphones and a defined area for the journalists. This process was made easier by gating off Downing Street from the public, for security reasons. The process also destroyed, of course, the distinctive 'on the hoof' quality of such encounters, with their implied (though possibly spurious) spontaneity. They were distinctive now largely just because they were out of doors.

Doorsteps were a useful way of parading overseas visitors, and there was an echo of spontaneity in their convenience for breaking news. Thatcher gave doorstep conferences in 1987 both about the Zeebrugge ferry disaster in April and the Provisional IRA bomb on Remembrance Day in Enniskillen. Major gave one in the middle of the August coup attempt against Gorbachev in 1991, to say that he had just managed to make contact by phone with a besieged Boris Yeltsin in the Russian parliament building,[52] and another when Yeltsin visited Downing Street the following January (figure 8.2). Doorsteps were used several times during the Gulf War in 1991 and by Blair in November 1998 during the build-up to the bombing of Iraq.[53] Blair chose a doorstep conference in April 2001 as the method of announcing the controversial postponement until June of the general election planned for early May, because of the national foot-and-mouth disease outbreak. When Rudi Giuliani,

---

[50] Groves interview, 15 January 1988.
[51] Margaret Thatcher, *The Downing Street Years*, London: HarperCollins, 1993, pp. 208–9.
[52] Nicholas Jones, *Soundbites and Spin Doctors*, p. 99; Seldon, *Major*, p. 230.
[53] Nicholas Jones, *Soundbites and Spin Doctors*, pp. 37–8, for the Gulf War; *The Times* and others, 14 November 1998, for the Iraq bombing.

Figure 8.2: *John Major's 'doorstep' with Boris Yeltsin, 31 January 1992.*

Major and Yeltsin greet the press outside Number 10. Yeltsin is flanked by his interpreter (with typical interpreter body language). Behind are ranged assorted cabinet ministers (Norman Lamont on the extreme left; Tom King immediately behind Yeltsin) and members of Yeltsin's entourage. Major's press secretary, Jonathan Haslam, is second right in the back row.

Photograph: Glynn Griffiths/*Independent*.

New York's celebrated mayor at the time of the 2001 terrorist attacks, visited Britain in February 2002, it was at a doorstep conference that he met the press.

Overseas visits and *summits* are at the other end of the scale from Downing Street doorsteps. They take a wide variety of forms and happen all over the globe. Domestic journalists – chiefly lobby correspondents – started accompanying the prime minister abroad when large aircraft became routinely available about the end of the 1960s. The Downing Street press office, like the White House, took on a minor role as travel agent. Until then, overseas press conferences would be conducted according to local custom, perhaps with a few modifications suggested by the press secretary; and the primitive state of electronic technology meant they would not necessarily get much coverage back home. 'When Harold Macmillan met the American President, which was frequently,' noted his press secretary Harold Evans, 'one had to confront the full battle array of the White House Press corps.' Evans thought these conferences were 'in part a façade', for the benefit of agencies and TV networks: 'the serious talking still went on behind the scenes after the conference was over'.[54] Earlier Anthony Eden had bridled at the very idea that the BBC might report one of his press conferences in the United States.[55]

Away from domestic pressures prime ministers often charmed the local press. Churchill, adamant against press conferences at home, delighted journalists on his several post-war visits to America. This was the main reason why the lobby felt he should meet them occasionally too.[56] Macmillan, similarly, was 'splendidly urbane and persuasive' on a visit to recently independent Ghana in 1960.[57] Both Heath's press secretaries thought Heath was better on foreign soil and in settings not dominated by the lobby correspondents. He got on particularly well with French and American journalists, whom he thought more intelligent and serious than the lobby and less likely to misrepresent him.[58]

In that earlier period the first chance the lobby had to quiz the prime minister about a trip was when he arrived home. An early and dramatic example was Neville Chamberlain's return to Heston Airport from seeing Hitler in Munich in September 1938, when he fluttered the scrap

[54]   Evans, *Downing Street Diary*, p. 79.
[55]   William Clark, Diary, 2 February 1956.
[56]   Martin Gilbert, *Never Despair: Winston S. Churchill 1945–1965*, London: Heinemann, 1988, pp. 182, 190; Francis Boyd interview, 10 February 1988.
[57]   Harold Evans, *Downing Street Diary*, pp. 91–2.
[58]   James Campbell, *Heath*, London: Pimlico, p. 503.

of paper promising 'peace for our time'.[59] That phrase haunted Chamberlain, and post-war press secretaries encouraged prime ministers to prepare carefully for such encounters. Macmillan, for instance, agreed to a televised London Airport conference on his return from a key United Nations meeting in 1960, on condition that he could see the questions in advance. Returning from a crucial meeting with president-elect Kennedy about a British nuclear deterrent, in Nassau at the end of 1962, Macmillan reportedly spent six hours (most of the flight home) preparing for a news conference on arrival. He had also given an airport conference on the way out.[60] It is noteworthy that these televised airport press conferences preceded the development of prime ministers' studio interviews, perhaps because the latter might have meant conceding a 'right of reply' to the opposition, under the broadcasting rules of the time.[61]

By the end of Macmillan's premiership, travelling journalists were beginning to become a nuisance. Evans noted that press conferences in Helsinki and Stockholm in August 1963 were both 'hogged' by non-locals, especially Americans, and that 'the questions were chiefly aimed at British politics and the PM's own future'. Macmillan was correspondingly peevish and grumpy.[62] Blair, in contrast, found that all the American journalists were really interested in, during a joint press conference at the White House on 6 February 1998, was Bill Clinton's affair with the intern Monica Lewinsky. This experience was not unusual for visiting statesmen at the White House, even in less stressful times.

The era of routine in-flight conferences began in the mid-1960s. This did not mean the end of airport conferences: Callaghan's 'Crisis? what crisis?' exchanges in 1978 are an example. But prime ministers increasingly needed to have reasons not to talk to journalists in-flight, and it became normal to do so. News organizations spent large sums specifically to take advantage of the opportunity – including, often, greater contact with the prime minister at the other end than they could expect at home. From the prime minister's position, one of the disadvantages of the arrangement was that the journalists remained absorbed with domestic issues. They wanted to quiz the prime minister about these,

[59] Chamberlain actually spoke the words outside 10 Downing Street – but the crowd did not include just journalists, so it does not count as a pioneering 'doorstep'.
[60] Harold Evans, *Downing Street Diary*, pp. 122–3, 241. On the former, Evans comments: 'It went more smoothly and with less irritation than most airport occasions, and his opening statement dominated the TV evening bulletins.'
[61] Geoffrey Cox, *Pioneering Television News*, London: John Libbey, 1995, p. 126. Cox was editor of ITN, 1956–68.
[62] Harold Evans, *Downing Street Diary*, pp. 289–90.

rather than the overseas objectives. In an example as long ago as 1961, Macmillan squashed a domestic question by the television journalist Robin Day at a Moscow press conference with a put-down that would have been difficult at home. 'That is a question from the wrong man in the wrong place.'[63] John Major had problems of this kind on a trip to Japan in September 1993, when his leadership was under threat.[64] At a press conference in Moscow after talks with President Vladimir Putin in 2000, Tony Blair angrily directed his opening remarks at the subject of British press criticism of his European policy the previous day.[65]

Summits should be differentiated from overseas trips, since they sometimes take place in Britain. They deserve attention in their own right – and far more than the brief remarks offered here. Until Britain joined the (then) EEC in 1974, the regular (but infrequent) meetings of Commonwealth heads of government were much more significant examples than they became later. One of Attlee's few press conferences was on the occasion of the Commonwealth Conference in 1948, when he met thirty selected correspondents at Downing Street.[66] Eden did the same sort of thing in 1956.[67] Alec Douglas-Home gave an open conference at Central Hall, Westminster, at the end of the meeting in 1964.

Since then, summits have multiplied hugely, in number and variety, due partly to such cyclical meetings as the EU heads of government and the G7/G8 economic summits.[68] Foreign, trade, finance and defence ministers are frequently involved in addition to the prime minister. Being so often multilateral, summits provide opportunities for media diplomacy, and press conferences range from the platitudinous or abstruse

[63]   Macmillan's visit to Moscow was the first by a Western leader since the end of World War II. Day's question, in a conference of three hundred journalists, was about the date of the next general election. 'I was well and truly slapped down,' he recalled later. Anthony Cockerell, *Live From Number 10*, p. 65.

[64]   On Major and Japan, Anthony Seldon heads the relevant section in his biography, 'Far East: Journey to Hell'. Thirty political reporters were at the rear of his plane, twelve business leaders in the middle and the Downing Street contingent at the front. Major talked to the press on the record during the flight but refused to be interviewed on camera. For the BBC's benefit he talked on camera at the British Embassy. The atmosphere was strained and got worse. Anthony Seldon, *Major: a Political Life*, London: Weidenfeld and Nicolson, pp. 394–7.

[65]   The *Guardian*, which led with the story, commented: 'Travelling prime ministers are used to foreign trips being subsumed by domestic conflicts.' 22 November 2000.

[66]   Attlee papers, Bodleian Library. Box 73, memo dated 8 October 1948. These occasions, one must remember, were for prime ministers of independent Commonwealth states, so numbers were small until the 1960s. In 1956 there were nine.

[67]   25 June 1956, PREM 11/1540.

[68]   Mrs Thatcher attended 32 European Councils, 12 G7 economic summits, 7 Commonwealth Conferences and 3 NATO summits. Ingham, *Kill the Messenger*, p. 246.

to the highly significant. A communiqué may be issued at a joint conference, followed by leaders giving separate, perhaps competitive, briefings of their own. Thus, at the crucial Maastricht summit leading to the treaty on European Union in 1992, for example, 'what appeared at the time on television or in the newspapers', one journalist recalled, 'was dictated largely by what the national delegations . . . chose to impart in their news conferences.' Journalists who went to other countries' conferences 'were viewed with evident suspicion'.[69] Similarly at the rather less historic G7 meeting hosted by Britain in 1991, John Major had supplemented the official communiqué with a briefing aimed at the British press.[70] In 1998 Britain's six-month presidency of the EU began and ended with ritualistic press conferences: a launch by Tony Blair in the shiny surroundings of Waterloo station's Eurostar terminal (5 December 1997), and a conclusion with a joint conference in Cardiff (16 June 1998). Perhaps because they are inescapable, intensely focused, cocooned, or distanced from domestic politics in some other way, summit press conferences, like other overseas conferences, seem often to have shown prime ministers at their most effective as performers. Many of Mrs Thatcher's most direct encounters with the press were after European summits.

Election campaign press conferences, lastly, need singling out. Although it is true only in a rather technical sense, general elections are fought by the prime minister principally as a party leader. Thus Downing Street press secretaries have almost always steered clear – even Bernard Ingham, despite his very close association with Mrs Thatcher. Only Joe Haines and Alastair Campbell, as acknowledged partisans, could regard government and electoral business as a more or less seamless web.

The organization, content, style and purpose of campaign press conferences are all affected by the short-term, partisan context. Before 1959, when conferences in the now familiar sense were introduced, journalists had little opportunity to question the party leader in public at all. There were routine briefings about the leader's movements, but nothing more. In 1959, which was not a leader-dominated campaign, Macmillan took no part in the conferences, and even ministerial colleagues appeared only in the last ten days. In 1966 Wilson, who wanted to stay aloof and statesmanlike, did not take part until the last week.

In the 1970s the daily conferences began to be treated as an opportunity to shape the midday and early evening broadcast news agenda.

---

[69]   Alan Watkins, *Independent on Sunday*, 19 November 2000.
[70]   See papers for 17 July 1991. The conference was held in Lancaster House.

Party leaders gave them higher priority. Wilson appeared daily in 1970, chaired by the party general secretary and supported usually by Denis Healey. In the 1974 elections he followed the same kind of pattern; so did Heath in February 1974.

Mrs Thatcher took part in most election press conferences and dominated them. In 1983 she notoriously slapped down the Foreign Secretary, Francis Pym, for making electorally naive remarks about the negotiability of Falklands sovereignty (a year after the war to win back the islands) and the disadvantages of a large parliamentary majority.[71] Her abrasiveness had caused party managers to discuss in advance the possibility of the party chairman, Cecil Parkinson, chairing the conferences, but Mrs Thatcher preferred to do it herself. In 1987, again, she was 'visibly at odds' with her Education Secretary and got herself into tangles about housing policy and private health insurance, through ill-chosen remarks.[72]

John Major, who took part in seventeen out of nineteen press conferences in 1992, preferred to be chaired by the party chairman, Chris Patten. A one-hour briefing took place at 7.30 a.m., with the conference at 8.30. The rules of exchange were tightly controlled: no supplementaries were allowed, which is a particular disadvantage to journalists in a campaign setting, and implicit preference was given to TV reporters. In 1997 the prime minister was again heavily involved. Perhaps inevitably now, broadcast and broadsheet journalists dominated the proceedings.[73] Early in this campaign the Conservative pension policy was launched at a press conference in Downing Street. It was organized by the press secretary but with heavy party involvement. In the days when party and government business were more easily distinguished than they had become through the ubiquity of television, this event would probably not have happened. In 2001 Labour chose Birmingham for their manifesto launch. The mainstay of their regular press conferences was Gordon Brown, with Blair taking part only from time to time.

With devolution, European parliamentary elections and the occasional referendum, prime ministers have more opportunities than in the past for partisan campaigning during the course of their government.

---

[71]   For her own account, see Margaret Thatcher, *The Downing Street Years*, p. 294.
[72]   David Butler and Dennis Kavanagh, *The British General Election of 1987*, London: Macmillan, 1988, pp. 106–7.
[73]   David Butler and Dennis Kavanagh, *The British General Election of 1997*, London: Macmillan, 1997, p. 93. 'The questioning was quite aggressive but, since supplementaries were seldom allowed, it was hard to pin the parties down and very few gaffes were spotted.'

As we have seen, John Major's garden press conference was partly inspired by the results of the European parliament elections, and his pleasure in what was only a less bad result than expected may have reflected his own involvement. During the campaign he had chaired three press conferences. Tony Blair, similarly, took part in the final London press conference of the Scottish parliament campaign on 5 May 1999.

Campaign press conferences, in sum, provide a glimpse of what might have been. But it is no more than a glimpse, for prime ministers behave rather differently from how they would be likely to in a regular 'presidential' conference.

Conclusion: Prime Ministers and the 'Presidential' Press Conference

Prime ministers have given a variety of press conferences, as this selection shows. Only two have regularly used the discreet Roosevelt type – Neville Chamberlain and, for a short period, Harold Wilson. Blair, in his second term, decided to adopt the televised Kennedy type. Why were prime ministers in general so reluctant to follow the presidential example, and why did Blair do so?

The first reason for reluctance was precisely that the example is presidential. For roughly half the period between 1945 and the end of the century, the conventional wisdom that Britain had a collective cabinet government remained undisturbed. The government machine was barely penetrable by outsiders; there were neither journalists nor audiences with resources and curiosity to bother poking around. In a collective system, ministers are responsible for media relations in their own departments, subject to overall coordination and control from Downing Street, and the Downing Street press office is organized on that basis. If a prime minister spoke regularly to the press, he would either trump his ministers (to their annoyance), get things wrong, or talk waffle rather than hard news.[74] In cabinet government, on this argument, there is no place for a prime ministerial press conference. In good times his colleagues will resent it. In bad, he will want to share the grief. But in the

---

[74]   There is an echo here of the problem with 'overlord' ministers – grandly named individuals (including 'deputy prime ministers') who have occasionally been given overarching portfolios but no actual department. Without a department and budget, they have lacked real influence and the appointments have almost never worked. For an early sceptic, see Lord Morrison of Lambeth, *Government and Parliament*, London: Oxford University Press, 3rd edn, 1964, pp. 58–70.

second half of the post-war period the machinery of government, as chapter 1 indicated, was gradually stripped bare. Greater openness provided evidence to support claims of prime ministerial dominance and presidential tendencies. These became commonplace under Thatcher and Blair. The objection to a prime ministerial press conference on grounds of collective responsibility therefore carried less and less conviction, and it would have been unlikely to cause Blair more than a moment's hesitation.

A second piece of conventional wisdom, reiterated by successive Speakers, has been that the House of Commons, rather than a press conference or a broadcasting studio, is the place where prime ministers (and other ministers) should announce important news and be held to account. Prime ministers themselves took this argument very seriously, until the spread of electronic media. Churchill used it to brush off the lobby at Southampton, and it weighed heavily with Macmillan.[75]

Macmillan's example is particularly interesting, because of his interest in following Kennedy's example in 1961. Conservative party headquarters, the Downing Street press office and the prime minister himself all considered it, but 'we always came to the conclusion that the big difference between us and the Americans was the House of Commons', according to the deputy press secretary.[76] In 1962, when 'the going was getting rough', Oliver Poole, the party chairman, pressed Macmillan to hold regular televised conferences, on the grounds mainly that he was at his best in question-and-answer sessions. The fact that he was 'beholden to the legislature' was again the chief objection.[77]

The growth of political broadcasting made this second historic argument against press conferences crumble like the first. It crumbled too because of the prime minister's declining involvement with the Commons on a day-to-day basis, towards the end of the twentieth century. Blair was a particularly bad offender. The less answerable the prime minister becomes to parliament, the stronger is the case for holding him answerable in such forums as a press conference. The justification for the Kennedy-type conference in the United States has

---

[75] The extreme case of this attitude was the 'fourteen days rule', which banned broadcast discussion about any item of forthcoming parliamentary business in the fourteen days before the business took place. The rule was abandoned in 1956. See Colin Seymour-Ure, *The Political Impact of Mass Media*, London: Constable, 1974, pp. 140–3.

[76] Interview, John Groves, 15 January 1988.

[77] Even so, Macmillan had half made up his mind to adopt the proposal by the spring of 1963. Evans thought it full of hazards and was relieved that it never happened. Evans, *Downing Street Diary*, pp. 38, 260. John Campbell, *Edward Heath*, London: Pimlico, 1994, p. 503.

always included the simple argument that it is needed because the separation of powers removes the president from public scrutiny in the legislature. A press conference is thus the president's 'Question Time'.

The prime minister's own Question Time was increasingly important as an instrument of scrutiny, symbolically at least, as prime ministers reduced their parliamentary participation in general. The introduction of television to the Commons in 1989 made it an even more prominent occasion. On the other hand, it can also be argued that this last development worked against the case for a press conference in addition. For if a press conference is the president's Question Time, has not Question Time become the prime minister's press conference? MPs play the role of journalists to the prime minister in a Kennedy-type format. The division into government and opposition provides sympathetic and hostile questioners, as at a press conference. The priority for frontbenchers and Privy Counsellors echoes that of network and national journalists. The majority of MPs, as of journalists (such as the ninety at Blair's first 'regular' conference), are observers – though noisier than journalists. They follow proceedings from the back rows, like the unseen audience beyond the television screen or radio. The content is a mixture of the predictable and the unexpected, with the ever present possibility of a prime ministerial blunder. Meticulous preparation is undertaken, both by the prime minister and the questioners. The rules of exchange are strictly regulated, permitting few supplementaries. The entire occasion is chiefly an opportunity to evaluate the prime minister as a performer in a choreographed production. Is he up, is he down? Is he perky, is he tired? Is he in command of his brief, or floundering? The performance is the 'information' at Question Time, much as it eventually became in a presidential press conference.

It is worth noting that Tony Blair dropped a revealing hint that he himself viewed Question Time as a kind of press conference. During a TV programme about his press secretary Alastair Campbell, Blair referred to Campbell's lobby briefings as 'his equivalent of Prime Minister's Questions'.[78] Since the secretary's briefings resemble a Roosevelt-type conference and the secretary himself is sometimes a surrogate for the prime minister, Blair was indirectly likening his own parliamentary routine to a press conference.

The two great differences between the conduct of Question Time and a press conference, however, are the roles of the opposition – especially its leader – and of the Speaker. The performance of the opposition leader is under comparable scrutiny to that of the prime minister, while the

---

[78] *News from Number Ten*, BBC2, 15 July 2000.

Speaker's role as moderator has no press conference counterpart. Even if Question Time overall bears comparison with a press conference, the two certainly cannot be regarded as sufficiently similar to be substitutes for one another. Blair could reasonably argue that they should be complementary.

The potential for the Downing Street press secretary to act as a surrogate supplies a rather different argument against prime ministerial press conferences. Most of the best press secretaries before Bernard Ingham were technicians, in the sense that they managed the lobby and, as civil servants, kept clear of party politics. Ingham, though not a party politician, became so close to Mrs Thatcher that he was widely regarded as speaking her mind. Alastair Campbell lacked even the formal element of non-partisanship in his closeness to Tony Blair. These two prime ministers, especially, could feel that they did not need to have press conferences themselves, so long as their press secretaries were holding them.

That argument, individual cases aside, was weakened, like the first two, by television. The press secretary was an adequate substitute in a Roosevelt-type conference but no substitute at all in a Kennedy-type televised conference. Even a senior cabinet minister would be a dubious substitute; for why should not the prime minister be holding the broadcast conference himself? This difficulty helps to explain the extreme and unrealistic reluctance of Alastair Campbell to be quoted by name rather than by a title ('Prime Minister's Official Spokesman'), once his lobby briefings began to be put on the record, and also his refusal to permit the briefings to be broadcast. A prime ministerial clone is effective as an inconspicuous intermediary with journalists: direct broadcasts need the original.

Before the growth of television, the lobby certainly pressed for Roosevelt-type conferences with the prime minister. Their lack of success reflected their poor leverage and the progressive degeneration of the lobby system from the 1960s, through large scale and turnover. The best lobby correspondents, moreover, never set great store by conferences, precisely because they were collective occasions and did not reward individual resource, contacts and industry. In general one may expect the lobby not to object to regular Kennedy-type conferences but to see little benefit in them.

That argument is a reminder that the objectives of reporters are not sufficiently close to those of the prime minister anyway for a regular press conference necessarily to be a reliable method of getting the prime minister's message across to the public. Experience suggests that such meetings can easily become sparring matches, not information exchanges; that they are artificial creations (especially if orchestrated for television), not genuine news events; and that frequent meetings devalue the prime minister's office. Lacking hard news, a press conference can be little more than a chancy demonstration of the incumbent's continuing fitness for office. Blair's crisis conferences in 2000 and 2001 worked because the prime minister did have hard news, wished to give it direct to the country, and wished also to give media an opportunity to quiz him.

One further argument should be added, lastly, because it appeared to contribute to the decline of the traditional presidential press conference in Washington. This is the claim that developments in electronic technology, both for news-gathering and for dissemination, make the Kennedy-type conference format look slightly primitive, however subtle might be its rules and procedures and despite such aids as PowerPoint presentations.[79] To illustrate the point, the 'electronic town meetings' held by Bill Clinton make a good contrast. The town meeting, a historic New England nod to Athenian democracy, gave effect to the idea that the best form of information exchange was for everyone to meet in the same place at the same time. In small New England settlements this was a practical possibility. Clinton's electronic versions removed the imperatives of place and created complex patterns of interaction, without sacrificing the basic idea of exchange.

What reasons, in sum, may have led Blair to start holding Kennedy-type press conferences at a time when American presidents were letting them lapse? As we have seen, several formerly problematic quasi-constitutional factors and limitations of media technology, which caused his predecessors to hesitate, no longer carry much weight. Blair's reasoning may therefore have been principally short-term. After four years in office, his government was being battered by the media, frequently about issues of news management and spin. Press conferences would bring him in touch with media directly, showing off his skills as a performer, to repair relations damaged by political advisers and spin doctors. More broadly, and for the somewhat longer term, regular press conferences fitted in with the stress on accountability at the start of Blair's second term. For example, much was made of Blair's agreement to appear occasionally before the Commons Liaison Committee, a body comprised of the chairmen and -women of the backbench committees monitoring the work of government departments.

---

[79] At Blair's conference on 25 July 2002 the head of the Downing Street Delivery Unit gave a PowerPoint presentation about the government's progress in meeting its detailed domestic policy targets.

Such short-term and arguably symbolic aims were hostages to fortune. At root, it is the *regularity* of the Roosevelt and Kennedy types of press conference which creates risks for a prime minister. For their regularity dictates much of the conferences' form and content. Some of these risks were outlined in the early sections of the chapter. They pose a threat to his control of the content and outcome of press conference communication. Like much else in political communication, regular press conferences are an opportunity for the prime minister – including an opportunity to fail. To introduce a long-term device for a short-term purpose is intrinsically risky. In Washington, where presidents have no constitutional forum for public communication, there is a logic to the regular press conference – even though the Roosevelt and Kennedy forms have been largely superseded. The logic is less plain in Britain. For prime ministers, the regular press conference is not like trousers or a skirt, which are something they simply have to have. It is more of an accessory, like a necktie or scarf, to be worn according to occasion. So we should not be too surprised if Blair's successors do not automatically follow his example.

9

Grapevine Politics:
Political Rumours

What did survivors think had happened when the atom bomb fell on Hiroshima? They knew about carpet-bombing: they were expecting it. But the atom bomb was unheard of. On that August morning in 1945 they were aware only of a blinding flash of light. This was followed by gradual darkness with raindrops the size of marbles. Large areas of the city were flattened. People dropped dead for no apparent reason. Everyone was thirsty; but if you drank from the river you felt nauseated and were sick. There was a strong smell of ionization.

What caused this devastation? The answers came as rumour. There had been a self-scattering cluster of bombs. Or a single plane had sprayed the city with petrol and ignited it. Or the plane had sprayed magnesium powder, which exploded upon contact with power cables, or with the tramlines. Or American paratroopers had done it. Or – this one, which surfaced after about a week, seemed wholly implausible – there had been a bomb using the energy released by splitting in two the smallest known particles of matter.[1]

Rumour is a highly distinctive form of communication, probably common to all cultures and all times. It thrives in war but also in everyday politics. It is a staple of mass media and the internet, and it can travel as fast as mass media just by word of mouth – on the grapevine.

---

[1] The classic account of the Hiroshima bomb, first published in the *New Yorker*, is John Hersey's *Hiroshima* (Harmondsworth: Penguin Books, 1946). A succinct discussion of the rumours is in Tamotsu Shibutani's authoritative general survey of rumour, *Improvised News* (New York: Bobbs-Merrill, 1966). A later general discussion is Ralph L. Rosnow and Gary Alan Fine, *Rumor and Gossip*, New York: Elsevier, 1976. Both remain excellent introductions, paying due credit to the seminal work by G. W. Allport and L. J. Postman, *The Psychology of Rumor* (New York: Holt, Rhinehart and Winston, 1947). A later summary of Rosnow's ideas is in Ralph L. Rosnow, 'Psychology of rumor reconsidered', *Psychological Bulletin*, 87.3, 1980, pp. 578–91. A more recent survey is Jean-Noel Kapferer, *Rumors*, New York: Transaction Publishers, 1990.

Students of politics seem to underestimate it, and surely this is a mistake. For rumour is one of the rubbish tips of politics. Just as you cannot have the glory of a garden – lawns and flowerbeds, order and harmony – without a rubbish tip for weeds and cuttings, so you cannot limit political communication to the routines of news schedules and media organizations. The Chinese call rumours 'by-road news'.[2] Mass media, by comparison, are limited-access highways. To get about, you need both.

Rumour thus deals in disorder and the non-routine – in *uncertainty*. (Hence the correct rumour in Hiroshima was no more plausible than the others.) The purpose of this chapter is to explore how rumour works and how it fits into (mainly) British politics. For political leaders, the particular challenge is to *control* it. How can a damaging rumour, either about yourself or about people and events with which you are involved, be anticipated, evaluated and stopped (or encouraged)?

Conditions for Rumour

The essence of rumour is that its content is unverified and perhaps unverifiable. Rumour is not necessarily false: it may turn out either true or untrue. Often it is widely shared. Indeed the sharing is important, for rumour is a process – active, yeasty – and not just a type of information. Rumour differs from gossip in having potentially significant consequences, where gossip is usually a trivial and mutually rewarding social exchange. It differs also from speculation, which is conjecture about the future, often well grounded. Much research has been done by psychologists and sociologists on the conditions in which rumours arise, but little by political scientists. Work on their consequences seems mainly inspired by the desire to control them, especially in wartime.

Psychologists typically explore rumour in relation to individuals. Here, rumour is 'distortion in serial transmission' – the children's game of Chinese Whispers. A message is quickly passed along a line and its final version is compared with astonishment to the original. A simple example – but no game – can be quoted from the Falklands War in 1982. Preparing to line up for the assault on Port Stanley, two units of troops were strung out in a column two miles long and were passing messages by word of mouth, not radio. 'One damp afternoon the message came down, "Air raid warning, Red". And as the leaders got

---

[2]   Andrew Higgins, *Independent*, 25 October 1988. Cf. Ivan D. London and Miriam B. London, 'Rumor as a footnote to Chinese national character', *Psychological Reports*, 37, 1975, pp. 343–9.

down in hollows . . . they saw the men bring up the rear a mile away, jumping up and throwing their rifles in the air, and the echo of "Air raid warning, Red" came back as "Hurray, Galtieri's dead!".[3]

An entirely different kind of rumour, which exploded onto the front pages of the national press in January 1993, concerned an alleged adulterous affair between the prime minister, John Major, and a Downing Street caterer. The rumours had been surfacing opaquely (no names, no details) for a couple of years previously, in such places as *Private Eye* and the 'Mr Pepys' column in the London *Evening Standard*. They even featured in a pop song by the band Soho, which the distributors released in the United States but did not risk releasing at home.[4] When the story came fully into the open, a reader gave her own account, in 'serial transmission' form, in a letter to *The Times*: 'A 73-year-old lady has had her street cred raised at Wirral coffee mornings this week. She has been able to pass on the fact that one of her sons had heard the gossip about John Major over a year ago from my son. My son learnt it from me; I was party to the tale from a lady while playing bridge, shortly after John Major became Tory Party leader. She did not reveal her source, merely that it was neither political nor press. My son also heard the gossip from friends at college who heard it from parents or at parties. The gossip was alive and well in Berkshire, Hampshire and Lincolnshire.'[5]

Where the psychologist studies how people fit rumours into their individual worlds, sociologists see rumour as a collective activity concerned with social stability and control. Members of a group pool information

[3] Robert Fox, 'The radio man's war', *Listener*, 1 July 1982. General Galtieri was the Argentine president.
[4] *New Statesman and Society*, 29 January 1993; *Independent*, 8 November 1992.
[5] *The Times*, 1 February 1993. The caterer Clare Latimer met John Major when her company catered parties for the Conservative Whips' office. Rumours started after he employed her when Chancellor after October 1989, and they grew in strength following the 1992 election. For example, the author (a political innocent living in a small cathedral city) first heard them when told that Ms Latimer had been drawn as a statuette on the Downing Street mantelpiece in a national daily paper cartoon. Major was advised to ignore allegations in the insignificant magazine *Scallywag*; but a feature in the *New Statesman and Society* was too strong a provocation. Major sued both publications, taking the decision while on an export-boosting trip to India. The case was settled in July 1993, with no admission of libel and both sides able to claim victory. Major said he had no wish to take the case through the courts or to bankrupt the magazine. *New Statesman and Society*, 29 January 1993; *The Times*, 29 January 1993; Anthony Seldon, *Major: a Political Life*, London: Phoenix, 1998, pp. 355–7; John Major, *John Major: the Autobiography*, London: HarperCollins, 1999, pp. 553–4. At no time, apparently, did the rumours feature the MP Edwina Currie, with whom (she disclosed in 2002) Major did have an affair before he became prime minister. So – no smoke without fire, but attention focused on the wrong flame.

to try and make sense of something, just as the survivors of Hiroshima did. People make distinctive contributions, perhaps supplying new 'facts', or explanations, doubts, arguments and suggestions about what to do. This process suits the internet, being interactive, rather more than newspapers. It is a sort of verbal milling, like cattle milling when a storm brews.[6] In this way, the stories circulating among journalists and politicians, or among web users, gradually acquire a common shape.

Either process, linear or lattice, can advance with astonishing speed. For example, a famous rumour swept Britain during four or five days after the outbreak of war in August 1914. One hundred thousand Russian troops were said to be passing through the country on their way from Archangel to the front in France. They were travelling in trains with the blinds down. They demanded vodka at Carlisle and Berwick-on-Tweed and jammed a slot machine with roubles at Durham. Most memorably, they stamped the snow off their boots on station platforms. Reports came from all over the country, almost entirely by word of mouth.[7] More mundanely, word-of-mouth rumours of fuel shortages swept Britain in September 2001 and caused panic-buying at petrol stations. A disruptive blockade of refineries by delivery drivers had ended the previous week, but the rumours claimed a new blockade was starting.[8]

The efficiency of word of mouth was demonstrated after the deaths of Franklin Roosevelt and John F. Kennedy. Roosevelt's unexpected death on 12 April 1945 was announced in the United States in a radio newsflash. People who heard it each told on average seven others, and each of the latter told one more (who had not already heard). More than eighty per cent thus heard by word of mouth, the majority within ten minutes of the broadcast. When Kennedy was shot, there was a gap of an hour between news of the shooting and of his death. Half of those who heard of the shooting first, and two-thirds who heard only after he was dead, did so from another person. Most of those who heard of

---

[6] James Deakin writes of 'the milling-around area' at the White House in the Eisenhower era. 'The milling-around area is any area where reporters are confined while they wait to be told something. When newsmen enter an auditorium or hotel where an important event is to take place, a senior correspondent sometimes demands to be taken immediately to the milling-around area. That is what is going to happen anyway, so it saves time. There is nothing worse than milling around waiting to be taken to the milling-around area.' James Deakin, *Straight Stuff*, New York: William Morrow, 1984, p. 33.

[7] Arthur Ponsonby, *Falsehood in Wartime*, London: Allen and Unwin, 1928, ch. 5; C. W. C. Oman, *Transactions of the Royal Historical Society*, 4th series, vol. I, London: RHS, 1918, pp. 16–18.

[8] See, e.g., *Guardian,* 20 September 2001.

the shooting did so within thirty minutes. TV and radio were used to confirm and supplement the news. The assassination, of course, created a lasting rumour industry.[9]

Regardless of the means of transmission, the progress of rumours has common features. They need a climate of *anxiety*, a *suggestible audience*, and *ambiguous content* about *a matter of importance*.[10] It is easy to see, then, why rumours are rife in war. War is an extreme case of anxiety and uncertainty, with people in a suggestible and credulous state (prepared briefly to believe that Russian boots could be snow-covered in an English autumn). Near-war, such as rioting, is similar. Indeed Allport and Postman claimed it was almost a 'law' that riots are preceded by a rumour.[11] The attacks on New York and Washington on 11 September 2001 not surprisingly produced a spate of rumours.[12] Ordinary political crises and conflicts are frequently visualized in warlike terms – battles, campaigns, troops, 'big guns', 'secret weapons'. The fighting may be metaphorical, but the conditions for rumour still arise; the rumours themselves are simply less horrific.

These four features of rumour are succinctly illustrated for ordinary times, though not in warlike terms, by the example of a comment in *The Times* during a crisis in John Major's premiership. A year after the rumours about Major personally, when Conservative morale was at an especially low ebb, a succession of minor sex and financial scandals had hit the party's parliamentary ranks, exactly as the prime minister was promoting a 'back to basics' policy of probity and family values. 'The current mood of puritanical witch-hunting is highly unstable,' wrote *The Times*'s political editor. 'After three resignations [of ministers] in a week and events ranging from the comically bizarre to the tragically

[9] Delbert C. Miller, 'How our community heard about the death of President Roosevelt', *American Sociological Review*, 10.5, 1945, pp. 691–4; Bradley S. Greenberg, 'Diffusion of the news of the Kennedy assassination', *Public Opinion Quarterly*, 28.2, 1964, pp. 225–32.

[10] See Rosnow and Fine, *Rumor and Gossip*, esp. chs 4 and 5.

[11] 'The evidence at hand is so convincing that we may advance it as a law of social psychology that *no riot ever occurs without rumors to incite, accompany, and intensify the violence.*' Allport and Postman, *The Psychology of Rumor*, p. 193.

[12] Rumours in Washington on 11 September claimed (wrongly) that explosions occurred at the State Department, the Capitol and offices adjoining the White House, and that a second hi-jacked plane was heading below radar for the White House or the Pentagon. Many workers left their offices. On the next day, rumours of petrol shortages (false) caused queues at thousands of garages across the United States. The day after, rumours (false) that five firefighters, trapped in the rubble of the World Trade Center since Tuesday, had been rescued alive, were reported around the world. Times Newspapers website, 16 September 2001.

fatal, wild rumours are circulating at Westminster about the private lives of politicians: what will be revealed next about whom?'[13]

As rumours run, they are likely to share three other features: *levelling, sharpening* and *assimilation*. Levelling and sharpening involve elimination of some details and selective emphasis on others; while assimilation adjusts the new rumours to an existing pattern of information and understanding.[14] Thus the particular variations in the Conservative sex scandals in the 1990s were played down and the whole lot were encapsulated, with the financial scandals, in the notion of 'sleaze'. 'Sleaze' proved a potent weapon against a party in office for fifteen years. The prime minister's attempt 'to dismiss sleaze story after sleaze story as unrelated and minor matters', wrote the *Independent* columnist Andrew Marr, 'has failed. The Government has lost control of the political agenda.' Control was never regained, and 'sleaze' was a leitmotiv of Labour's campaign in the 1997 general election.[15]

If they can spread like wildfire, what makes rumours end? Proof or disproof by a credible source is the most conclusive way. For example, Anthony Eden's parliamentary private secretary wrote to him in Jamaica, while the debacle of the Anglo-French invasion of Suez was being sorted out at the end of 1956, saying: 'Some papers have carried rumours of your impending resignation. This was beginning to snowball, but announcement of your return, coupled with heavy background work, has reversed this.'[16] Again, rumours that a leading Conservative ex-minister, Michael Portillo, was gay, stopped in 1999 when he admit-

---

[13]   Peter Riddell, *The Times*, 11 January 1994. Between September 1992 and June 1996 nine members of the government resigned and a tenth died in circumstances of sexual scandal. Five of these events happened in the early months of 1994. In the same period seven members of the government resigned or were officially criticized for financial 'sleaze'. Altogether there were more ministerial resignations in 1992–7 than in any previous parliament in the twentieth century. Similar scandals embroiled several Conservative backbenchers too, right up to the 1997 election campaign. See David Denver, ch. 1 in Anthony King (ed.), *New Labour Triumphs: Britain at the Polls*, Chatham, N.J.: Chatham House, 1998; David Butler and Dennis Kavanagh, *The British General Election of 1997*, London: Macmillan, 1997, esp. chs 1 and 6.

[14]   Rosnow and Fine, *Rumor and Gossip*, p. 36.

[15]   Andrew Marr, *Independent*, 26 October 1994. Sleaze ranked second out of twelve issues in ITV's news coverage during the election campaign, and third in BBC1's. The majority was in the early weeks. David Butler and Dennis Kavanagh, *The British General Election of 1997*, pp. 138–40.

[16]   Robert Allan to Anthony Eden, 7 December 1956. Quoted by Robert Rhodes James in *Anthony Eden*, London: Weidenfeld and Nicolson, 1986. Eden did in fact resign, almost exactly one month later, on 9 January 1957.

ted homosexual experiences as a student.[17] The previous year, Tony Blair's Secretary of State for Wales, Ron Davies, set rumours racing when he resigned following a late-night encounter on Clapham Common. Although he did not give details, his televised admission on the following Friday that it had been 'a moment of madness' made the rumours die away.[18]

Those are simple cases. Denial of a rumour's truth is more difficult. Bill Clinton categorically denied on TV, face to camera and jabbing his finger emphatically, that he had had sex with Monica Lewinsky, the White House intern with whom he eventually admitted that he had had an affair. But the authority of his office was insufficient to stop the rumours for long – and all the less, probably, because they had originated on the internet, where they spawned an enormous trade in jokes.[19] John Major's patience ran out when the New Statesman published the catering manageress rumours: that magazine had a reputation, whereas Scallywag, the magazine on which the article partly drew, was insignificant. Suing the insignificant can risk giving new life to a rumour in the scotching of it. (This was a problem that used to face victims of the young Private Eye.) Major expected – rightly – that his decision to sue would 'knock the story on the head'.[20]

Sometimes the mere threat of legal action is sufficient. Before and during the 1964 general election, a widespread word-of-mouth rumour claimed that when Wilson became Labour party leader on the unexpected death of Hugh Gaitskell a year earlier, he and his wife had been on the point of divorce. Wilson let it be known that any reference to the rumour in subsequent publications about the election campaign would bring writs. Where rumours involve a range of people or libel is not a reliable remedy, prime ministers have set up inquiries under credible authority figures. Harold Macmillan appointed a senior judge, Lord Denning, to make a report intended as the last word on rumours

[17] New Statesman, 20 September, 1999.
[18] Independent on Sunday, 1 November 1998. 'The rumour mill began its inevitable churning,' the Guardian had noted on 28 October, the day after Davies's resignation. Davies described being robbed at knifepoint in his car by a stranger he had picked up on Clapham Common, and two of the stranger's friends. After the three dumped him in the street, Davies went to a police station. He gave no indication of what type of behaviour his 'madness' had consisted in.
[19] For the story of Clinton's involvement with Monica Lewinsky and his impeachment, see Peter Baker, The Beach: Inside the Impeachment and Trial of William Jefferson Clinton, New York: Scribner, 2000.
[20] Major, John Major: the Autobiography, p. 554. He described the rumours as 'swilling around' Fleet Street.

involved in the Profumo affair of 1963 (the first major post-1945 political sex scandal).[21] Clement Attlee set up an inquiry, similarly, after financial scandal involving ministers in 1948 (the Lynskey Tribunal).[22] The appointment by John Major in 1994 of a standing committee on Standards in Public Life, initially under Lord Nolan, can be seen also as an attempt to reduce rumour-mongering through the examination of 'current concerns' about standards, and through the establishment of clear guidelines for the relations between personal and public conduct.[23]

Rumours sometimes simply fade away. People become bored; their attention switches. Lord Denning's report drew a line under the Profumo affair (and became the highest-selling official publication of all time, up to that date). But within months Macmillan himself had resigned because of ill health anyway, and a year later the entire political landscape had changed, with the election of the first Labour government for thirteen years. Rumour depends on public appetite. If there is no appetite, there will be no rumours. When it was announced in 1994 that former president Ronald Reagan had Alzheimer's disease, the report by the medical editor of The Times remarked that 'rumours abound' that Harold Wilson also had the disease. But Wilson's premiership had ended eighteen years earlier, so the rumours (apart from being denied) made no waves.[24]

General Explanations of Rumour

The conditions for rumour go some way towards explaining why as well as how it arises. But explanations can go further. For individuals, rumour is a means of enabling us to share information which will express anxieties, hostilities, jealousies and other feelings we may be reluctant to admit. We can legitimize (and therefore perhaps intensify)

[21] John Profumo, minister for War, had an affair in 1961 with Christine Keeler, a call-girl who was also involved with Stephen Ward, a society osteopath and artist and something of a pimp, and with Eugene Ivanov, Soviet assistant naval attaché. After rumours developed at the end of 1962, Profumo categorically denied in parliament any impropriety in the relationship, on 22 March 1963. The rumours continued to gain strength (including about a possible security risk), and on 5 June Profumo admitted the truth. The prime minister then set up the Denning inquiry. See Lord Denning's Report, London, HMSO, 1963, Cmnd. 2152; Alan Doig, Westminster Babylon, London: Allison and Busby, 1990, chs 5 and 6.

[22] A good account is by John Gross in Michael Sissons and Philip French (eds), Age of Austerity, Harmondsworth: Penguin Books, 1964.

[23] Independent, 26 October 1994.

[24] The Times, 8 November 1994.

such emotions by displacing them onto other people, the implied rumour sources. We can claim the rumour as fact, while disclaiming responsibility for its veracity and for its consequences. Thus rumour is rich soil for the grubs of racism, homophobia and claims about dole scroungers and bogus asylum seekers.

At the same time, rumour-spreading can be an attempt to gain esteem. In 1984 a Brighton taxi-driver taking participants to a conference, not long after an IRA bomb aimed at Conservative ministers destroyed part of the Grand Hotel, regaled his passengers with stories about an alleged massive post-bomb cover-up. He personally (being in the ambulance service at the time) had helped bring out nineteen bodies; he had passed Mrs Thatcher on the stairs; there were one hundred dead in all.[25] (The number of dead in fact was five.)

For groups, as has been indicated, the general motive of rumour-sharing is to provide a kind of solution to a puzzling and stressful predicament. In October 1999 the *Sunday Times* aired rumours that the former Treasury minister, Geoffrey Robinson, possessed compromising photos of 'a senior cabinet minister'. 'After almost a week of nudge-nudge journalism', wrote the *Guardian*, 'it is worth asking what's going on and why?' The *Guardian*'s answer was that the rumours were a crude attempt by one government mini-faction to browbeat another.[26] These particular rumours evaporated. But when rumours persist and acquire a common meaning, this can lead to action.[27] The crescendo of 'sleaze story after sleaze story' in October 1994 provoked the prime minister's sudden, constitutionally far-reaching, appointment of Lord Nolan's committee on standards in public life.

The various motives for rumour can be tidied into three categories: *pipe dreams, bogies* and *wedge drivers*.[28] Pipe dreams are wish fulfilment: 'Hurray! Galtieri's dead!' The Russian troops rumour is of this type too. Rumours about unpopular political leaders are full of pipe dreams. In 1974, when Richard Nixon was in travail in the later stages of the Watergate scandal which brought him down, Washington buzzed with optimistic rumours of his imminent resignation.[29] In the run-up to

[25]   This author, also a conference participant, was soon told these rumours by his colleagues – and helped circulate them to others. Five people died (including the wife of cabinet minister John Wakeham) and thirty-two were injured in the explosion, which took place during the Conservative party annual conference.

[26]   *Guardian*, 25 October 1999.

[27]   Rosnow and Fine, *Rumor and Gossip*, p. 56.

[28]   R. H. Knapp, 'A psychology of rumour', *Public Opinion Quarterly*, 8.1, 1944, pp. 22–37.

[29]   Pressure built up so much that on 10 May 1974 Nixon's press secretary, Ron Ziegler, phoned a statement to the *New York Times*: 'The city of Washington is full of rumours.

the 1992 presidential campaign, serious worries about management of the American economy fuelled pipe-dream rumours that George Bush would not seek re-election: he would stand down 'for health reasons' at the last minute in favour of the highly competent Secretary of State, James Baker. As Bush's campaign faltered in the summer of 1992, 'an old rumour has resurfaced' – that the accident-prone vice-president, Dan Quayle, would be dropped from the ticket.[30]

Sometimes the pipes contain substances more mind-blowing than tobacco. An account of rumours in Argentina in 1990 contained bizarre examples, mostly appealing to the extreme right wing. For instance, President Menem was dying of cancer as the result of spells cast by an occult sect. A government minister had been caught trying to steal the ring of the dictator Juan Peron from his tomb; inside the ring was inscribed the number of a Swiss bank account containing enough wealth to wipe out Argentina's debts.[31]

Bogie rumours reflect fear of the future, most obviously in war. But bogies can be very deep-seated too. A curious case is channel tunnel rumours. During the Napoleonic wars the French were rumoured to be planning an invasion by tunnel. So were the Germans in World War II. Rumours about IRA sabotage, rabies and inundations accompanied the construction of the tunnel in the 1980s.[32]

Wedge drivers may be motivated by anxiety, but their distinguishing feature is an aggressive attempt to divide a group. The rumours about Geoffrey Robinson are an example. Not long after those, the cabinet minister Mo Mowlam suffered a similar fate. According to prominently reported rumours, a brain tumour operation before the 1997 general election had left her 'without the intellectual rigour' to carry on her job. 'There are people that want to put the knife in', she riposted, 'and this story enables them to do it. It is very difficult to answer.'[33] At much the same time, the fight for the Labour party candidacy for election as Mayor of London saw wedges hammered in. 'The word is', wrote a *Guardian* columnist, that Ken Livingstone had been saying in various places 'that Frank Dobson is "clinically depressed".'[34]

All that have been presented to me today are false, and the one that heads the list is the one that says President Nixon intends to resign. . . . he will not be driven out of office by rumour.' Bob Woodward and Carl Bernstein, *The Final Days*, New York: Avon Books, 1976, p. 170. Nixon resigned on 9 August.

[30]   *Independent on Sunday*, 29 September 1991; *Independent*, 23 July 1992.

[31]   *Independent on Sunday*, 23 July 1992.

[32]   Rosnow and Fine, *Rumor and Gossip*, pp. 109–10.

[33]   *Independent on Sunday*, 30 January 2000; *The Times*, 2 February 2000; *Guardian*, 4 February 2000.

[34]   Polly Toynbee, *Guardian*, 8 December 1999.

After the debacle of Britain's ejection from the European exchange rate mechanism on 'Black Wednesday', 16 September 1992, John Major was a victim on a larger scale. The claim was that he nearly 'cracked up' during the crisis. The rumour was itself rumoured to be 'part of a Thatcherite-inspired dirty-tricks campaign' against the prime minister. The Downing Street press office took pains to correct factual inaccuracies in the claim, such as that he had lost weight and was tinting his hair. A couple of months later, the catering manageress rumours were attributed to the prime minister's enemies in his own party as much as to the opposition.[35]

Overall, then, we can see that the incidence and force of specific rumours are unpredictable, though we can be fairly sure rumours of some kind will arise where the conditions can be predicted. The elements of anxiety and credulousness give rumour an irrationality and bushfire potential which may not be easily controlled. John Profumo's lies to the Commons 'so shook the confidence of the people of this country that they were ready to believe rumours which previously they would have rejected out of hand', claimed Lord Denning in 1963.[36] About the rumour climate in early 1994, *The Times* political editor commented, 'What started off as just an adulterous affair by a middle-ranking minister has turned into an unpredictable storm which has threatened John Major's survival strategy.'[37] Prime ministers have to manage or accommodate such episodes – in some of which they themselves are the focus. So how do rumours fit into the institutions and culture of British politics?

Rumour in British Politics

Rumour supplements artificially structured public information

Most public facts become available through mass media. We cannot verify them personally, but we accept their truth because we trust the journalist and/or the source to whom the facts are attributed. When that trust is put in doubt, uncertainty begins and the conditions for rumour develop. Yet even when a source is clear and trusted, media facts are intrinsically open to dispute. It is a commonplace that they are 'factoids'

---

[35]   *The Times*, 21 October 1992; *Independent*, 22 October 1992. Anthony Seldon, *Major: a Political Life*, p. 356.
[36]   *Lord Denning's Report*, p. 101.
[37]   *The Times*, 11 January 1994. The 'middle-ranking minister' was Lord Caithness, Transport minister in the House of Lords.

– manufactured deliberately, and located along a fact–fiction continuum. The characteristic rumour processes of levelling, sharpening and assimilation match closely the process of fashioning 'news'. The extreme case is the simplicities of tabloid language. During the Falklands War in 1982, for example, the *Sun* filled its front page with a one-word headline, 'GOTCHA!', over a picture of the sinking Argentine battle cruiser, the *Belgrano*. The word succinctly (and provocatively) encapsulated both an event and its interpretation.[38]

The same example illustrates the relation between the 'truth' of a media story and the recipient's preceding knowledge of its details and context. Media truth is necessarily relative, due to the selectivities involved. A story saying, 'the cabinet has decided . . .' will be literally untrue, if the real decision was taken by an informal group of ministers and civil servants. But it will fairly pass as a summary truth for a person unfamiliar with the organization of the cabinet system. The truthfulness of media 'facts' thus depends upon recipients' understanding of the journalistic conventions which produce them. In these circumstances, the conditions of rumour thrive. As Janet Daley wrote in *The Times*, the *New Statesman* article linking John Major and the caterer in 1993 was effectively saying, 'all of this has been well known gossip for ages. It has been so widely circulated that encrypted references are made to it right under your nose, but they are only decipherable by those in the know.'[39] There is a difference between ambiguity caused in a news story by oversimplification or sensationalism and by imposing on the story an interpretation set by preceding knowledge. But both are fertile ground for rumour.

Many media 'facts', moreover, are statements about motive and intention. We need such information, if we are to contextualize and evaluate concrete facts, such as a particular policy decision or appointment. The *Guardian*'s question about the Geoffrey Robinson rumours in 1999 – 'What's going on and why?' – typifies the political journalist's routine attempt to seek it out. Yet motive and intention are not easily verifiable. Those concerned may state them incompletely, wrongly, or not at all. The media's own motives, in addition, are equally open to doubt. Newspapers have their own political agendas, even (perhaps especially) if they are not partisan loyalists.

[38]   *Sun*, 4 May 1982. The editor, under pressure during a strike of journalists, quickly had second thoughts. The headline was replaced after the first edition (about one-third of the print run) with the more subdued 'DID 1200 ARGIES DROWN?' Robert Harris, *GOTCHA!*, London: Faber and Faber, 1983, p. 13.

[39]   *The Times*, 29 January 1993.

Those arguments can be further elaborated by exploring the differences between oral and newspaper rumours. The very idea of newspaper news contains, in ambiguity, one of the conditions of rumour. But a newspaper rumour can take varying forms. A story can be reported explicitly as a rumour. 'POUND RISES ON ERM RE-ENTRY RUMOURS' was the headline to an *Independent* story not long after 'Black Wednesday' in 1992.[40] Secondly, an item can be reported as a rumour implicitly, by not citing a clear source. For example, the claim that Mo Mowlam's brain tumour had left her 'without the intellectual rigour' to do her job was sourced vaguely to 'senior government aides'.[41] These were 'concerned *that*' (author's emphasis) she was incapacitated. This language itself is ambiguous. Does it mean they were concerned *whether* she might be incapacitated? Or concerned because they knew definitely that she was?

In the first of those two forms of report, the journalist states as a fact that rumours are circulating. In the second, the 'concern' of government aides is stated as a fact, but the accuracy and the precise nature of their concern are left implicit. The aides being unnamed, the claim is unverifiable independently by the reader.

A third variant is illustrated by the quotation earlier from Janet Daley's *Times* article about the Major–caterer rumours. A newspaper reports an item as fact, and a reader infers from it an encrypted (or a contextual) meaning which, unverified, introduces extra information in the form of rumour. Where the inference is correct, the rumour is likely perhaps to be more credible to the reader than to the journalist. For all the 'facts' in the paper have a consistent credibility to the reader, conferred by the journalist's authority. The journalist, in contrast, is constantly adding to a stock of private information from sources of varying reliability. At intervals some of it will be published, when the journalist is satisfied about its veracity and when it has enough news value. The remainder, unless it is published explicitly *as* rumour, is likely to stay unpublished, and the journalist will perhaps share it as oral rumour.[42]

---

[40] *Independent*, 26 September 1992. The story began: 'The Treasury yesterday denied rumours on the foreign exchange markets that the Government was about to spring a surprise on the world and take sterling straight back into the European exchange rate mechanism.'

[41] *Independent on Sunday*, 31 January 2000.

[42] 'For every Ministerial resignation, there are many other "scandals" that never see the light of day. . . . There is a sense of achievement and glee when newspapers are able to substantiate and publish "stories" held in their scandal queues – special database files containing all sorts of gossip and rumour about [leading politicians].' Anthony Bevins, political editor, *Independent*, 9 January 1994.

Readers too, of course, can spread and add to the written rumours orally.

Rumour, in sum, enables us to read between the lines of published news. Oral and published rumours (internet publication included) work in tandem. Rumour (typically, one suspects) starts orally. Upon publication, it enters the public domain. Publication in the press, as distinct from the internet, gives it definition or precision and accelerates it, arguably, by legitimating its circulation. Publication probably tends to legitimate the substance of the rumour too: 'if it's in the papers, it must be true.' Finally, publication probably increases the rumour's potential to cause substantial effects – but at the same time lays the basis for attempted disproof and termination.

Rumour fits political news values well

The appropriateness of *Improvised News* as a title for Shibutani's text on rumour is well illustrated by listing the characteristics which studies repeatedly show to be typical of news. Events are more likely to make news if they are unpredictable (within a range of what may be expected), unusual, close to home, personally affecting, about elites (individuals, groups, nations), reaching a certain volume (goals scored, numbers dead), clear and unambiguous, negative, and fitting the cycle of the medium (hourly, daily, weekly). The less there is of one, the more is needed of another. Many of them overlap with the conditions for rumour.

Moreover, rumour-mongering fits the journalistic attraction to 'exclusives' (scoops). These provide a measure of competence and a source of professional esteem, and they are believed to sell newspapers. What better way is there of being 'first with the news' than being ahead of it – to report it before it happens? (Hence the attraction to media of opinion polls.) Exclusives can avoid being mere speculation (about a cabinet appointment or the contents of a parliamentary report, for instance), by being hedged or by being sourced to someone who knows – and who effectively provides verification in advance.

More important in some ways than being first with the news is not being last with the news. Journalists dislike late-night calls from the office asking why every paper has a story except their own. Partly to avoid this, political journalists (among others) operate as 'competitor–colleagues', sharing information with carefully selected colleagues.[43]

---

[43]   See Jeremy Tunstall's pioneering works, *The Westminster Lobby Correspondents*, London: Routledge, 1970, and *Journalists at Work*, London: Constable, 1971.

Beyond that, many of the locations in which they work are good 'milling areas', involving a certain amount of hanging around.

Overwhelmingly, however, rumour fits the specific values of British political journalism through the latter's tolerance of imprecise sources. This tolerance is often criticized but is impossible to eliminate. If journalists can get extra news off the record, sourced anonymously or to a metaphor ('informed circles'), then they will do so. The practice is institutionalized in the lobby correspondent system (described in earlier chapters), which has survived in modified forms for about 120 years. The system originally rested on the assumption that the reader would trust the journalist and not worry about the source. 'Verification' of today's soggy story attributed to 'sources close to the prime minister' lay in the proven accuracy of yesterday's story (vindicated, hopefully, by events).

The lobby system retained respect so long as institutional politics stayed rooted at Westminster, while the lobby group stayed small and had a slow turnover (membership for up to thirty years was not unknown), and while broadcast media were not a serious force in political news. By the early 1960s, all those conditions were changing. A young recruit, John Whale, working for ITN, recorded his dismay at how well informed his competitors were. Then he noticed they attended the same briefings, had the same contacts. The difference was just that they wrote with more confidence and licence.[44] With increased size and turnover, and with the ephemeral nature of broadcasting (compared with print), the system became sloppy and degenerate. In a caustic analysis of the *Independent on Sunday* story about Mo Mowlam's alleged mental decline, Simon Jenkins illustrated these weaknesses by cataloguing the feeble attributions of the paper's claims. They were sourced to 'a senior government aide', 'senior government aides' (plural), 'one adviser', 'an insider', 'a Labour insider', 'Downing Street', 'a senior party source', 'some ministers' and 'a Downing Street spokesman'.[45]

The machinery of political journalism is adaptable, and the lobby is long past its heyday. But the conventions of source anonymity were not at all contingent on its existence. The lobby was (and is) essentially a method of distributing news collectively. The dynamics of political journalism still make source anonymity important.

---

[44] John Whale, *Journalism and Government*, London: Macmillan, 1982, pp. 80–1.
[45] *The Times*, 2 February 2000. By the 1990s, membership of the lobby was nominally up to 250.

Rumour is well suited to communicating about the private spheres of politics

This is where the rubbish tip analogy becomes particularly apt. By 'private sphere' is meant those activities and attitudes which the dominant values in a political system exclude formally or informally from the free flow of information. Such activities and attitudes may help the system work, but for one reason or another they cannot be acknowledged publicly. The unverified, clandestine, oral and irresponsible qualities of rumour make it possible to communicate about them privately.

Getting behind the conformity of collective behaviour and shared values

Public conformity contrasts most strongly with private dissent and diversity in authoritarian regimes which enforce a rigid official ideology. The more totalitarian the ideology, the greater the political role of rumour. Communist China, the USSR and the satellites in the Soviet bloc are or were obvious examples. Steven Sampson, arguing that Ceauşescu's Romania was an extreme case, claims that rumour evolved from being a supplementary system of communication, as in open political systems, to a parallel system competing with the official media. Rumour and gossip were politicized, as the state tried alternately 'to censor, stigmatize or criminalize all channels of information which it [could not] control – from letter-writing to telephone conversations to social clubs to any informal oral channels'. Even samizdat publications, Russian examples of which were often quoted in Western media, were almost non-existent. Oral rumour acquired great popular authority. People whose jobs linked them to the political elite (maids, repairmen, waiters) were key rumour-mongers, while truck drivers and chauffeurs spread and embellished the findings.[46]

Totalitarian systems are only the extreme case. Rumour plays a comparable role in open or 'constitutional' systems. 'If the demand for news in a public exceeds the supply made available through institutional channels,' Shibutani observes, 'rumor construction is likely to occur.'[47] Most constitutions are written down. Their rules and principles are prescriptive. Even if they are not ignored or distorted purposely, their practice will adapt with time. A literal reading of the United States constitution gives a most imperfect idea of the system of government today. Formal and informal rules – for instance, about the role of the president – diverge.

[46]   Steven Sampson, 'Rumours in socialist Romania', *Survey*, 28.4, 1984, p. 144.
[47]   Shibutani, *Improvised News*, p. 57.

An unwritten constitution such as the British, with its emphasis on intrinsically soggy concepts such as convention, is even more flexible. But the scope for rumour arises in particular because of the collectivist elements in the British system. Rumour can reflect the inevitability of private dissent and compromise within a collective enterprise – and all the more, no doubt, in one which claims to be democratic. In the executive, the key principles of collective cabinet responsibility and individual ministerial responsibility, with their corollaries of cabinet secrecy and civil service confidentiality (see chapters 1 and 2), demand a conformity in government which is politically unrealistic.

In the legislature, the demands of party discipline – necessary to keep the executive in office – have the same implications. Rules restricting access to the premises at Westminster reflect the exclusiveness of the membership. (Hence the old analogy to a 'gentlemen's club'.) Peers are appointed for life. In the Commons, Members from safe seats stay for years. They work long and sometimes eccentric hours. Their business is talking and listening, sometimes formally in the chamber or a committee, and sometimes informally and sociably at meals and in bars. Within each party they adjust their differences in pursuit of an agreed interest. But because parliament is a competitive arena, both within parties and between them, the conditions for rumour flourish. 'The solitary individual caught in a crisis is anxious and restless, and actively engages in restructuring activities aimed at finding out what will happen next.'[48] That summary of 'verbal milling' fits parliament very well. Anxiety and uncertainty about something, even if at a low level, are never far away, and the rumours blow.

Competition at Westminster between the parties is channelled into debate and divisions. It is for that very reason that the enforcement of conformity within each party can reach, so to speak, Romanian levels. Members thus use rumours, leaks and private briefings with journalists, to advance or demolish a reputation, a following or a policy, in an endless jostle for position. Rumour, in sum, is an integral part of the dynamics of parliamentary politics and government.

Fitting humans to offices: private frailties, public principles
Rumour does not simply communicate the tensions within a collectivity. It also fits the vagaries of individual personality to the needs of specific offices, acknowledging again the imperfect fit between theory and reality.

---

[48] Rosnow and Fine, *Rumor and Gossip*, p. 56, citing R. H. Turner and L. M. Killian, *Collective Behavior*, Englewood Cliffs, N.J.: Prentice-Hall, 1957.

Public offices are designed for perfection. We cannot in principle accept that generals should be incompetent, judges prejudiced, policemen corrupt and political leaders stupid. So these persons are housed in special places, whisked around in special cars and clothed (in some cases) in uniforms and wigs. The person fades into the abstraction, the imperfect realization into the ideal. Much of that involves elements of privacy and concealment – creating physical and psychological distance from the rest of us. Some of the privacy, moreover, is uncontested. An officeholder may embody an ideal but will enjoy areas of private life protected by law and custom.

Distance breeds mystery – a condition which can help a prime minister to acquire the appearance of statesmanship. But citizens will not be content with information just about the 'perfect' prime minister. We know perfection is impossible. We know too that the distinction between public and private life is spurious, in the sense that experiences and feelings in private may affect a prime minister's behaviour in office – and by extension, our own wellbeing. During the last thirty years of the twentieth century, the public thirst for knowledge about this private sphere increased – and fed the competitive appetites especially of the tabloid press. A prime minister's private life has therefore become less an entitlement than a concession. Apart from round the fringes (family and friends) the concession is readily made, because without it suitable persons would be unlikely to accept the job. (In the United States, indeed, this is already a problem in finding candidates for the presidency.) But the feeling of moral right to knowledge about the private sphere can be used by media to justify a traffic in dubious rumours.

People want to know, then, both about the imperfections of officeholders and about the areas of arguably legitimate privacy in their lives. Rumour is a means by which these public and private worlds are bridged: the pretence of the public ideal is maintained, while the private person is exposed. The best and possibly the most common examples are reductive rumours about core features of humanity: health and sex. Stripping away the trappings of office, rumour shows the powerful as ordinary mortals like the rest of us. So it has a special power to bring a miscreant leader down.

Rumours about health
Health makes a nonsense of the boundary between public and private life, for it affects someone's behaviour all the time. Prime ministers are by definition healthy (in the sense of clearly up to the job) at the moment of taking office. We become concerned only when their health appears to affect performance adversely, at which time it becomes 'bad' and the

institutional premiership (to use the categories of chapter one) has to accept that the personal prime minister is ill. Only when it is unavoidable will a prime minister's colleagues want to admit the incapacity publicly, for it creates an immediate threat to the stability of the administration. To quote from the case of an Australian prime minister, Malcolm Fraser, rumoured in 1981 to be much more ill than in fact he was, 'The prime minister's health is no longer simply a medical problem. It is a political problem.'[49] (The same might have been said of Churchill after his stroke in June 1953; see below.) In presidential regimes the problem is greater, for a single chief executive has no cabinet colleagues sharing his responsibilities and able to carry on seamlessly in his absence. Partly for this reason, presidents tend publicly to be highly explicit, compared with prime ministers, about the nature of their ailments – once these are admitted.[50]

But how do we know an officeholder's health is bad? Since you are by definition fit when you take office, your health can go in only one direction – downhill. Almost any reference to health at all is likely to start rumours that something may be wrong. 'If everything is fine', wrote a Russian columnist about the ailing Boris Yeltsin in July 1995, 'why announce he was in hospital?' Many Russians were said to be convinced he was already dead.[51] Some Americans thought the same about Woodrow Wilson in 1919: he had had a stroke and his wife was keeping visitors away.[52] Again, rumours swept Beijing in November 1990 that Deng Xiaoping was seriously ill. Deng, 86 but still 'the anchor of China's fragile balance', had been out of public view for four months.[53] When Fidel Castro disappeared for three weeks in 1997 people thought he too was dead.[54]

Good health is relative anyway, particularly in people who have reached middle age or beyond, which most political leaders have. Much

[49] *Sydney Morning Herald*, 26 August 1981. Fraser was rumoured (wrongly) to be suffering from stomach cancer, and enemies in his party sought to destabilize his leadership through them. Colin Seymour-Ure, 'Rumour and politics', *Politics*, 17.2, 1982, pp. 1–9.
[50] In a celebrated early example, Lyndon Johnson thrust his abdomen at the TV cameras in October 1965, to show the scars following his gall bladder operation.
[51] Alexander Minkin, *Moskovsky Komsolomets*, quoted in the *Independent*, 16 July 1995. On the death rumours, see *Independent*, 22 July 1995.
[52] John M. Blum, *Joe Tumulty and the Wilson Era*, Boston, Mass.: Houghton Mifflin, 1951, pp. 214–15. Other people thought Wilson might have gone mad. Mrs Wilson became for a while almost *de facto* president.
[53] *Independent*, 10 November 1990.
[54] The period included his 71st birthday. A spokeswoman confirmed Castro was 'in excellent health'. She gave a general wedge driver explanation for rumours to the contrary. *U.S.A. Today*, 19 August 1997.

illness, too, is more like flu than a broken leg. Flu creeps up on you: the moment at which you define yourself as ill is arbitrary. There is not much doubt, by contrast, when you have broken a leg. Moreover medics speak a specialized language, which increases the scope for 'spinning' an illness. Churchill's stroke on 23 June 1953 was translated for the media (after a delay of three days) into an announcement that 'the prime minister has had no respite for a long time from his very arduous duties and is in need of a complete rest'.[55] When Eisenhower had a heart attack in 1955 it was announced initially as a 'digestive upset', and his ileitis in 1956 was called an 'upset stomach'. His stroke in 1957 was called a 'chill', and as the rumours circulated, one news agency was so confused that it put out a bulletin saying the president had suffered 'a heart attack of the brain'.[56] Boris Yeltsin's spokesman explained his boss's cancellation of all engagements for ten days in July 1995 as due to 'stress because of the war in Chechnya'. Later, Yeltsin admitted he had had a heart attack.[57] Poor health, lastly, is often a cover for the real reason why an officeholder has declined to do something or has resigned. Anthony Eden, for instance, was easily able to cover resignation after the Suez debacle in 1956 with the cloak of ill health, since he had a poor medical history.

All those factors tend to create conditions of anxiety, ambiguity and suggestibility. So rumours about the health of prime ministers and presidents are quick to take off. The same factors encourage colleagues to try and hush up an illness. This can simply accentuate the rumours, as in the Wilson case. Similar problems may arise when an illness ends, for recovery is not always easy to demonstrate.

Regardless of recovery, health rumours are difficult to scotch. React too quickly or angrily, and suspicion is fuelled. Delay too long and people think the worst. Authoritarian regimes try to scotch them through their control of institutional media. With photographers in

[55] Martin Gilbert, 'Never Despair': Winston S. Churchill 1945–1965, London: Heinemann, 1988, p. 851. Churchill's private secretary, Jock Colville, then persuaded three press barons, Lords Camrose, Beaverbrook and Bracken, particular friends of Churchill, to gag Fleet Street. This no doubt encouraged rumours. A month later, an American lunch guest at Chartwell noted that 'rumours of all kinds had been flying around London about [Churchill's] health, so I did not quite know what to expect'. Gilbert, 'Never Despair', pp. 852, 866.

[56] Ileitis is an inflammation of the small intestine which can lead to gangrene of the bowel. Eisenhower's stroke was eventually described as a 'cerebral occlusion', but the press office persistently refused to use the word 'stroke'. James Deakin, Straight Stuff, ch. 1. Deakin gives a lively account of the White House press corps milling, as they tried to get at the truth behind official obfuscations.

[57] Independent, 15 July 1995, 19 July 1995.

attendance, the 73-year-old Mao Tsetung, in a famous example, demonstrated his fitness in 1966 by swimming the two-miles-wide Yangtse river at Wuhan, when he was rumoured to be seriously ill.[58] In 1995 the old totalitarian methods failed Yeltsin, however, when his entourage sought to quash the rumours referred to above by doctoring old photographs. An official photo supposedly showing Yeltsin at work in a Moscow clinic in July was exposed as a doctored still from a holiday video the previous April. Only then did Yeltsin admit on TV that he had suffered a heart attack.[59]

Apart from Churchill, British prime ministers in office have suffered few rumours about their health. The rumour that John Major came near to 'cracking up' during the ERM crisis is the best example in recent times, and it was of only minor significance. Like that one, health rumours are a mixture of pipe dreams and wedge drivers. Even where media do not share the motives of the latter, the claim of a public interest in a leader's health is ample justification for rumour-mongering.

Rumours about sex

Many of the uncertainties which fuel health rumours are about definition and measurement. These do not apply to rumours about sex in the same way – although Bill Clinton memorably tried to defend his claim that he had not had sex with Monica Lewinsky by arguing that there had been no penetration. Like health, sexual behaviour can affect the capacity to perform public office. The Conservative cabinet minister David Mellor allegedly said (but perhaps not seriously) that his love life with his mistress left him too 'knackered' to carry out all his duties efficiently. But it is arguable that an extracurricular sex life might actually improve someone's performance in office, if it acted as recreational therapy. Certainly Lloyd George was an effective wartime prime minister, while having a permanent mistress.[60]

The threat to political officeholders from sex rumours is of disqualification for immorality, not for incapacity. Betrayal of trust, lack of

---

[58]   At Wuhan the Yangtse's current is strong, and provided the swimmer sets course downstream and stays afloat, a safe crossing is normally assured. C. P. FitzGerald, *Mao Tsetung and China*, London: Hodder and Stoughton, 1976, pp. 114–15; Stuart Schram, *Mao Tsetung*, Harmondsworth: Penguin Books, 1967, p. 338.

[59]   *Independent*, 15 July 1995, 16 July 1995, 19 July 1995, 22 July 1995.

[60]   Lloyd George married Frances Stevenson in 1943. She had become his mistress in 1912, following him as private secretary from the Treasury into Downing Street (1916–22). She was originally employed as tutor to Lloyd George's daughter Megan. A. J. P. Taylor (ed.), *Lloyd George: a Diary by Frances Stevenson*, London: Hutchinson, 1971.

integrity, 'bringing the office into disrepute': these are the charges. They make the victim a political liability. If the person's private life is inconsistent with his public principles, he (it is usually a he) will obviously seek to conceal it, and it is the resulting ambiguity which provides the condition for rumour.

In the case of sex, then, the problem is whether rumoured behaviour corrupts. Compared with health rumours, this decision is more in the hands of public opinion – interpreted and evaluated by and through the media and then weighed – in the British system – by parliamentary and party leaders. If a colleague is the subject of plausible rumours but does not immediately resign, a prime minister will often wait and see how the wind blows. In the United States, during the events culminating in the impeachment proceedings against Clinton in 1998–9 (he was found not guilty), the media played an important part in developing public opinion about the president's behaviour with Monica Lewinsky. Clinton argued his case through television, when both denying impropriety and later admitting it. He used the media as a lever to try and influence Congress, with whom the final judgement lay.

Compared with health too, there seems greater variability in the standards of unacceptable behaviour associated with sex rumours. In the high Victorian age, William Gladstone's position as prime minister and party leader could have been seriously threatened at times by rumours about his nocturnal so-called 'rescue work' with London prostitutes.[61] These encounters were high-minded and respectable compared with the serial womanizing of Lloyd George ('the Welsh goat'). Lloyd George's behaviour certainly fed rumours. Potentially the most damaging, perhaps, was during his time as Chancellor in 1909, when he successfully sued the Conservative Sunday paper, the *People*, over innuendoes in which he was not in fact named.[62]

Homosexual rumours illustrate this variability of standards clearly. By the 1990s gay relationships which would have destroyed a political

[61]   During much of his life Gladstone undertook solitary late-night rambles, during which he sought out prostitutes, with the intention of winning them away to a better life. His success rate seems to have been unhappily low. The political implications of the work were a frequent concern to his colleagues, especially at election times. Richard Shannon, *Gladstone: Heroic Minister, 1865–1898*, Harmondsworth: Allen Lane, the Penguin Press, 1999, e.g. pp. 1, 450, 486.

[62]   Lloyd George, according to his son, pleaded with his wife to appear at his side in court, claiming that otherwise his career would be ruined. In the previous year the *Bystander* compensated Lloyd George, without the need for legal action, for publishing rumours about his womanizing. B. B. Gilbert, *David Lloyd George*, London: Batsford, 1987, p. 376.

career before the law was reformed in the 1960s posed no formal threat. But gay rumours abounded at Westminster, and by inference they were often still intended to be damaging. 'The real target in Fleet Street's sights', wrote the *Observer* about tabloid coverage of one of the "sleaze" cases in 1994, 'is what has become known as a "gay ring" of Tory MPs.' The existence of this was entirely a matter of rumour.[63] Again, when the former cabinet minister Geoffrey Robinson was rumoured in 1999 to possess photographs of a senior ministerial colleague, allegedly gay, the language in which they were discussed was that of 'attempted blackmail' and 'compromise'.[64]

More than health, lastly, sex rumours lead their victims into tangles. John Profumo was destroyed as a minister in 1963 because the rumours of poolside sex romps surfaced publicly; but his complete political destruction was the result of lying about them in the Commons chamber. Similarly David Mellor was on the run as a result of the climate created by rumours about his sex life, but the catalyst for his resignation from John Major's cabinet was the prominence given to the discovery that he had accepted a holiday from a friend who was the daughter of the treasurer of the Palestine National Council.[65]

Tangles may have become more likely, perhaps, because of the double standards in late twentieth-century British life. The public appeared to expect of their politicians greater integrity and more traditional values than they had themselves. Mellor failed to carry conviction when he argued that an adulterous affair should no longer be regarded as a disqualification from cabinet office.[66] In the United States, by contrast, Bill Clinton was shown to be a sexual adventurer and liar, but he did not suffer for it in the opinion polls. The French have been similarly insouciant. The existence of President Mitterrand's 'second family', for instance, was known to the political class for years. When a picture of his illegitimate daughter was published in *Paris-Match* in 1994, there was said to be more public concern about her exposure than her existence.[67]

---

[63]   *Observer*, 13 February 1994.
[64]   *Guardian*, 25 October 1999.
[65]   Anthony Seldon, *Major: a Political Life*, pp. 323–4.
[66]   Alan Doig and J. Wilson, 'Untangling the threads of sleaze', *Parliamentary Affairs*, 48.4, pp. 568–9.
[67]   *Independent*, 4 November 1994. When similar rumours surfaced six years earlier, the same paper's then correspondent wrote, tongue partly in cheek: 'It is of course essential for informed circles in Paris to know that the President of the Republic has a mistress, and usually one is given the names of about three different mistresses.' Patrick Marnham, *Independent*, 7 December 1988.

A final point about sex rumours is that, where specific, they are easier to scotch than health rumours – for instance, by recourse to the courts (although at the risk of amplification).

Rumours about money

Rumours about money deserve mention briefly. The problem is again principally about agreed standards of acceptable private behaviour by public persons. Rumours run when the two seem to conflict. The process is probably assisted by the ambiguities resulting from the technical and legal complexities of the financial world.

Money rumours have been a problem *for* more than about prime ministers – as they were for John Major in his problems with 'sleaze'. Several prime ministers have got into financial scrapes, but only Lloyd George seems to have been the victim of serious rumours. When Chancellor of the Exchequer, Lloyd George in April 1912 bought 1000 shares in the American Marconi Company. So did two other ministers. They paid a pre-issue price of two pounds. The shares doubled on the first day. Lloyd George kept his shareholding secret. By October rumours had escalated to such an extent that a parliamentary committee was established. A minority report criticized the three ministers for grave impropriety, but the government majority ensured that they were absolved. The support of the prime minister, H. H. Asquith, was crucial, and an opposition censure motion in the Commons was defeated with the help of a three-line whip. Lloyd George was an asset the Liberals could not afford to lose.[68]

Harold Wilson was entangled in the complicated 'slagheaps affair' in the 1970s, through land reclamation deals by relatives of his secretary Marcia Williams. Some of the allegations were based on forgeries, but the whole affair was not driven particularly by rumour. Mrs Thatcher had to cope with media and opposition needling about the financial affairs of her son Mark. The issue was whether he received 12 million pounds in commissions from a huge arms deal negotiated by his mother with Saudi Arabia. Rumours of his role 'have been circulating in the media for years', commented one paper when the story surfaced again briefly in 1994. But the issue was never a serious difficulty for Mrs Thatcher.[69]

Rumours about money, in conclusion, like the two previously discussed 'human frailty' types, fit well the idea of rumour as problem-

---

[68]   A summary of the scandal is in Alan Doig, *Westminster Babylon*, pp. 38–40.
[69]   *Independent*, 10 October 1994. The deal involved a £20bn sale of aircraft and equipment to Saudi Arabia in 1985.

solving. They help us to satisfy our curiosity about persons who may have power over us but who are human beings just the same.

Conclusion: the Implications of Political Rumour

What does this analysis suggest for the significance of rumour in British politics, especially for the prime minister? Rumours are clearly a useful ingredient in our individual perceptions of reality. They either supplement or embellish the public record provided in mass media. They supply information and they touch our emotions. Part of the price we pay is that this extra information may be wrong.

More specifically, rumours are a distinctive method of reconciling our desire for information about powerful people with our acceptance of the fact that there are areas of political life which either are unavoidably secret or are legitimately protected. Some of these areas sustain myths and conventions which help to make institutions function properly. In this process, moreover, rumour can also help to make unwelcome submission to authority tolerable. This is especially true in repressive and authoritarian societies. (Political jokes have a comparable effect.)

Rumours can go further. As a form of exposure, when they bubble over publicly after seething in the Westminster pot, they can enforce popular accountability on political leaders and even bring them down. To that extent, they give people a share in power. The press grabs the chance to play its historic self-appointed role as the people's tribune: 'The real feather in the cap is a resignation,' wrote the political editor of the *Independent*, when discussing the media's role in the 'sleaze' rumours in 1994; 'nothing less than a scalp on the belt will satisfy most editors.'[70]

In all those ways rumours can be positive for a political *system*. But they will not serve the needs of all within it – including sometimes, as the previous paragraph indicates, those of a specific leader. They may threaten a leader's personal position: it seems unlikely, for example, that John Major would have survived if the catering manageress rumour had been proved true. More often they threaten a prime minister's purposes or the persons and ventures with which he deals. For, if the press is a tribune, it is surely a selective one. Some scalps will be more desirable than others. It stretches belief to think that there are not, at any time,

---

[70]   *Independent*, 9 January 1994.

persons in public life who are the subject of unpublished rumours yet who remain unharassed by the press.

Even though the outcome may be positive at the end of a particular rumour process, the process itself will have been disturbing. As a consequence of their connection with anxiety and uncertainty, rumours always involve some degree of political instability. In extreme cases, rumour may presage a major shock to the entire political system, through riot, revolution and war. In lesser cases, rumours about leaders typically destabilize them. The *Daily Mail* apparently heard the catering manageress rumours about two weeks after John Major became prime minister. 'It was a massive attempt to destabilise Major,' one of their journalists was quoted as saying; '. . . a quite deliberate attempt to undermine the new prime minister.' Unfortunately for the hypothetical destabilizers, they picked the wrong woman.[71]

Destabilization need not mean the threat of major scandal. To return to an earlier image, it is more often, surely, flu than a broken leg. Voters are periodically invited to pass judgement on a leader's reputation, performance, competence and personality. Rumour will play its part in forming that judgement.

Destabilization is encouraged also by the irrational and emotional elements in rumour, and by their proneness to error. Rumours are 'irresponsible' in a British political system traditionally described in textbooks as 'responsible government'. It is perfectly possible that a leader may be destroyed by an erroneous rumour, or by actions pumped up out of proportion. The resources of the internet are likely to increase this possibility, since websites are subject to even fewer checks on the accuracy of their content than newspapers. Provided the conditions are right, rumour can be used deliberately and aggressively in leaks and negative campaigning.[72] All the while, a political leader has to judge their importance, gauge their potential and try to keep them in proportion.

Most of those propositions imply difficulties of control for a leader over the rumour's consequences. To take an extreme example, how was an inexperienced prime minister to react to the climate of rumour after the death of Princess Diana in 1997? The princess herself was semi-

---

[71] *New Statesman*, 29 January 1993. For Clare Latimer's reaction to the disclosure of Edwina Currie's affair with John Major, see, e.g., *The Times*, 30 September 2002. Currie's disclosures are in her *Diaries, 1987–92*, London: Little, Brown, 2002.

[72] 'The drip drip drip of rumour, innuendo and allegation [against Ken Livingstone] has begun,' wrote the *Independent on Sunday* (12 March 2000), as Ken Livingstone defied the Labour party and began his campaign for the London mayoralty as an independent. In the London political climate of the times, it was unlikely that such rumours would take off. Livingstone duly romped to victory.

detached from the monarchy; her current boyfriend and his father (Mohammed al-Fayed) lived very largely at an angle to British society. The principal persons were thus already in an 'ambiguous' situation before the tragedy happened – and it happened abroad. How should the government behave (and advise the Queen to behave) in such circumstances? How, and how emotionally, would public opinion and the media behave? As with the assassination of President Kennedy, the rumours about Princess Diana's death were unlikely ever quite to go away, although surviving at a low level of public curiosity.

The problem of control is perhaps at its worst and most distinctive with oral rumour. How do you nail a whisper? You have to identify it, weigh it, work out how to counter or disprove it. It is quite likely to concern delicate matters in an uneasy climate. But whatever form they take, guarding against and coping with rumours will surely continue to be a challenge to a prime minister's communications management.

10

Drawing Blood? Prime Ministers and Political Cartoons[1]

How have cartoonists dealt with prime ministers – and prime ministers with cartoonists? We should not assume that cartoons are frivolous because they may be funny, nor that frivolous things necessarily have frivolous consequences. A cartoon can skewer a politician as effectively as the written or spoken word. Just as rumours are a special kind of news, political cartoons are a special kind of comment. They are 'editorials in pictures' (indeed Americans commonly refer to them as 'editorial cartoons'). They deserve a kind of wary respect. So how much and what kind of attention do cartoonists pay to prime ministers? What images do they use, and how do prime ministers react?

Like an editorialist, the cartoonist decides what is worth attention among the day's goings-on, tells us what he (still very rarely she[2]) thinks it signifies, and gives us his critical opinion of it. Like editorials, too, the cartoon has a familiarity of style, form and 'language'. It tends to be a regular size, in a regular place and on a regular page – usually quite close to the editorials.

Beyond that, however, a cartoon has qualities that make it more subtle and complex than a written editorial. Cartoons essentially work by comparison and imagery: elections are like horse races or battles, prime ministers behave like acrobats, puppets or gorillas. These images cannot argue: they only assert. Cartoons do not deploy evidence: the image *is* their evidence. 'So the prime minister is like a gorilla? He's that primitive, is he?'

[1] The traditional title for discussions of the political cartoon is 'Drawn and Quartered'. 'Drawing Blood' is fresher and just as good. I had never thought of it nor seen it used, until Steve Bell published *Bell's Eye: Twenty Years of Drawing Blood* (London: Methuen, 1999). Due acknowledgement is hereby given.
[2] During the 2001 general election only one of nearly thirty cartoonists drawing for the national daily and Sunday press was a woman – Nicola Jennings of the *Guardian*.

The use of imagery necessarily throws upon the reader the task of deciding what the cartoon means – and in particular, how far it is intended critically and how strongly felt. This makes cartoons doubly ambiguous, and for the reader it may be part of the fun. Is the use of a gorilla image, to continue with that example, meant contemptuously? (Its connotations of savagery may seem old-fashioned.) Is the cartoonist indicating what he himself thinks, or simply what he believes other people think? Further ambiguity can arise, moreover, if people do not know about the circumstances to which the image is being applied. The point of the gorilla image may be lost on them. Cartoons cannot give us the news; they can only react to it, and they need to be topical.

While ambiguity brings the risk of misunderstanding, assertiveness heightens the appeal of cartoons to the emotions. They may produce 'a shock of prejudice', as one cartoonist put it, 'that can be incised on the beholder's mind'.[3] Their method is that of 'road rage' – assertion followed by abuse. They can express the unsayable, too. Images which cause no difficulty within cartoon conventions would be unacceptable in a reasoned leading article (Scarfe depicting Harold Wilson licking Lyndon Johnson's arse; Bell showing John Major surfboarding on a giant turd; Brookes drawing William Hague as the livid rear end of a Blair baboon). Moreover, if a cartoon is interpreted, say, as sexist, racist, ageist, or obscene, the cartoonist may protest that his intention was quite otherwise, he was drawing ironically, and that the interpretation is all in the reader's mind.

The nature of their work thus gives cartoonists altogether very little control over how it will be understood. For so graphic a medium, its appreciation is paradoxically private, for it depends heavily on the reader's imagination. For this very reason, perhaps, political cartooning seems quite a conservative genre, in that it sticks to a fairly narrow and traditional range of imagery, with which the artists who introduced cartoons to the daily press a hundred years ago would feel perfectly comfortable in the new millennium. (Another reason may be that cartoonists tend to have long working lives. The average age of cartoonists for the national press during the 2001 general election was 56.) Where the genre is less conservative is in cartoonists' individual styles of drawing and in their genius for finding new ways of applying traditional images.

All these qualities make the cartoon powerful in attack. For a prime minister seeking to manage his public communication, cartoons must be at least as dangerous as hostile editorials. Nor is there an obvious method

---

[3]   Michael Cummings, Foreword to Michael Wynn Jones, *The Cartoon History of Britain*, London: Tom Stacey, 1971, p. 13.

of counter-attack. To object to a cartoon is to invite ridicule, even if the original did not poke fun. If it did, then Harold Macmillan, for one, accepted that 'it is a good thing to be laughed at. It is better than to be ignored.'[4] In fact, political cartoons are by no means always funny. One editor of *Punch* in its heyday, Kenneth Bird ('Fougasse'), wrote an entire book on humorous art without discussing political cartoons at all.[5]

Prime ministers have had to cope with cartoons more or less since the office came into existence. In the eighteenth century, the golden age of Hogarth, Gillray and Rowlandson, cartoons were generally published as prints. In the nineteenth century, magazines took over. *Punch* popularized the term 'cartoon', hitherto used only as a technical term in design, when it submitted mock entries to a competition for decoration of the new House of Commons in 1843.[6] The first newspaper staff cartoonist, Francis Carruthers Gould ('FCG'), was hired in 1888 by the *Pall Mall Gazette*, a London clubland evening paper with a bite-sized circulation in the low thousands.

Political cartoons took off with the popular daily press, which grew rapidly after the foundation of Alfred Harmsworth's *Daily Mail* in 1896. The London-based, metropolitan press turned progressively into a nationally circulating group of papers, which swamped the provincial press. By the 1930s, titles such as the *Daily Mail*, *Daily Express* and *Daily Herald* had circulations in millions, where their counterparts in the 1900s had hundreds of thousands at most. To achieve these, papers had to be light, entertaining and well illustrated. A political cartoonist was an obvious attraction – and stars such as David Low and George Strube eventually commanded very high salaries. In 1904 Harmsworth, foreseeing the trend, appointed W. K. Haselden the first cartoonist on a national daily paper and made him a key contributor to the relaunch of the struggling *Daily Mirror*. Haselden stayed for thirty-six years.

In addition to drawing for a much larger readership, cartoonists progressively lost their custody of the prime minister's likeness. When a contemporary wrote of Gould that 'most of our leading men are better known to the public at large through the cartoons of FCG than by their photographs', this was not mere flattery.[7] Until newspaper photography

---

[4]   Harold Macmillan to the Postmaster-General (Reginald Bevins), 10 December 1962, PREM 11 files, Public Record Office. The memo referred not to a cartoon but to the ground-breaking TV sketch show, *That Was The Week That Was*.
[5]   Fougasse (Kenneth Bird), *The Good-Tempered Pencil*, London: Max Reinhardt, 1956. The author's justification for excluding political cartoons was that humour, even if used, is not their principal purpose or weapon.
[6]   R. G. G. Price, *A History of Punch*, London: Collins, 1957, pp. 43–4.
[7]   J. A. Hammerton, *Humorists of the Pencil*, London: Hurst and Blackett, 1905, p. 32.

developed widely and in quality, the cartoonist (and the 'straight' illustrator) had no rival. Thereafter their precedence declined, in the face of cinema newsreels and, from the 1960s, of television.[8] Gould could give a face a particular expression, and so long as readers knew it was meant to be the prime minister, the resemblance could be minimal. Gould could concentrate on his cartoon's idea and on the metaphor conveying it – Balfour as Humpty Dumpty, for example (figure 10.1). The likeness was secondary. But one hundred years later, the balance has shifted. A cartoonist draws in the knowledge that readers can compare his version of the prime minister with the photo-realism of other media. The cartoonist's version needs a credibility which Gould did not have to worry about. This must be a significant complication. For, as later pages argue, cartoonists wish to depart from literal likeness just as much as in Gould's day. They want to express an 'inner' personality or to use the prime minister as a symbol. Yet they have to keep more closely in touch with the 'real' prime minister.

Readers came at length instinctively to expect a cartoon in their paper – but not, oddly, if they read a broadsheet. Only from the 1960s did the broadsheets, diversifying and brightening their contents, take political cartoons as seriously as had Lord Beaverbrook, say, in the mid-century heyday of his middle-market *Daily Express*, *Sunday Express* and London *Evening Standard*. By the 1990s the majority of imaginative and celebrated cartoonists were to be found in the *Guardian*, the *Independent*, the *Daily Telegraph* and *The Times*, and in their Sunday counterparts. The artists gained space and a more educated readership, but at the cost of reduced penetration. At the beginning of the new millennium, 'Mac' (Stan McMurtry) reached in the tabloid *Daily Mail* as many readers as the combined stable of nine or ten regulars on *The Times*, the *Daily Telegraph*, the *Guardian* and the *Independent*.

Prime Ministers in Cartoon

If Tony Blair asked for the original of all the national newspaper cartoons in which he appeared, he would need a stadium-sized lavatory (a

---

[8]   Television, for a decade or so, provided a hugely popular direct rival in the form of the satirical series *Spitting Image*, which used latex puppets of politicians and celebrities. First broadcast in February 1984, it became the inspiration for similar programmes worldwide. But the scripts had their roots in TV comedy traditions owing more to music hall, light comedy and revue than to the conventions of political cartooning. At its peak, *Spitting Image* attracted an audience greater than the readership of all daily papers except the *Sun* and the *Daily Mirror*.

Figure 10.1: *Humpty Dumpty up to date. Francis Carruthers Gould,* Westminster Gazette, *25 January 1905.*

Gould's imagery is instantly recognizable a century later, even if his cartoon's subject is not. One of the most familiar of all nursery rhymes is used to show the dangerous position of the Conservative prime minister (1902–5), Arthur Balfour. Balfour's government was drastically split on the issue of free trade and was defeated at the 1905 general election. He himself tried to avoid commitment – so the cartoon combines Humpty Dumpty with a second familiar image, 'sitting on the fence'.

conventional place for celebrities to hang them). He featured in more than 300 cartoons in 1998; and many others made allusion to him without including him in the drawing. This total is one in five – surely much more than for anyone else. In the broadsheet papers, as table 10.1 shows, the total is one in four. In the tabloids he appeared in fewer than one in ten, confirming the impression that tabloid cartoons are more likely to be illustrated jokes and wisecracks, which rely less on caricature or complex imagery. A few broadsheet cartoonists put Blair into forty per cent or more of their drawings.[9]

[9] In general elections, as one might expect, the focus on the prime minister and opposition leader is even greater. In the 1997 election, for example, twenty-nine per cent of

Table 10.1 *Cartoons of Tony Blair 1998: broadsheet and tabloid papers*

Cartoonist	Paper	Broadsheet Total cartoons	% depicting Blair
Bell	Guardian	159	22
Brookes	The Times	223	27
Brown	Independent/ Ind. on Sunday	66	24
Garland	D. Telegraph	163	32
Heath	Observer	52	6
Priestley	Independent	132	6
Riddell	Observer	49	22
Rowson	Guardian	77	29
Scarfe	Sunday Times	43	21
Schrank	Ind. on Sunday	64	40
Trog	S. Telegraph	49	43
Willson	Times/S. Times	55	56
Total		1132	26

Cartoonist	Paper	Tabloid Total cartoons	% depicting Blair
Gaskill	Sun	91	10
Griffin	Sun/D. Mirror	73	12
Johnston	D. Mirror	86	15
Mac	D. Mail	144	3
Thomas	D. Express	109	6
Total		503	9
Total broadsheet and tabloid		1635	21

Note: Totals are probably incomplete. Period is 1 January–31 December 1998.
Source: University of Kent Cartoon Centre Database. For a note about the Cartoon Centre, see the end of this chapter.

Blair's prominence in 1998 gains perspective from a comparison with John Major's last twelve months as prime minister and with the attention paid to Blair and William Hague as opposition leaders (table 10.2). Major was cartooned the most frequently – three cartoons for every two of Blair as prime minister. Indeed Blair appeared almost as often when opposition leader in 1996–7 as in 1998 when prime minister. But the most dramatic measure of all three party leaders' dominance in table

cartoons featured John Major. The majority of these also included Tony Blair. Colin Seymour-Ure, 'What future for the British political cartoon?', *Journalism Studies*, 2.3, 2001, p. 340.

Table 10.2   *Cartoons of government and opposition members, 1996–7, 1998*

Total cartoons, 1996–7 % depicting:				Total cartoons, 1998 % depicting:			
PM (Major)	30	Oppn leader (Blair)	20	PM (Blair)	21	Oppn leader (Hague)	6
Clarke	7	Prescott	4	Brown	6	Thatcher	2
Heseltine	5	Cook	3	Cook	5	Heseltine	1
15 others	15	12 others	8	Prescott	4	13 others	5
				18 others	12		

Notes
Numbers are of depictions, not of cartoons: more than one person may appear in a single cartoon.
   Total number of cartoons 10 May 1996–10 May 1997: 1828. 1 January–31 December 1998: 1726.
Source: University of Kent Cartoon Centre Database.

10.2 is the contrast with their colleagues. Each was depicted four or five times as often as even their most senior colleagues, such as Chancellors of the Exchequer and deputy prime ministers. Major and Blair featured more often in 1996–7 than all their cabinet and shadow cabinet colleagues together. Blair did not achieve quite the same predominance as prime minister, nor William Hague as opposition leader. In fact Hague and his entire team were comparatively inconspicuous – and might well have taken Harold Macmillan's remark to heart. Margaret Thatcher, eight years into retirement, actually appeared in more cartoons than any of Hague's shadow cabinet.

   Corresponding figures for earlier prime ministers are not readily available. But the long run of cartoons by Nick Garland (figure 10.2) for the *Daily Telegraph* and the *Independent*, catalogued by the University of Kent Cartoon Centre, does allow comparison with Margaret Thatcher. Over more than ten years in office, she appeared in a quarter of his cartoons. In table 10.3 these are divided into the periods when she faced different opposition leaders. James Callaghan, the first, appeared only one-third as often as she did; Michael Foot and Neil Kinnock did rather better. None did as well as Blair in opposition, but each did much better than Hague. Thatcher's dominance over her colleagues, shown in table 10.4, is both consistent and at a similar level to that of her successors. In each parliament, five cabinet colleagues were depicted ten times or more, compared with around 250 for herself. Seven ministers during her first parliament managed only twenty-five cartoon appearances between them, and nine did not appear at all. In her last parliament the non-appearers were even more numerous. From start to finish of her

TEAM SPIRIT

Figure 10.2: *Team spirit. Nicholas Garland,* Daily Telegraph, *9 October 1991.*

Garland uses an image from one of the cartoonist's staple categories – sport – to high-light divisions in the Conservative government about European policy. John Major, in office less than a year, fumbles the ball, while former prime minister Edward Heath tackles Margaret Thatcher – a member of his own team. Heath and Thatcher enjoyed famously bad relations, especially over Europe. Chris Patten and Norman Lamont, min-isterial colleagues, look helplessly on. To fit the rugby image, Garland had somewhat to 'masculinize' Thatcher, which he manages neatly with the headband. In a few lines round the eye and mouth, he also conveys economically Major's general uncertainty of touch.
Copyright Telegraph Group Limited 1991.

Table 10.3   *Mrs Thatcher and opposition leaders, 1979–90: cartoons by Garland*

| Dates | Cartoons depicting: | | | | Total cartoons |
	Prime minister	%	Opposition leader	%	
3 May 1979–2 November 1980	Thatcher	29	Callaghan	10	271
3 November 1980–1 October 1983	Thatcher	23	Foot	17	590
2 October 1983–28 November 1990	Thatcher	24	Kinnock	15	1599
Average		25		15	2460

Notes
The cartoons were published in the *Daily Telegraph*, except for the period September 1986–January 1991 when they were published in the *Independent*.
    The three time periods are differentiated by changes in the opposition leader.
Source: University of Kent Cartoon Centre Database.

Table 10.4 *Mrs Thatcher and cabinet colleagues, 1979–83 and 1987–90: cartoons by Garland*

3 May 1979–10 June 1983			1 May 1987–28 November 1990		
	Cartoons			Cartoons	
Minister	Number	%	Minister	Number	%
Thatcher	251	29	Thatcher	236	29
Howe	69	8	Lawson	53	6
Whitelaw	40	5	Howe	49	6
Joseph	24	3	Hurd	26	3
Pym	16	2	Major	24	3
Carrington	10	1	Baker	17	2
7 others	25	3	11 others	38	5
9 others	Nil	–	18 others	Nil	–
Total cartoons	852			823	

Notes

Numbers are of depictions, not of separate cartoons. The dates cover the full period of Mrs Thatcher's premierships.

The cartoons were published in the national daily and Sunday press.

The maximum size of the cabinet was twenty-three.

Geoffrey Howe was the only cabinet survivor from the start to near the end, apart from Mrs Thatcher herself.

Source: University of Kent Cartoon Centre Database.

premiership, Mrs Thatcher outscored the combined appearances of her entire cabinet.

Going back further, the computer database does not allow systematic comparison, but there is enough in table 10.5 to suggest that a strong focus on the prime minister is nothing new. For example, Vicky (Victor Weisz), an acknowledged influence on Garland, featured Harold Macmillan, whom he famously drew as 'Supermac', on much the same scale as Garland drew Mrs Thatcher. David Low, by comparison, drew Winston Churchill much less during World War II. This was no doubt because Low concentrated on bashing the enemy: he drew Mussolini as much as Churchill, and Hitler nearly three times as often.[10] Before the war, in contrast, Low featured Neville Chamberlain quite frequently.

The star of table 10.5 is the Edwardian prime minister (1902–5) Arthur Balfour. Francis Carruthers Gould put him into more than half

[10] Leslie Illingworth, similarly, drew for the *Daily Mail* 309 cartoons that included Hitler between 1939 and 1945, but only 141 that included Churchill. Mark Bryant, unpublished Ph.D. thesis, University of Kent at Canterbury.

Table 10.5 *Prime Ministers in cartoon: selected prime ministers and cartoonists, 1903–63*

Prime minister (dates)	Cartoonist	Total cartoons	% depicting prime minister
Macmillan (1957–63)	Vicky (Victor Weisz)	1889	29
Churchill (1940–5)	Low	728	6
Chamberlain (1937–40)	Low	413	17
Balfour (1902–5)	FCG (F. Carruthers Gould)	304	55

Note: The cartoons cover the full period of each premiership, except for the first five months of Balfour's.
Source: University of Kent Cartoon Centre Database and Library.

the 300 cartoons analysed. Gould is included here as the historic benchmark. The cartoons are taken from his annual anthologies, which almost certainly overrepresented the prime minister. None the less, prime ministers clearly have been a – probably the – principal rogue in the cartoonist's gallery for as long as there have been cartoons in the national press.

In our own time, this prominence is not at all surprising, if only on the basis of claims that the prime minister so dominates the political scene as to be an unofficial president. But why the prominence in Gould's time, when the prime minister's position bore more resemblance than now to the term 'first among equals'? The answer may be that cartoonists find it useful for their own purposes to concentrate on prime ministers, irrespective of whether the result accurately reflects their importance.

Partly this concentration means no more than that cartoonists see the prime minister as a convenient symbol of his or her government. They can concentrate on developing a successful version of this one person, without having to worry much about versions of his colleagues. So familiar do the cartoon versions become, moreover, that it is surprising to learn that cartoonists have sometimes found the human versions unpromising material. Even now, surely, anybody can evoke Hitler just by drawing a smudge with a diagonal line over it. Yet David Low claimed Hitler had a dull and featureless face.[11] The trenchant *Daily Express* cartoonist Michael Cummings claimed that Harold Wilson was rarely drawn before becoming prime minister in 1964, 'because his face

[11] 'Whatever you do with his face his physiognomy is essentially weak to draw.' David Low, 'The cartoonist's job in war', *The Listener*, 2 December 1939.

had about as much variety as the underside of a soup plate'.[12] When Edward Heath became Conservative Leader, 'no one knew anything about him, outside political circles', writes Gerald Scarfe; but as prime minister, 'events began to influence his public persona'. Scarfe could draw him as Concorde or a cracked egg – and leave no one in doubt about who he was.[13] Part of Vicky's distinction, in Garland's view, lay in his ability to break down a face and construct a cartoon version – so that other cartoonists often took their lead from him.[14]

The symbolism of the cartoon prime minister, however, goes far beyond being the representative of a whole government. He will also be used to personify issues and attitudes which the cartoonist attributes to that government. The prime minister may be wisdom and decency personified, but if his government behaves foolishly or brutally, foolish and brutal he will be drawn. This is why a cartoonist can say, as Low characteristically put it, that 'often people do not look like themselves', or, to quote Cummings again, that 'we must make the politicians in our image rather than theirs'.[15]

Cartoonists thus frequently go beyond the tweaking and simplifying of faces and physique required in an easy likeness. Instead, they work away at a prime minister's image, with the aim of making it express their view of his character and the wisdom or morality of anything from his government's entire credo to the details of some ephemeral row. It is here that the ambiguities of the cartoon medium come into play. There are two extremes in the relation between the depiction of the prime minister as a symbol and the stuff of what he symbolizes, and there is a wide area of variation between them. At either end or in between, there may be uncertainty about the cartoonist's intentions: how far is his cartoon about the prime minister personally, and how far about something he symbolizes?

At one extreme, the prime minister – his character or behaviour – *is* the stuff at issue. For example, Steve Bell's device of showing John Major wearing underpants outside his trousers was intended as a comment on Major's general uselessness. Brookes achieved a compa-

---

[12] Michael Cummings, *On the Point of My Pen*, Portsmouth, Hants: Milestone Publications, 1985, p. 6. Alec Douglas-Home, Wilson's immediate predecessor as prime minister, spoke to Cummings about how difficult he too must be to caricature, not least because of the smallness of his chin. Cummings, Foreword to Michael Wynn Jones, *The Cartoon History of Britain*, London: Tom Stacey, 1971, p. 12.

[13] Gerald Scarfe, *Line of Attack*, London: Hamish Hamilton, 1988, p. 12.

[14] Interview with Nicholas Garland, March 2002.

[15] David Low, *Ye Madde Designer*, London: The Studio, 1935, p. 52; Michael Cummings, in Wynn Jones, *The Cartoon History of Britain*, p. 11.

ALL BEHIND YOU, WINSTON

Figure 10.3: *All behind you, Winston. David Low,* Evening Standard, *14 May 1940.*
Churchill replaced Neville Chamberlain as prime minister four days before this cartoon was published. Dunkirk and the blitz lay ahead. Low uses a 'flying wedge' of politicians to convey a sense of power, reinforcing the shirt-sleeved resolution of the new, 'national unity' government. Churchill, whose politics Low previously disliked (except on the question of European fascism), is already taking on a bulldog appearance. Beside him stride three Labour leaders, Attlee, Bevin and Morrison. Chamberlain is behind, to the left of a mixed group of Conservatives, Liberals and Labour.
Copyright Atlantic Syndication Partners.

rable effect of vacuousness by leaving Major's eyes blank behind his spectacles. During the Falklands War of 1982, 'masculinized images' of Mrs Thatcher increased alongside perceptions of her as 'a forceful, decisive leader of fighting men'.[16] Cartoon images of Churchill in World War II, similarly, emphasized qualities such as indomitability, which implicitly were attributed both to himself and to the British people. (See the heroic formation in figure 10.3.)

At the other extreme, the cartoonist wishes to comment on an issue or event with which in truth the prime minister may have had little if

[16] Christine Musk, *Platinum Lady, Iron Man?*, unpublished draft MA thesis, deposited in University of Kent Cartoon Archive, 1994, p. 51.

anything to do. Yet because it is the prime minister's government, he is the focus. At this extreme, cartoon versions of a prime minister may thus be more flexible. In the words of Gerald Scarfe, 'a character may appear a tyrant in one drawing, a weakling in another'. When Mrs Thatcher's popularity declined, the masculinized images mentioned above gave way to 'stereotypical sexist images'.[17]

The gentlemanly Francis Carruthers Gould said he was concerned 'only with the politics of a statesman, and with his personality only as far as it is inseparable from his political career'.[18] Would that the distinction were so simple. Gould may have intended to attack policy, not personality. But how can we necessarily detect the difference in the drawing itself, if people are drawn (as Gould typically drew them) as foxes or donkeys? If a policy is asinine, should not the reader believe the policy-maker is an ass?

Cartoonists, in summary, focus heavily on prime ministers both for the obvious reason that they are the single most important politicians of their day, and also because they can be used as flexible symbols of wider issues and attitudes. Having devised their prime ministerial likeness, cartoonists then apply it to, or embellish it with, an array of metaphors and images. The methods they use can now be explored.

The Cartoonist's Armoury

Likenesses themselves are created by exaggeration, distortion and simplification. Part of the trick is to find the best features for the purpose. With Macmillan it proved to be his moustache; with Wilson, bags under his eyes. With Major it was a distinctive lip: you can trace its development in Steve Bell's anthologies. Some cartoonists, such as Brookes in *The Times*, also picked on Major's hairstyle and thick-framed spectacles. With Blair, prominent ears and a toothy smile became dominant features. William Hague was diminished, as an inexperienced leader of a weak opposition, by being drawn much too short and schoolboyish. Alec Douglas-Home, unexpectedly thrust into office by Macmillan's illness in 1963, was similarly diminished (by Vicky in particular) through depiction as a sticklike figure. Mrs Thatcher's force of character was often indicated by a sharp nose. Bell later gave her a manic, circular eye (her 'psychotic glint') – an expression he eventually gave to Blair too.

---

[17]   Gerald Scarfe, *Scarfe by Scarfe*, London: Hamish Hamilton, 1986, unpaginated; Musk, *Platinum Lady, Iron Man?*.
[18]   Quoted, Hammerton, *Humorists of the Pencil*, p. 26.

David Low wrote of such conventions in an evocative phrase as 'tabs of identity'.[19] They condense a likeness, and often aspects of personality too, into a few telling features. These are not necessarily parts of the body. Gladstone was recognizable by his collar, Neville Chamberlain by his umbrella, Thatcher by her handbag. Churchill, during his fifty-year political career, was labelled successively by headgear (with his connivance), cigars, the V-sign and a bulldog expression (as wartime prime minister); and, as elder statesman, by his penchant for the flamboyant robes of a Knight of the Garter.[20]

The outstanding tab of identity in the 1990s was John Major's cellular Y-front underpants. What on earth will later generations make of them? Steve Bell relentlessly drew them worn outside the prime minister's trousers (figure 10.4). Bell describes the idea's origins as a mixture of Superman (who wore sleek briefs over tights) and hearsay about Major tucking his shirt inside his underpants. He had already drawn Major as 'Superuselessman', and the shirt/pants relationship struck him as an apt sign of stupidity. Bell's citation for a cartoon award in 1993 claimed the image had 'all but become the universal standard'.[21] If the implication is that it was widely copied, this is not true: cartoonists probably respected its originality too much to borrow it.[22] But the image became common knowledge (just like Low's reactionary character Colonel Blimp), and there were rival claims about who inspired it. Bell's genius elaborated it with wonderful imagination. The pants could turn Major into something else, such as a self-propelled rocket launcher. Or they could detach themselves from him altogether, while remaining an instant means of identification – even when appearing in the form of a tugboat, tea strainer, hammock, nosebag, tennis net, parachute or Christmas stocking.[23]

Tabs of identity thus not only identify the cartoon prime minister, but in addition they help a cartoonist stretch the metaphorical circumstances into which he may be placed. If a cartoonist wishes to show him 'behaving like a pig', he can simply put the prime minister in a pigsty.

---

[19] David Low, *Ye Madde Designer*, p. 18.

[20] Harold Nicolson, introduction to Fred Urquhart, *W. S. C.: a Cartoon Biography*, London: Cassell, 1955, pp. viii–ix.

[21] Quoted by Anthony Seldon in *Major: a Political Life*, London: Phoenix, 1998, p. 204.

[22] 'That fellow,' David Low recalls the caricaturist E. T. Reed complaining to him about a colleague, 'he's a thief. He stole my Winston's [Churchill] eye.' *Low's Autobiography*, London: Michael Joseph, 1956, p. 146.

[23] Bell's account of the development of the underpants is in Steve Bell, *Bell's Eye*, London: Methuen, 1999, pp. 110–11. The pants are also anthologized in Steve Bell and Simon Hoggart, *Live Briefs*, London: Methuen, 1996.

Figure 10.4: *Election 97. Steve Bell,* Guardian, *4 February 1997.*

Unlike the imagery of Gould's Humpty Dumpty cartoon (figure 1), Bell's depiction of John Major wearing cellular underpants over his trousers may take some explaining to later generations. The image was intended to suggest the prime minister's inability quite to get the hang of things. It proved a highly flexible device. In this example, Major hopes the pants will launch him like a rocket into the 1997 general election campaign. On polling day, 1 May, Major's party suffered a catastrophic defeat.
Copyright Steve Bell.

Alternatively, he can draw the prime minister literally as a pig – but still recognizable as himself. It is in this latter case, especially, that strong tabs of identity help us to recognize whom we are looking at.

Making people look like animals is one of the oldest types of cartoon image. The art historian Ernst Gombrich called it the 'political bestiary'.[24] 'I saw Wilson as a crafty old warty toad, puffing and swelling with self-congratulatory pleasure,' wrote Gerald Scarfe. 'Thatcher was a pterodactyl, razor-sharp beak, swooping down onto her victims with leather wings and blood-red talons. John Major was a dull grey tortoise trudging slowly through the mire of unpopularity.'[25] A common image

[24] E. H. Gombrich, 'The Cartoonist's Armoury', *Meditations on a Hobby Horse*, London: Phaidon, 3rd edn, 1978, pp. 127–42.
[25] Caption notes for a National Portrait Gallery touring exhibition of Scarfe's work, 2000–1.

Figure 10.5: *'Oh look, he's dreaming!' Chris Riddell, Observer, 4 August 2002.*
Riddell, who often uses animal imagery, draws Tony Blair as President George W. Bush's poodle, in a lather of curls and ringlets. Blair had slavishly followed Bush's aggressive line towards Iraq – hence the vicious claws. But in his sleep the poodle dreams of a world where he is boss. This dream-bubble Blair is no poodle. To help us recognize him in back view, Riddell uses the familiar Blair ears as a tab of identity. Note the naked, kneeling figurine of Bush on Blair's shirt cuff. Riddell has mimicked press photos of Blair's vacation outfit, which featured a designer shirt with tasteful nudes on the cuffs. This is the kind of topical detail which can enrich a cartoon but quickly fades.
Copyright Chris Riddell.

for Blair, until his tougher side emerged, was the wide-eyed Disney fawn, Bambi. The bestiary had been a favourite device of Carruthers Gould. Peter Brookes was making a speciality of it in *The Times* a hundred years later, and so, to some extent, was Chris Riddell (figure 10.5).[26]

Other kinds of conventional imagery are categorized in table 10.6. Cartoonists have sought metaphors in occupations, inanimate objects, everyday images and figures of speech, history, literature and the visual arts. Not only do they copy well-known pictures and statues (Rembrandt's *The Anatomy Lesson*, Rodin's *The Thinker*); they do pastiches

[26] See, for example, Brookes's anthologies, entitled *Nature Notes, Nature Notes: the New Collection* and *Nature Notes III*; London: Little, Brown, 1997, 1999, 2001.

Table 10.6   *Cartoon images of Tony Blair, 1 January–31 December 1998*

Type of image	Total different images	%	Total images	%
Common cultural reference	56	20	72	20
Occupational	30	11	56	16
Everyday image/Figure of speech	45	16	51	14
Everyday activity	40	14	44	12
Theatre/Literature/Visual arts	34	12	40	11
Sporting	18	7	25	7
Animal	17	6	23	7
Topical non-political events	14	5	18	5
Historical	14	5	14	4
Inanimate object	8	3	11	3
Total	276	100	354	100

Note: The categories overlap and so there is some double counting of cartoons. Percentages are rounded.
Source: University of Kent Cartoon Centre Database.

of famous predecessors such as Tenniel and Low. Inevitably these various categories overlap, so the figures in table 10.6 involve double counting. They list both the total number of images applied to Tony Blair in each category in 1998, and – since images recur – the number of different images. Roughly one-third of the images were used more than once; substantially more in the occupational category (lots of soldiers and doctors).

The commonest images (one in five) were *common cultural references*. Like common knowledge, which is 'what everyone knows everyone knows', these are images of anything in our culture from acrobats to zoos, passing cowboys and the man in the moon *en route*. The difference is narrow between these and another big group, *everyday images* – stabs in the back, heads in nooses, walking on air. With a third group, *occupational*, these two made up about half the 1998 total. Sporting images were numerous enough to have a category of their own. The frequency of *everyday activities* (shopping, driving, walking the dog) shows cartoonists emphasizing the underlying ordinariness of a prime minister. *Topical events* (showbiz awards, the World Cup) similarly place the non-political in a political context. Turning Blair into an inanimate object did not happen often, but it sometimes showed cartoonists at their most ingenious. Bell's drawing of Blair as an electricity pylon (figure 10.6) is an outstanding example. The table does not separate broadsheet and tabloid papers, since the distribution of images was

ECO-BLAIR STRIKES AGAIN

Figure 10.6: *Eco-Blair strikes again. Steve Bell, Guardian, 7 March 2001.*

The dot at the centre of the cartoon draws the reader's attention and turns into Blair's eye. Round it assemble the main features of the cartoon version of Blair's face: sticking-out ears and exposed teeth. Bell's success in encapsulating Blair so clearly within the skeleton of an electricity pylon is a mark of his skill. Never mind the context (an issue about the environment). This is a master cartoonist at work.
Copyright Steve Bell.

much the same. The exception, predictably, was the 'arts' category, which tabloid cartoonists used less often.

If cartoons rely on familiarity, enabling the reader to catch on quickly, then one should expect that much of their imagery will be traditional. 'Traditional' is a sufficiently vague term to mean that different people might score them differently. But perhaps as many as eighty per cent of the 1998 cartoons depicting Blair were drawing on the traditional (see table 10.7). They could have been used just as well a hundred years ago or more.[27] Few occupations, for instance, were 'modern', in the sense

[27] In his *Gladstone in Contemporary Caricature*, London: Review of Reviews, 1899, W. T. Stead reproduces cartoons showing Gladstone as (among other things) a lion, an ostrich, a chicken, a squid, a gardener, a policeman, a surgeon, a strongman, a stiltwalker, a statue, a comet, a whirligig, a Red Indian and Saint George.

Table 10.7 *Cartoon images of Tony Blair, 1 January–31 December 1998: traditional imagery*

Type of image	Traditional images		Total images
	Number	Percent	
Common cultural reference	61	85	72
Occupational	42	75	56
Everyday image/Figure of speech	43	84	51
Everyday activities	39	88	44
Theatre/Literature/Visual arts	27	68	40
Sporting	20	80	25
Historical	10	71	14
Inanimate objects	7	64	11
Total	249	80	313

Note: Omits 'animal' and 'topical non-political events'. For definition of terms, see text.
Source: University of Kent Cartoon Centre Database.

that, say, a computer scientist is modern. Some (wagon driver, huntsman) were positively archaic. Few everyday images had the topicality of 'fat cats', 'cloning' or even 'vandalism'; and 'modern' everyday activities, such as 'clubbing' and 'appearing on TV', were rarer still.

As one trawls through the cartoons, from which further examples are listed in table 10.8, it soon becomes plain how many of the images are more than traditional: they are clichés. A writer would have looked for something fresher. For a cartoonist, however, this is an advantage. His skill lies not in having hit upon the image in the first place, but in having found a fresh and graphic way of applying it. The tiredness typical of cliché can be avoided, while the usefulness of familiarity remains.

The categories in table 10.8 were selected chiefly, however, because they seem to tap into particularly deep and enduring associations. Many of the images, for instance, though very familiar, are beyond people's direct experience. They are halfway to fantasy already. How many people have played the bagpipes, rattled a skeleton, met a circus trainer or a cowboy or an executioner, heard a barrel organ, walked a tightrope, fondled a dove or been on a wild goose/pig chase? Even the schoolroom idea of a 'dunce' has no place in a world of dyslexia and Attention Deficit Disorder. These are activities and roles that are (in some cases always were) rare or uncommon, or are buried in myths of popular culture. For most of us they work principally in the imagination, and to that extent we have started to do the cartoonist's work of make-believe for him, before we even look at his cartoon.

Table 10.8 *Traditional imagery in cartoons of Tony Blair, 1 January–31 December 1998: selected categories and images*

Common cultural references	Everyday images/Figures of speech
Bagpipes	Puppet
Circus trainer	In (someone's) pocket
Dragon	Casting a shadow
Slave driver	Sitting on the fence
Gangster	Executioner
Acrobat	Knight on a charger
Cowboy	Walking on air
Chamber of Horrors	Beggar
Unicorn	Head in a noose
Court jester	Getting a bouquet
Man in the moon	Dunce
Leprechaun	Stab in the back
Britannia	Miracle worker
St Valentine's Day	Skeleton
Organ-grinder's monkey	Wild pig (goose) chase
Christmas	Looking into the abyss
Judgement of Solomon	Walking a tightrope
Huntsman	Dove of peace

Historical
Oliver Cromwell
Crusaders
French Revolution
Old Testament prophet
Samurai

Note: These are not complete lists. Some images are used repeatedly.
Source: University of Kent Cartoon Centre Database.

Not all the images have this largely figurative existence: Christmas is an inescapable reality, and the Chamber of Horrors in Madame Tussaud's museum is a major tourist attraction. But both these last examples illustrate an intriguing further point: they have a strong association with childhood. Many other examples can be found, mainly in the four categories listed in table 10.9. They are images less *of* childhood than of events, activities, persons, animals, plays, pictures and books, which become familiar *in* childhood and to the child's imagination, and which continue to resonate, often fondly, in adulthood. Nearly three-quarters of the 'common cultural references' and 'animal'

Table 10.9   *Cartoon images of Tony Blair, 1 January–31 December 1998: childhood imagery*

Type of image	Childhood images		Total images
	Number	Percent	
Common cultural reference	52	72	72
Theatre/Literature/ Visual arts	19	48	40
Animal	17	74	23
Historical	6	43	14
Totals	94	64	149

Note: Totals include repeated images: they are not of separate images. Some images appear in more than one category.
Source: University of Kent Cartoon Centre Database.

categories in 1998 were of this type, and not far from half of the other two types listed in the table. Many of them obviously also count as 'traditional', as can be seen in the specific examples in table 10.10. Here we have plainly entered a world of child's play and fabulists, laughter and tears, and simple moral judgements. It is a jumble of circuses, fun-fairs, party games; back-garden pets, creatures half-extinct (gorillas), half-imaginary (Godzilla) or wholly fantastic (Bugs Bunny); nursery rhymes, pantomimes, witches, cowboys and Indians; books and TV pro-grammes to lose yourself in (Alice, Sherlock Holmes, *Dr Who* and *ER*); and a cluster of 'every-schoolchild-knows' references to crusaders, French Revolutionaries, Oliver Cromwell and kamikaze pilots. Such a list could feature in an essay about myths of Britishness – or have formed a planning brief for the Millennium Dome.[28] It is a potent mixture – which reflects the fact that cartoonists choose such images precisely because people can engage with them so directly, when they are used to make a political point.[29]

[28]   Something similar did constitute a brief for the Hungarian immigrant Vicky, whose editor subjected him to 'a prolonged, patient process' of familiarization with Britain. This included *Alice*, Dickens, Shakespeare, cricket and football. Russell Davies and Liz Ottaway, *Vicky*, London: Secker and Warburg, 1987, pp. 38–9, quoting Gerald Barry, *Observer*, 27 February 1966.

[29]   Compare Jackie Wullschläger's comment on the nature of some of the best-loved Victorian and early twentieth-century children's literature: '[The] books are all great children's fantasies. Alice's Adventures in Wonderland and Through the Looking-Glass, Edward Lear's nonsense verses, Peter Pan, The Wind in the Willows, and the

Table 10.10   *Cartoons of Tony Blair, 1 January–31 December 1998. Childhood imagery: selected categories and images*

Common cultural references	Theatre/Literature/Visual arts
Computer games	Flash Gordon
Pop stars	Bugs Bunny
Cowboy	Godzilla
Egg-and-spoon race	Alice in Wonderland
Seesaw	Pop singers
Musical chairs	ER (TV series)
Witch	Sherlock Holmes
Big dipper	Jeremy Fisher (Beatrix Potter)
Dalek	Kipling
Juggler	The Owl and the Pussycat
Red Indian	Punch and Judy
Man in the moon	Cinderella

Animals	*Historical*
Rabbit	Crusader
Cat	Old Testament prophet
Pig	French Revolution
Squirrel	Kamikaze pilot
Sheepdog	Oliver Cromwell
Tortoise	
Cuckoo	
Fox	
Reindeer	
Tiger	
Gorilla	

Note: See table 10.9.
Source: University of Kent Cartoon Centre Database.

Winnie-the-Pooh stories are fabulous, mythical works set in bizarre, enchanted places and peopled by peculiar creatures such as nursery-rhyme characters, playing cards, toys, talking beasts and fairies . . . The fantastical worlds these writers created have a lasting power; Wonderland, Neverland, are physical, tangible realities from which it is hard to tear oneself away.' Jackie Wullschläger, *Inventing Wonderland*, London: Methuen, rev. edn, 2001, p. 3. It is worth pointing out, too, that John Tenniel, illustrator of the Alice books, and Ernest Shepard, illustrator of *The Wind in the Willows* and the Pooh books, both worked as principal editorial cartoonist for *Punch*. Contemporary cartoonists who have worked as children's book illustrators include John Jensen, Chris Riddell, Posy Simmonds and even, once, Martin Rowson.

What Affects how Cartoonists Use their Imagery?

His likenesses and his imagery comprise, in Gombrich's phrase, the cartoonist's armoury. Exactly how he uses it depends on the state of popular taste, the scope allowed by his newspaper, and his own feelings about prime ministers. The extent to which popular taste can change is sweepingly illustrated by the contrast between political cartoons of the late eighteenth and mid-nineteenth centuries. The bums and breasts of Gillray and Rowlandson gave way to Victorian modesty and discretion. Some of the most astonishing examples of the former, to twenty-first century eyes, depicted the Royal Family – defecating, farting, pleasuring their mistresses. Political leaders got the same treatment.[30]

The earliest twentieth-century newspaper cartoonists were still affected by this fastidiousness. Gould said, 'I etch with vinegar not vitriol', and he liked to quote Izaak Walton's advice to the angler: 'Put your worm on the hook as if you loved him'.[31] Haselden had 'two very plain obligations – firstly to amuse; secondly to do so without offending'.[32] In the 1920s these attitudes were becoming part of a more general blandness associated with the enormous circulations achieved by the popular press. For David Low – an irreverent New Zealander – mass circulation made cartooning soft. Cartoonists had to 'generalize their points until they practically disappear'. Facetiousness replaced 'the strong meat of satire'; caricature was 'emasculated and stultified'.[33] A prime example was the amiable George Strube, who seemed 'to translate the average opinion of the *Daily Express* reader with an aptness

---

[30]   See, for a variety of examples, Kenneth Baker's two anthologies: *The Prime Ministers*, London: Thames and Hudson, 1995; *The Kings and Queens*, London: Thames and Hudson, 1996. Victorian modesty was well illustrated right at the end of the period by a famous cartoon in the French satirical magazine, *Assiette au Beurre* (28 September 1901). A shameless Britannia ('L'impudique Albion') flaunts her bare buttocks – drawn to resemble the jowls of King Edward VII. After publication, the publishers pasted over the buttocks with a variety of patches. The occasion was French criticism of British use of concentration camps in the Boer War. R. J. Goldstein, *Censorship of Political Caricature in Nineteenth-Century France*, Kent, Ohio, and London: Kent State University Press, 1989, p. 251.
[31]   Quoted by Ann Gould in 'The picture-politics of Francis Carruthers Gould', *20th Century Studies*, 13/14, December 1975, pp. 26, 24.
[32]   W. K. Haselden, *Daily Mirror Reflections*, vol. II, London: Daily Mirror, 1909, pp. 1–2.
[33]   David Low, ' "These vulgar cartoons" ', *Evening Standard*, 20 December 1929; Foreword, H. R. Westwood, *Modern Caricaturists*, London: Lovat Dickson, 1932, p. xiv; *British Cartoonists, Caricaturists and Comic Artists*, London: Collins, 1942, p. 43.

and an accuracy which a mere writer of articles could hardly hope to emulate'.[34]

Politicians and proprietors certainly continued to see papers as important political weapons, but it is true that they were 'depoliticized' in comparison with the late Victorian papers for which Gould worked. Their cartoonists were encouraged to concentrate on entertainment and avoid giving offence. They still did so in the decades after World War II, even while party divisions were comparatively wide. For instance Stanley Franklin, recruited to the Labour *Daily Mirror* in 1959, was instructed to take 'a more light and humorous approach' than his partisan predecessor, Vicky. He did so, there and at the *Sun*, for nearly forty years. Similarly JAK (Raymond Jackson), political cartoonist for the London *Evening Standard* from 1966 to 1997, told an interviewer in 1994: 'The *Evening Standard* is a very moral paper, and I can't do some of the things I see other cartoonists doing.'[35] One result of this light approach was that the mass circulation cartoonists usually did not – and still do not – expect to have decisive control over their cartoon's content. They drew a selection of 'roughs', from which the editor made a choice.

By the start of the new millennium, the tabloid press was freely cartooning the Royal Family again – but with a decorum which showed that the wheel of taste had not come full circle since the uninhibited eighteenth century. Cartoonists on the broadsheet papers were given more freedom. Gerald Scarfe and Ralph Steadman were the pioneers, taking advantage of the relaxation of social conventions in the 1960s. Scarfe, significantly, proved too 'strong' for the mass circulation *Daily Mail* and flourished on a weekly broadsheet, the *Sunday Times*. Steadman drew mostly for magazines. Not until the confrontational politics of the Thatcher era, therefore, did the daily broadsheet cartoonists push the boundaries of taste much closer to Gillray and Rowlandson. At the *Guardian*, Steve Bell, followed by Martin Rowson, reintroduced scatological imagery, some of which made Bell's motif of Major's underpants look positively salubrious – perhaps because the underpants were used for so many things apart from underpants. Garland at the *Daily Telegraph*, or Brookes at *The Times*, could not have got away with such images. Garland, in a rare (and therefore celebrated) example, had a cartoon rejected by his editor because it showed Mrs Thatcher with her knickers round her ankles.

---

[34] H. R. Westwood, *Modern Caricaturists*, p. 28.
[35] Stanley Franklin interview, *Political Cartoon Society Newsletter*, Autumn 2001, p. 2. JAK quoted in John Harvey, *Stiletto in the Ink*, Reuter Foundation Paper No. 8, Oxford: Green College, 1994, p. 14.

The limitations imposed on the cartoonist's armoury by 'taste', then, vary both between and within the different types of paper. The chief influences are the make-up of the readership and the preferences of the proprietor or editor. Within this context, the cartoonist can follow his inclinations. Broadly, cartoonists have tended to be either herbivorous or carnivorous – nice or nasty. One may use imprecise words for these distinctions, because the judgements involved are so subjective. Sometimes cartoonists themselves believe they are the one, but are thought by their victims to be the other. Low thought himself a herbivore, but Baldwin thought him 'evil and malicious' and Churchill called him 'a green-eyed young antipodean radical'.[36] Cummings may have thought himself more benign – certainly more even-handed – than his drawings suggest, for there was a sneer in his line and his imagery could be vicious. (The example in figure 10.7 shows him at his most benign.)

Judgements about niceness and nastiness can be made, firstly, on the evidence of the cartoonist's apparent sympathy or hostility towards the subject of his drawing; secondly, on the evidence of his imagery (is it cruel? unfair? shocking?); and thirdly on the evidence of his line. The inherent ambiguities of the first and second have been discussed earlier. But for the present purpose the third is especially difficult to assess, not least because emotions (including laughter and anger) can be produced by the drawing as well as by the image itself. Thus a Gould crocodile, though unmistakable, looks absurd rather than vicious, just because of the way it is drawn. Most of Low's wild animals, too, while making their point (a tiger striped with swastikas, for instance), are at the soft-toy end of the scale. So, in our own generation, are those of Chris Riddell and Peter Brookes. The same imagery, from another artist, such as the young Gerald Scarfe, could be cruel and ugly.

The potential for nastiness is increased by the 'deniability' inherent in a cartoon's dependence on metaphor: 'No, I didn't mean that comparison literally, and I didn't mean it personally either.' The potential is increased yet further by the cartoon's inability to argue. For the main way in which cartoons can indicate strength of opinion is by strength of imagery. An image may seem 'unfair', because the cartoonist has exaggerated it in order to show the extent of his outrage. Or he may choose an obscene or disgusting image as a measure of contempt and dislike for the person depicted. 'Stripped down to its essentials', writes Rowson, 'I think all humour can be defined as laughing at farting and

[36] Baldwin's remark is reported in Arthur Christiansen, *Headlines All My Life*, London: Heinemann. 1961, p. 155. Churchill's description of Low is in Winston Churchill, 'Cartoons and cartoonists', *Strand Magazine*, June 1931, p. 588, reprinted in Churchill, *Thoughts and Adventures*, London: Macmillan, 1932.

Figure 10.7: *The empties. Michael Cummings,* Daily Express, *14 May 1978.*

The prime minister as milk bottle. Cummings uses an everyday image – 'putting out the empties' – which has become less familiar with the decline of home milk delivery. But readers would have known exactly what he meant and who the politicians were. Even though he does not have the whole face to work with, Cummings's deftness makes James Callaghan (prime minister), Denis Healey (Chancellor of the Exchequer), Michael Foot (leader of the Commons) and Tony Benn (Energy secretary) instantly recognizable. Callaghan had no obvious tabs of identity, unlike Benn, whose staring eyes neatly symbolized for critics his 'loony left' policies. (Later, a psychologist discovered that Benn had a lower blink rate than most orators. Max Atkinson, Our Masters' Voices, *London: Methuen, 1984, pp. 91–2.)*
Copyright Express Newspapers.

the people you hate.'[37] Wally Fawkes (Trog) makes a good distinction between imagery about what comes out of the top half of a politician and imagery about what comes out of the bottom.[38] Rowson, clearly, enjoys being a below-the-belt carnivore. Trog, in contrast, always stayed above the belt, following in the path of his mentor at the *Daily Mail*, Leslie Illingworth.

[37]   Martin Rowson, 'Seriously funny', *Index on Censorship*, 6, 2000, p. 25.
[38]   Interview with the author, May 2001.

Illingworth had 'as much interest in politics as I have in thermodynamics', a colleague remarked; and he mistrusted 'zealots of any party or persuasion'.[39] But he could draw beautifully (he trained at the Royal College of Art), capture a likeness and be funny. He was thus herbivorous by all three measures – sympathy, imagery and line. He was a classic mass-circulation cartoonist of the post-1945 era. Trog, on the other hand, was strongly committed politically: he remained firmly anti-Conservative throughout his long career. In this respect Trog exemplifies the fact that cartoonists can be herbivores in one way and carnivores in another. The majority, probably, have been herbivorous in their imagery and style, but many (like Trog) have been carnivorous in their opinions. Illingworth was not personally partisan, but he was perfectly content to draw anti-Labour cartoons at the *Daily Mail*.

Cartoonists do seem to be more comfortable when they can draw against somebody or something. What happens, then, when their favourites are in office? One possibility is that they just trudge uncomfortably on. Low wrote in 1932 that a satirist has no moral obligation to his fellows but to throw bricks at them.[40] But when he found himself cartooning, after 1945, a Labour government with which he was in broad sympathy, he fretted. So uncomfortable was he at the Labour-controlled mass-circulation *Daily Herald*, to which he moved in 1949 for a change of scene, that he soon resigned.[41] Vicky, in the same way, had much more fun attacking Harold Macmillan than Harold Wilson.

Cartoonists are not normally so loyal to a party, however, that their urge to criticize is stifled. Herbivores criticize without causing their victims offence. Carnivores go on crunching anyway. Cummings, whose opinions were strongly anti-Labour (for instance about trade unions), regarded himself as not attached to any label – 'Right, Left, Centre or anything else'. Gerald Scarfe told an interviewer, 'The whole point of employing political cartoonists is that they make a statement and are not there to support the line of the paper.'[42] In the 1990s cartoonists on

[39] Quoted in Draper Hill, *Illingworth on Target*, Boston, Mass.: Boston Public Library, 1970, p. 9.
[40] Foreword to H. R. Westwood, *Modern Caricaturists*, p. x.
[41] For a time in the 1930s the *Daily Herald* had the largest circulation of national daily papers – more than two million. It was relaunched as the *Sun* in 1964 and sold to Rupert Murdoch in 1969. Low moved to the *(Manchester) Guardian* in 1950. Will Dyson, an Australian carnivore who started drawing anti-capitalist cartoons for the *Daily Herald* before World War I, left the paper in 1921 for similar reasons to Low's. John Jensen, *Will Dyson*, Canterbury: University of Kent for the Australian High Commission, the University of Kent and Kent County Council, 1996, p. 24.
[42] Michael Cummings, Foreword to *These Uproarious Years*, London: MacGibbon and Kee, 1954; Scarfe quoted in John Harvey, *Stiletto in the Ink*, p. 13.

all sides took advantage of the scope for attacking John Major's weak and accident-prone government. Blair, in his turn, found himself attacked caustically by the left-wing *Guardian* cartoonists Steve Bell and Martin Rowson after 1997. 'In my time', wrote Rowson, 'I've drawn, I hope, some truly cruel, offensive and totally unfair cartoons of British and international politicians.'[43]

Rowson's provocative comment does not suggest going to absolute extremes. He would agree with the counterclaim, widely endorsed by cartoonists, that (as Low put it) malice clouds the judgement and 'brutality almost invariably defeats itself'.[44] Mockery and ridicule are more effective. Propagandist cartoonists do not fit national daily papers. They risk being counter-productive, through predictability and losing their sense of proportion. Thus Dyson, a deeply committed socialist, was much happier on the infant *Daily Herald* in 1912, when it was a propaganda sheet, than after he returned in the 1930s. He found it had become a bourgeois mass-circulation paper – and it wanted him to be funnier. Vicky, in the 1960s, was arguably at his weakest in occasional cartoons drawn in his so-called 'Oxfam style'. These sentimentalized Third World issues in images of abject poverty and despair. In the London *Evening Standard* they jarred.[45] Once again Gould, the pioneer, sums up the argument in words which would be equally applicable a century later: 'a cartoon pushed beyond legitimate lines does more harm than good to a cause.'[46]

Cartoon Effects

What can prime ministers do about cartoons? Cartoons face them with criticism which is eye-catching, instantly understood (or misunderstood), emotive, often funny; and which is also – as they may see it – rude, oversimplified, unfair, impossible to contradict, and of uncertain but potentially worrying influence over readers.

There are three alternative reactions. The simplest is a real or simulated disdain. John Major is quoted as saying of Bell's underpants image, 'It is intended to destabilize me and so I ignore it'. His biographer, even

---

[43] Martin Rowson, 'Seriously funny', *Index on Censorship*, 6, 2000, pp. 25–6.
[44] David Low, *Ye Madde Designer*, pp. 11–12. Correspondence with Martin Rowson, February 2002.
[45] Cf. Russell Davies and Liz Ottaway, *Vicky*, London: Secker and Warburg, 1987, pp. 60–1.
[46] Gould, unpublished autobiography, quoted in Ann Gould, 'The picture-politics of Francis Carruthers Gould', p. 24.

so, claims that it was 'most unpleasant and offensive to him'.[47] Edward Heath, asked why his collection of originals included no unfavourable cartoons, remarked: 'I can't think of any. If they were unfair, I would not remember them'. Mrs Thatcher, too, was said to be impervious: hostile cartoons 'never got to her – probably because she never saw them'.[48] Such comments are of a piece with the claims by some prime ministers, Attlee being a much quoted example, that they never bothered to read the papers. Nor do prime ministerial memoirs usually have anything to add.

Those disclaimers sound unconvincing. Other comments suggest a more human mixture of resignation, grumbling and even a perverse satisfaction. As Churchill pointed out, years before he was in Downing Street, cartoons are an index of a politician's importance.[49] Prime ministers are surely bound to be curious about how, and how often, they are depicted. Echoing Macmillan's remark about it being better to be laughed at than ignored, Gerald Scarfe observed fiercely that politicians 'would rather be drawn as a yellow gob of phlegm hanging on a barbed wire fence than ignored'.[50] It is a short step from curiosity to collecting – which is an index of politicians' vanity. Robert Peel was one of the earliest and most eager collectors. There can be few prime ministers who have accumulated none. 'I propose to have this framed and kept where I shall see it constantly,' wrote Ramsay MacDonald to David Low, thanking him for an original in 1932.[51] Whether it had been solicited or not is unrecorded. But comparable letters must have been written often across the decades.

Churchill's own vanity was touched to the quick in old age by a rare documented example of a cartoon causing a prime minister distress. Illingworth drew for Punch, at the editor's request, a caricature which mocked the pretence that the 79-year-old prime minister was fit for office. The drawing looks gentle enough now, but it seemed carnivorous to traditionalist readers at the time. 'The eyes were dull and lifeless,' Churchill's doctor, Lord Moran, noted. 'There was no tone in the flaccid muscles; the jowl sagged. It was the expressionless mask of extreme old age.' Churchill was upset: 'Yes, there's malice in it. Look at my hands

[47]   Anthony Seldon, *Major: a Political Life*, London: Phoenix, 1998, p. 204.
[48]   The Heath and Thatcher comments are both from Kenneth Baker, *The Prime Ministers*, pp. 18, 17.
[49]   *Strand Magazine*, June 1931, p. 588, reprinted in Churchill, *Thoughts and Adventures*.
[50]   Gerald Scarfe, wall caption for National Portrait Gallery touring exhibition, 2000.
[51]   MacDonald to Low, 22 February 1932. Low family archive.

– I have beautiful hands . . . *Punch* goes everywhere. I shall have to retire if this sort of thing goes on.'[52]

Churchill was too old at that age to join in the cartoonist's game. But this – the second option – is a more positive alternative to disdain. Prime ministers can put the famed British sense of humour on show and turn fine compliments to the cartoonist's art. They can play up to the cartoonist's image: wartime Churchill with his cigars and V-signs, languid Macmillan with his hats (notably a huge furry one for a then exceptional Cold War trip to Moscow), Wilson with his pipe, Margaret Thatcher as the 'Iron Lady'. If people do grow to look like their drawings, 'playing up' could be one reason. The major reason, though, is presumably that we superimpose the cartoon image upon previously familiar versions.

Joining in has a material side too. Cartoonists can be flattered by being asked for originals. (Did Ramsay MacDonald really hang that cartoon where he could 'see it constantly'?) Tenniel, Gould, Bernard Partridge (*Punch* editorial cartoonist, 1899–1945) and Low were given knighthoods. More recently honours were given to Garland, Heath and Matt (Matthew Pritchett). This sort of compliment does not suit every cartoonist, but the capacity to criticize without wounding makes it possible for cartoonists to get quite close to politicians, if both sides want it.

The third alternative is riposte. Walpole, conventionally the first prime minister to whom the title applies, replied to attacks in the 1730s by commissioning cartoons which showed him favourably, and William Pitt paid Gillray a salary for the same reason. Except in the sense that partisan papers tend to have cartoonists who are either broadly sympathetic or herbivorous, that has not been an option in the twentieth century. Beaverbrook used to be pressured by his political friends to tone down Low's cartoons in the 1930s, particularly on the subject of appeasing Nazi Germany. Very occasionally he did so, although he liked protesting that Low's contract tied his hands.[53] The obvious risk of such pressure, if made public, is that the prime minister looks even sillier than before; disdain would have been better. There is always the option of private psychological satisfaction instead, by hanging a copy of the cartoon in the lavatory and thereby diminishing the cartoonist to the level of common humanity, in a kind of reversal of 'the Emperor's clothes'.

[52]   Lord Moran, *Winston Churchill: The Struggle for Survival 1940–65*, London: Constable, 1966, pp. 523–4.
[53]   Colin Seymour-Ure and Jim Schoff, *David Low*, London: Secker and Warburg, 1985, pp. 45ff.

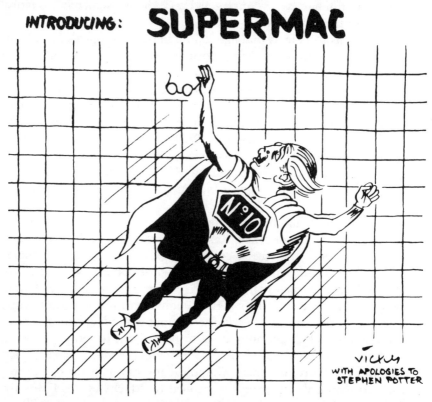

Figure 10.8: *Introducing: SUPERMAC. 'Vicky' (Viktor Weisz), Evening Standard, 6 November 1958.*

The dangers of irony. Vicky's image of Harold Macmillan as an ageing Superman (note the glasses) was intended as ridicule, at a time when Macmillan dominated the government and the opinion polls. Vicky quickly dropped it, when he saw how the Conservatives could turn it to advantage – which they did.
Copyright Atlantic Syndication Partners.

More practically, cartoonists have occasionally given prime ministers an unintended opportunity to turn the tables. The outstanding example is Vicky's depiction of Harold Macmillan as 'Supermac' (figure 10.8). This pastiche of Superman was obviously intended ironically. As well as from the comic book hero, it borrowed from the humorist Stephen Potter, who had recently published *Supermanship*. Potter's subtitle was

'How to continue to stay top without actually falling apart'. In his intro-
ductory Supermac cartoon Vicky changed this to '. . . without actually
having been there'. Even if it registered with readers, Vicky's irony was
easily taken at face value as a compliment. Supermac was seized on by
Conservatives with delight, and it was a helpful image in their victorious 1959 election campaign. Vicky admitted that it had boomeranged,
and he evidently never heard the last of it from his friends.[54] One
measure of its success, purely as an image, is that although Vicky quickly
stopped using it and portrayed Macmillan in very many occupational
guises, it was the Supermac image that caught on. Mrs Thatcher had
similar good fortune with the Russian description of her in 1976 as an
'Iron Lady', when she still had a reputation to make as opposition
leader. But cartoonists did not use the image intensively: in the 1979
general election, for instance, it was used only once.[55]

The most direct riposte by a prime minister to a cartoon, almost certainly, was Churchill's reaction to a *Daily Mirror* drawing by Philip Zec
in 1942 (figure 10.9). Here, prime minister, not cartoonist, was the carnivore. The cartoon did not depict Churchill himself, but he had a
grudge against the paper and had already accused it of a 'spirit of hatred
and malice towards the government'. The paper no doubt saw itself in
the role of candid friend. The cartoon is an excellent example of how
strongly an image depends upon the reader's choice of interpretation.
Its caption was: ' "The price of petrol has been increased by one penny."
Official.' The drawing showed a merchant sailor clinging to a raft in
rough seas. The *Daily Mirror* thought the point was to warn that petrol
should not be wasted, as its import cost lives. Churchill and the cabinet
thought it meant the government was allowing sailors to die, so that
petrol companies could profiteer. Polling evidence showed the majority
of the public saw it the paper's way. But Churchill had a cabinet

[54]   Mark Bryant, *Vicky's Supermac*, London: Park McDonald, 1996, p. 17. See also
Colin Seymour-Ure, 'The afterlife of cartoons', *British Journal Review*, 8.1, 1997, pp.
17–23; Russell Davies and Liz Ottaway, *Vicky*, pp. 134–9. Stephen Potter's books
appealed to educated middle-class taste and therefore to a big section of *Evening Standard* readers. They are now largely forgotten, although they gave the terms 'gamesmanship' and 'oneupmanship' to the language. They are: *The Theory and Practice of
Gamesmanship*, *Lifemanship* and *Supermanship*, London: Rupert Hart-Davis, 1947,
1950, 1958.

[55]   Mrs Thatcher comments in her memoirs, 'Some apparatchik . . . , his imagination
surpassing his judgement, coined the description. [The Russians] had inadvertently put
me on a pedestal as their strongest European opponent.' Margaret Thatcher, *The Path
to Power*, London: HarperCollins, 1995, p. 362. The description was provoked by a
speech in January 1976, criticizing the Soviet Human Rights record and banging a Cold
War drum.

Figure 10.9: *'The price of petrol has been increased by one penny.' – Official. Philip Zec, Daily Mirror, 6 March 1942.*

What was Zec trying to tell us? Cartoons mean what readers make of them, and this one was unclear. Zec claimed it was a patriotic warning not to waste petrol, which cost lives. But Winston Churchill, already suspicious of the Daily Mirror, *took it to mean his government was letting men die so that oil companies could profiteer. The fuss died down only after a debate in the Commons.*
Copyright Mirror Syndication.

committee explore the possibility of using it as a pretext to shut the paper down. Zec's background (and dodgy surname) were 'investigated'; so was the *Mirror*'s shareholder list. After a Commons debate, in which MPs urged caution and common sense, the matter lapsed.[56]

---

[56]   The most detailed account of the 'price of petrol' episode is by David Kellett, *Philip Zec: Cartoonist in a Propaganda War*, MA thesis, University of Kent at Canterbury, 1999. Partial and published accounts are in Cecil King, *With Malice Towards None*, London: Sidgwick and Jackson, 1970, pp. 163–7, and Hugh Cudlipp, *Publish and Be Damned*, London: Andrew Dakers, 1953, chs 24–8. Zec was born in London of Russian Jewish immigrant parents.

That was an episode from dark days of a world war. But are prime ministers, at the worst or best of times, right to worry about the possible effects of cartoons? Low used to tell a story about a cartoonist who was invited by an emperor to caricature him – and did so with such success that 'they buried him the same afternoon'.[57] At the very least it is sensible to acknowledge the potential of cartoons. For a prime minister who does not seek to manage his public communication, as earlier chapters have argued, ignores one of the levers of power. The claim is particularly strong for cartoons because of their emotive quality. This can in principle produce effects quite disproportionate to the cartoonist's efforts and which are difficult to counter. Again, however, the familiar argument about media in general applies: cartoons clearly do not manipulate us, nor yet are we likely to be wholly indifferent. The problem for a prime minister is to judge where, between those extremes, the point of influence lies.

Certain cartoon images, we have seen, take on a life of their own: Supermac and Major's underpants in the second half of the twentieth century, with the bulldog images of Churchill in earlier years and – perhaps the defining case – Hitler's forelock and moustache. (Does anyone, even decades later, sport a toothbrush moustache?) These images have become public property, and that in itself is evidence of a particular kind of influence. The concentration by contemporary cartoonists upon the prime minister to the exclusion of other ministers is an influence too: in this case, over the balance between depiction of a 'prime ministerial' and a 'collective' form of government.

Both those examples illustrate the power of media to help set 'the agenda of politics'. What a prime minister must chiefly worry about, surely, is the elusive influence of these agenda effects upon his fortunes: in the last resort, do cartoonists win votes? Yet these effects are almost impossible to measure precisely. Cartoonists themselves seem modest in their expectations. Day to day, they are probably right. Like the rest of the media, cartoons no doubt reinforce attitudes more than they change them, and the changes are gradual. But there remains the bloody-mindedness of the cartoon (herbivorous or not). 'All political caricature', writes Dorothy George at the start of her authoritative study of its golden age, 'tends to be radical, oppositionist, disruptive.'[58] Macmillan was lucky to be identified with a very strong cartoon image that

---

[57]   David Low, *Ye Madde Designer*, p. 30.
[58]   M. Dorothy George, *English Political Caricature*, Oxford: Oxford University Press, 2 vols, 1959, vol. 1, p. 3.

worked in his favour. Mrs Thatcher too, given the scope implicit in her long premiership and her unique status as a female British prime minister, was fortunate not to become stuck with a damaging cartoon image. Prime ministers may not always be so lucky. Certainly they should keep cartoons in proportion (even if that means using the lavatory strategy). But they should keep their fingers crossed, for if they do become victims of the cartoonist's art there is precious little they can do about it.

A note about the University of Kent Cartoon Archive Database

The Centre for the Study of Cartoons and Caricature, founded at the University of Kent at Canterbury in 1975, holds some 85,000 original drawings and large collections of clippings. The drawings date back to 1904 and were mostly published in British national newspapers and periodicals. They include, for example, work by Haselden, Dyson, Strube, Low, Lee, Shepard, Gabriel, Vicky, Emmwood, Cummings, Horner, Trog, Gibbard, Smythe, Steadman, Jensen, Garland, Riddell and Bell. Images are also stored on microfilm and there is a continuing programme of scanning material into the computer database. An increasing amount of the database is searchable (for example by artist, date, person or subject) through the Centre's website at http://library.ukc.ac.uk/cartoons/. Advice about copyright clearances, research visits to the archive, etc. can be obtained from the Director. The Centre, as 'CartoonHub', is the base for collaborative projects with collections held in other libraries. In addition the Centre undertakes research commissions, organizes and lends to exhibitions, and produces publications.

Index